Everything You Need to Know About...
PIKE FISHING

By
Neville
Fickling

First Published 2002

Published by Lucebaits Publishing
The Tackle Shop, Bridge Road,
Gainsborough, Lincolnshire.
DN21 1JS

Acknowledgements

It is easy to skim over the names and give thanks to all of those who have inspired me over the years. I'm not going to do this; instead at the risk of seeming like a namedropper I'm going to name everyone! The person who started me fishing my father Neville A Fickling followed by the man who put me on the right track in 1966, Harry Nelson of Magdalen. The authors of Fishing for Big Pike, the late Ray Webb and Barrie Rickards for the education! Fred Buller for his Domesday Book of Mammoth Pike, which was and still is truly inspirational. My wife Kathy and children Elizabeth and David for not asking who are you when I come in from yet another trip. Kathy also for a days research in Norwich on Broadland. There are the people who I talk to and fish with. Dave Moore my longest standing fishing friend going back to the early seventies. Nige Williams who because he catches 30lb pike when I do not is best classed as a nuisance! ET for the endless abuse. Jim the owner of Masons for making old age easier! Derek Mac for opening my eyes to the potential of lure fishing. The people who run the shop inspite of my efforts, Sue, Carole and Bob. Bill Giles and Reg Sandys for the interview and Mark Ackereley for his support at times of crisis and his chapter on Mask and Corrib. Lastly all the pike anglers who have been supportive over the years and have taken me at face value. No thanks at all to all those through ignorance or stupidity have made life difficult for fellow pike anglers and myself. That includes the fisheries managers, "scientists" and governments who seem to have difficulty listening to advice! Thanks to you the reader for buying the book!

Neville Fickling

Contents

INTRODUCTION

Pike fishing books tend to have a short life. This is not because the majority of books are unworthy of anything other than an ephemeral existence. It is because of the economics of printing! The first 2000 will be printed in one lot and it is rarely economic to produce another 500 to keep the book in print. The book therefore becomes obtainable only on the secondhand stalls and generally the better the book the harder it is to get hold of a copy. For example the classic Fishing For Big Pike by Rickards and Webb is a book you rarely see secondhand. In order to keep the few friends I have left I'll not be mentioning the books you can get hold of easily.

Over the years I have written several pike books of my own and ghost written one or two for other would be writers. I enjoy writing, something I have been eternally grateful for over the years. Writing has been a part of my living since the first article was published in I think 1973 and though I enjoy it, the money has always been useful, sometimes vital! In order to sell a book it has to be worth reading. A pike book should do two things, inform and entertain. The balance between the two can be difficult to find. The best instructional books go into great detail, but tend to be rather hard going. Stories of notable captures though entertaining do not always convey the vital information the reader needs to go and make his or her own captures. I have always believed that the best pike books combine instruction with anecdotes and stories of significant captures. When I read a pike book that is what I'm looking for and if the opinions of friends are anything to go by they feel the same.

Now you will have had to live on the moon for the past ten years not to realize that the number one species at the moment is the carp. This intense interest in carp began in Great Britain and has spread rapidly to the continent. It would appear that even in countries where predatory fish are worshipped, the carp is about to take over. The only snag with carp is that for about 5 months a year in many waters it is a waste of time fishing for them! So perhaps as a spin off from carp fishing, pike appear to be gaining in popularity. Whether this is a good thing or not remains to be seen. One thing is certain, the standards of fish handling displayed by most carp anglers is very good. Given suitable advice there is no reason why carp anglers should not be able to deal with pike on the bank without detriment to the fish itself.

Having established that pike fishing has increased in popularity, I'm going to digress here and ask a few rhetorical questions. Please bear with me! Why go pike fishing, indeed why go fishing at all? I think if you look a little too carefully at any aspect of fishing you are in danger of talking yourself out of doing it! However if we are going to get to the bottom of this desire to go fishing we really have to work out some first principles. Fishing as we carry it out consists of catching a fish and putting it back. Now if you were an alien arriving on this planet for the first time and you saw a fisherman do just that, you'd have to ask what was going on? I think the same would apply if you watched a football match. 22 grown men kicking a hollow ball around on a grass pitch seems a terrible waste of time and effort. Yet we still fish and we still watch football matches. The fact is that we have a certain amount of time, which has to be spent constructively; presumably work takes up a fair chunk while sleep occupies some more. That leaves time for leisure and in most cases leisure involves non-constructive activities. It appears that we as a species cannot operate on a diet of work and sleep alone; we therefore go to great lengths to find things to amuse us. Fishing and in this case pike fishing is just another rather pointless activity, but those of us who do it get a lot of pleasure out of it. Because we enjoy it, it does not matter that it is rather pointless and as the reader will now no doubt be breathing a sigh of relief I'm only going to dwell on further pseudo-philosophical points briefly!

What then makes a pike angler take his or her fishing as seriously as I do? We are as animals instinctively imbued with the desire to hunt, though some vegans might dispute this! Fishing for pike is a form of hunting. Whereas in the wild the desire to hunt once the quarry has been captured is reduced, pike fisherman want to do it again as soon as possible! In fact not only do pike fisherman wish to capture pike on a continuous basis, most also wish to select the bigger fish. This invariably makes the pike angler less successful as far as pike caught is concerned, the absolute opposite of the hunting ethic where you'd expect success to be defined purely as fish and weight of fish caught. I hate using the word obsession because to my mind it seems so derogatory, but really it' s the only word that describes the behaviour of dozens of pike anglers. That some pike anglers are obsessive becomes clear when you realize that some have elected to lead a single solitary life, others while trying to lead a normal home life have been involved in marital breakdown. Others only survive because of independent and understanding wives. A few even cut corners and are involved in a certain amount of dodgy dealings, " 'ere did you still want that 30hp Yamaha motor………."

While most of you out there will (excuse the inverted commas) be "normal" pike anglers, going once a week with a few weeks holiday thrown in for good measure, there are also the fanatics who will be able to go pike fishing as much as 3 times a week plus holiday. Obviously the fanatic will in the long run catch more big pike than the "normal" pike angler. I for example will fish a couple of whole days in a week along with up to two mornings. Sometimes I fish five mornings. At other times, for example during October when the trout waters all open I'll do 15 whole days in a month. Because I work for a living I end up working lots of evenings and sometimes around the clock. It is little wonder that the state of preparedness of my fishing tackle sometimes leaves a lot to be desired. I tend to spend all my time working or fishing. Preparation ends up a long way down the list of priorities.

There is absolutely no doubt that time is a very useful commodity for any angler. We already have full time carp anglers scattered around the country with one or two pike anglers also giving it a go. Interestingly your pike fishing results do not improve pro rata to the amount of time you put in. Rather it soon becomes clear that much time is wasted when you have lots of time on your hands. Some of this is exploration and this has to be done if you are to find new productive areas. A lot of time however is wasted due to sheer bloody mindedness. The pike angler with time on his side may determine to bore the pike out! Reduce the available amount of time and you tend to fish more efficiently. I have proved this to myself. In 1973/74 I took six months off to pike fish in the Fens. The result was 4 over 20lbs with a total of 28 over 10lbs. The following season while at Hull University with far less time plus feminine distractions I managed the same number of twenty pounders plus a couple more doubles. These days I appreciate my fishing more because I'm restrained from doing everything I like. Make no mistake there are very few chances that go begging because I cannot fit them in, but all those casual local projects I'd love to mess about with usually go to the wall. The number of club books I carry around and do not use would depress me if it weren't for the fact that tackle shops get complimentary permits. Despite the freebies I still end up wasting money, usually on boat licences for places I never get to fish. I'll look at exploration and doing your own thing in a later chapter.

It is possible to go pike fishing strictly on your own terms. It is even possible to be so isolated as to not know what is going on in the outside world. There's nothing wrong with this attitude because there's plenty of joy to be had from pike fishing on your own terms. I have a different outlook because I am commercially involved. As soon as you say commerce or business these days many people think you have uttered a dirty word. However it is possible to make money at pike fishing without selling out. People tend to respect you a lot more if you avoid trying to sell them something they either do not want or which is not what they need. People ask me why Lucebaits does not sell lamprey flavour. The simple answer is because I do not think there is such a thing! There is an ET lamprey flavour, which the shop has sold from time to time. My personal views as to how near this has been to a lamprey are neither here nor there. We sell it because customers ask for it. No way will I try and promote it!

The commercialism does however mean that I do not hide my light under a bushel. I need to publicise my catches to some extent in order to help retain the part of the market that The Tackle Shop and Lucebaits have. I also enjoy talking about my or a friends catches. I think in the late seventies and early eighties I lived for pike fishing and it was always something I thought about throughout each day. As you get older many things distract you so though I make my living from pike fishing I do think about other things from time to time.

The degree of commitment you give to your pike fishing will tend to reflect in your results. Before I look at this aspect of pike fishing it would be useful to consider what makes for enjoyment. You will after all be doing this for entertainment and different people will have different criteria as to what is entertaining. Mick Brown for example spent much of 2001/2 lure fishing for pike and zander. He caught a stack of fish, but as I write few if any really big fish. However he enjoyed it, found it interesting and at one stage he was night lure fishing, which obviously added a whole new outlook to his fishing. On the other hand I was fishing for 30lb plus pike from a number of different venues. Apart from one nice surprise the fishing was a bit of a struggle. I enjoyed some of it and endured the rest. Who had the most fun from his sport? I suspect Mick did though I have no regrets, because I am focused on catching something big from waters, which have a big fish reputation. Give me the time and I'm sure I'd enjoy catching large numbers of pike and zander on lures. I always judge my own personal success by numbers, not everyone's cup of tea I know. If I catch 5 twenty pound plus pike in a year I know it has been a difficult year. I'll be pleased but not satisfied. If I catch ten twenty pounders it will mean that I have been on the ball, that itself being pleasing because it is always better to feel that you have performed well rather than below par. If I catch between 15 and 25 twenty pounders I'll have had an exceptional year and it gives me a buzz. To an outsider it means nothing, it is something that only keen pike anglers can relate too. These are my personal standards and not those that any readers *have* to aspire to. I talk to a lot of pike anglers who are limited in the time they can take off to fish. To catch one or two twenty pounders a season would be very pleasing for them and if they didn't catch anything that size they'd still be just as keen to pike fish the following year. Because this book is aimed at a fairly wide readership it is essential to show that there is a wide range of aspirations, but it is also sensible to make it clear that none of the extremes up or down the scale are compulsory. You should fish to please yourself. I once had a letter from a zander angler who said that he wanted to catch some big zander to increase his credibility in the big zander scene. What a sad person! Then we have a keen lure angler intent on showing the world that he can catch big pike on live and deadbaits as well. I honestly do not think any of this is very important. Though I'm keen on keeping records of important aspects of pike fishing such as pike over 35lb and the most successful pike anglers, I am not bothered with over analyzing the data I have. Neither should you!

Having looked at some annual results, lets consider what constitutes a good days pike fishing. I always used to feel that once you'd had a fish over 7lb you were making progress. I'm perhaps a little more ambitious now, but in reality a 10lb plus pike is still a good result on most waters. Catching a 10 pounder involves just as much effort or thought as catching a 20 pounder, it's just that there will be say five times fewer twenty pounders in a water stacking the odds against the angler. A good day might produce 4 or 5 pike with a couple being double figures. A day to remember would produce a twenty pounder and anything more than that means getting the whiskey bottle out! If you are lucky or you can find some exclusive fishing you might have an exceptional day. I once had 22 double figure pike plus two singles in a day. The venue was the private Cut Off Channel and others have made similar catches in the past. I was still very pleased! The day on the Thurne, which produced a 41-06, 19 and 16 was also very special and exceptional. As a pike angler you will live for the exceptional day. They do not happen to everyone, but it is the hope factor that keeps all of us going.

If like me you spend a small amount each week on the national lottery you will understand the mentality of pike fishing. There is a lot you can do to put the odds in your favour, but in the end there is an element of luck that none of us has any control over. Take for example 30lb pike. In the eighties I caught a 29-15 pike from Blithfield. One two-ounce roach and it would have been a thirty pounder. Mark Ackerley had caught a 29-08 I caught from Lough Mask the week before at just over 30lb. A Masons lake 29-08 was out of condition and should have weighed 30lbs. I'm a bit of a specialist at catching 29lb plus pike! Despite this you will not see me kicking the cat or going into a depression. Pike fishing can be very unkind, (I'd not rate a 29 as too much unkindness!) but if you are not prepared for disappointment there is a very good case for doing something less stressful!

Even if you the reader is a rational sensible human being/pike angler you will be influenced by what I will call Mr. Bull*******. Mr. B catches far more big pike than you do. He fishes all the right waters. Indeed he is usually on all the right waters though you'd be hard pressed to find him there on any given day. In short he is everyone's worst nightmare. How do you deal with this sort of person? Well it's difficult, but the best approach is to try and ignore him. If you start to worry about what you are catching in relation to what he claims to be catching you will be lost. When it comes to having to deal with plonkers, I've been there and done that. The amazing thing about these people is that some of them even manage to get sponsorship deals. Some lesser species of Mr. Bs also get magazine columns, but the people who give these people a soapbox do not realise what they are dealing with. They do not recognise that there is a problem. It shows a lack of interest in pike fishing or worse still a lack of interest in dealing with the real pike angling community. Luckily at the moment I do not write for any magazines with this problem.

While I am on the subject of moaning about other pike anglers lets look at a few other examples of undesirable behaviour you are bound to come across if you become a regular pike angler. Now pike anglers are by nature liars. Do not get me wrong because the lies are invariably the white lies we all tell. I catch a big pike from a private water and I use a code name for the water. Furthermore even if someone tells me he knows where it is and is right I still deny it! The simple way to avoid this behaviour is to not ask the wrong questions of your fellow pike anglers. Good pike fishing usually only stays good if competition from other anglers is reduced. If you really wish to keep a secret then it's best not to tell anyone what you've caught. However this is no fun so most of us tend to want our cake and eat it. We publicise what we catch, but avoid giving meaningful details of where it came from. Selfish and dishonest I know, but exactly the right wayto behave in this situation.

What is unforgivable in pike fishing is telling lies about what you catch. One or two moderately famous pike anglers have done this over the years. What is worse, when challenged most just keep lying while some do not even acknowledge that they have a problem. Some pike anglers also have an exaggerated idea of their importance. They tell us that other people are following them round. Now I'm sure that people follow pike anglers as often as I read Women's Own. There is always the chance that someone out there is really desperate to find where you are fishing, but even I during my most intense period of fishing never felt the need to go that far. So you can generally take it for granted that the chap who thinks he is being followed is suffering from delusions of grandeur!

We have pike anglers claiming to be experts of great importance who will not tell us what they have caught. Some do not keep records; others do not wish to be a number in a list. Yet they gladly take sponsorship money and basically pull the wool over some tackle firms eyes. It is sad for the genuine pike anglers who because of long-term efforts have won recognition of their achievements that the rogue element can manage to jump onto the same bandwagon. Nobody said life was fair, but you the reader will be the ultimate judge. You may not end up liking my methods, my morality, or me but you will hopefully accept that my records are genuine.

You may find my criticism of unnamed people unsavory, but you should know full well that only a fool puts things in print even if he knows he is right. Even an unsuccessful libel action against myself is something I'd be inclined to avoid! So not all pike anglers are nice people and not everyone plays the game. However in general pike angling is a wonderful self-indulgent occupation. I'm still enjoying it and I hope the by the time you've read this book, you'll be catching more pike and looking forward to the next trip.

CHAPTER 1
THE PIKE IN CLOSE UP

Examples of the family Esocidae have been identified from Cretaceous deposits, which means that a species of pike existed when the dinosaurs were at their peak. The fossil evidence also suggests that the *Esocidae* evolved before the separation of the land masses which were to become Eurasia and North America. It is something of a tribute to the adaptability of the family that it has survived the extinction of the dinosaurs. The pike *Esox lucius* is one of 5 fish in the same small genus. The others are the muskellunge *Esox masquinongy*, the redfin pickerel *Esox americanus*, the chain pickerel Esox *niger* and the Amur pike Esox *rechti*. The redin pickerel occurs as a sub species the chain pickerel *Esox americanus vermiculatus*. There also exists natural and artificial hybrids between pike and muskie, tiger muskie. The distribution of all the *Escocids* is confined to the Northern Hemisphere with the pike widespread in North America and Canada, Europe and parts of what once was the USSR. The muskie and pickerels are confined to the USA while the Amur Pike is only found in the former USSR and parts of China. This book is about pike so if the reader wishes to learn more about muskies in particular there are a number of books available in the states, many videos, magazines and web sites. In the appendix at the end of this book you'll find some useful contact addresses and references should you wish to pursue your enquiries into the family *Esocidae*.

The fish that interests us here, the pike is not easily mistaken for another species. It's bodyform has been duplicated elsewhere by other totally unrelated species. The gar pikes (family *Lepisosteidae*) and the barracuda (family *Sphyraenidae*) both have the characteristic elongated form of the pike with the anal and dorsal fins grouped close to the tail. In freshwater the pike has proved to be the most successful species to adopt this bodyform. The pike is designed for rapid acceleration and it must be significant that so much fin surface area is located towards the tail of the fish. The pike has generally been classified as an ambush pursuit predator. The pike utilizes whatever natural cover it can find to move into striking range of prey fish. It then use's it's rapid acceleration to overhaul the hapless prey. To suggest that pike spend all their time lurking in a weed bed would be to over simplify their behaviour. Pike spend a substantial amount of time moving around, if only from one ambush point to another one. Prey fish are not stupid and if there was a resident pike lurking in the same spot all the time you could be pretty certain that the prey fish would avoid that area like the plague. In any piece of freshwater there is an awful amount of empty water. Encounters between prey fish and predator will not happen every day. The prey fish have to feed and get on with the things they do from time to time such as reproduce. They will be alert to danger, but not on red alert to coin a military phrase. It's more a case of being on yellow alert until a threat materialises. A predator for success depends on making its move before the prey realise's what's happening.

All predators experience varied levels of success. I've not been able to find any information on the success of the pike's attempts to capture prey. Somewhere I'm sure there will be a research paper on the subject. For every 10 attempts to capture prey possibly only one result in a capture. You only have to watch cormorants feeding to realise that it may take several dozen dives to catch a fish. The failure rate is only of concern if energy expended in hunting food exceeds energy gained from the prey. The fact that the pike is still with us after millions of years suggests that the failure rate is low enough to ensure the survival of the species if not always the odd individual.

A number of aspects of pike biology have a bearing on angling success. I have already mentioned the pike's feeding strategy. Of great importance to us is the amount of natural feed available to the pike. It is a general rule that the more food there is available to the pike the harder it is to catch. This is fairly obvious when you think about it. As an angler your bait is competing with the natural food. There is a limit to the amount of food a pike needs to eat and if there is so much food in a water that your bait is literally swamped by the natural food your chances will not be good. A lure or a livebait may if fished correctly tempt a predatory response from an otherwise apathetic pike, while a deadbait will probably be a dead loss.

A look through the scientific literature and my own practical experience suggests that a pike's annual food requirement is around 3 times its bodyweight. Smaller pike have a higher metabolic rate and their annual food requirement may be a bit higher. Just to survive a pike probably requires around 1.2 to 1.5 times its bodyweight in prey. Pike are amazingly adaptable creatures and though fish is the most important part of their diet, virtually anything that swims is fair game provided a pike can get it into it's mouth. Water birds and small mammals are eaten, but generally only when conventional prey such as fish is unavailable. Young pike initially feed on invertebrates and then progress to fish. The growth of young pike is positively correlated with temperature, but is also influenced by prey availability. In some years prey fish may grow so fast so as to be too big for the young pike to eat.

Where there are a large number of invertebrates this may not present immediate problems. However cannibalism can be very important in reducing young pike numbers. These natural control factors are all part of what limits the numbers of pike in our fisheries. Another significant factor affecting pike numbers is the water level at the time of spawning, hatching and early growth. Fluctuating water levels expose eggs and can force pike to spawn on much less favourable spawning substrate. The absence of weed increases mortality of young pike due lack of cover and increased predation from other fish such as perch and predatory birds.

Going back to the amount of food a pike eats, if we calculate that a 20lb pike eats 60lb of prey a year and then guess that each of the prey fish weigh 4oz. Our 20lb pike then has 240 meals a year. That is not one a day. If we further consider that pike do not feed consistently throughout the year, you start to realize that as an angler it is quite easy to not be in the right place at the right time. The peak time for feeding is post spawning.

During the period April to June as much as 60% of the annual prey fish intake can be consumed. With another peak in September and October, it is easy to see that the rest of the year presents comparatively few feeding opportunities.

The size of prey eaten has been the subject of numerous studies. Much of this work has been carried out in North America by workers such as Diana and in the UK by Frost and Kipling. Frost and Kipling were responsible for one of the longest ever studies in the UK on Lake Windermere. That work continues today albeit at a reduced level by other workers. On the Dorset Frome, Mann did much research on pike and a whole host of other researchers have over the years contributed to our wealth of knowledge. Though much of this work is highly academic and on an initial inspection of little practical use, knowledge always finds a use. Much of the modern medical research may seem to be esoteric and of little relevance to problems such as curing diseases. However without the very basic information you cannot progress to more complex matters.

You would expect that the bigger the pike, the larger on average the prey would be. In fact though the maximum size of prey increases, as a pike gets bigger, a wide range of prey sizes are consumed. Pike generally eat in proportion to the availability of the sizes and species in a water. For example prior to the introduction of ruffe into Loch Lomond the staple diet of these pike was powan, a type of plankton feeding whitefish present in a number of our largest deep natural waters. With the explosion of ruffe, these became the most important part of the pike's diet. This was despite there being plenty of powan in the loch. Many studies have shown that pike have seasonal preferences and many of these are well known in the UK. On Lough Mask pike intercept trout on the way to and back from the spawning grounds. It is amazing how far these pike travel to intercept trout and how the same fish arrive at the same spot each year. When perch spawn pike are on the shallows feeding on them. Perch after spawning can be really exhausted and are easy prey for pike. The same applies to roach and bream, or any member of the carp family in the spring. We can also be pretty certain that the seasonal runs of lamprey and eels that ascend and descend our rivers are also fair game for pike.

Pike probably eat more live fish than dead ones, though there is probably no real way that we can tell. I would suspect that most sick fish do not get to the stage where they are dead simply because a pike bumps them off first! That pike take dead fish we know, deadbaiting being the single most popular approach used to catch them. The fact that pike gladly take baits they could never see in the wild, i.e. mackerel and sardines suggests that they are opportunist feeders prone to taking whatever easy meal is presented to them. It is not a case of weaning pike onto particular deadbaits. They certainly take baits such as mackerel on a first acquaintance. It also a fact that there have been plenty of occasions when mackerel have produced more runs than a "natural" bait such as a dead roach. Indeed mackerel have often out fished live roach! In general it is better not to look at pike expecting them to be logical and predictable and it is certainly unwise to suggest that their thought processes (such as they are) are like ours. A pike looks at a dead fish and if it is really hungry it will take anything. If it is only slightly peckish it might be a little more discerning and only take a certain bait. When not hungry at all you have no chance with a deadbait, the only hope then being by lure fishing or livebaiting.

The amount of food a pike has available to it influences how fast it grows. It is well known and also extremely obvious that the better the food supply and the lower the density of pike the bigger a pike can grow. A typical low-density pike water is the Thurne system in Broadland. For years now an algae called *Prymnesium parva* has wreaked havoc there because when it dies it releases a toxin, which kills fish. Pike, which tend to be more solitary than roach or bream do not benefit from warning behaviour from their brethren and therefore tend to get caught unawares. This means pike tend to have a fairly precarious existence. Prey fish stocks though from time to time depressed; generally end up to be out of proportion to the pike stocks. This results in some surprisingly large pike.

Where pike are being culled regularly can also lead to the odd big individual. It is amazing how one or two pike can evade capture for long enough to grow to 30lb or even bigger. A water local to where I live has been regularly stocked with carp and even barbel over the years. Needless to say any pike caught from this water have been removed, usually to a nearby lake. Yet out of the blue a 31 pounder turned up. Unfortunately this too was moved. Maybe another big pike will come through, but for a while there may not be another really big fish present.

There are natural waters, which produce very big pike, mainly because there is a good food supply and the pike are not that, successful due to limited spawning areas. One such water is Lough Mask in Western Ireland. Until the gill nets returned in the mid 1990s Mask was producing more 35lb plus pike than any other water in Britain and Ireland. The nearby Lough Corrib though over twice the size of Mask and with a run of salmon and sea trout as well as coarse fish such as roach and bream was not so prolific for 35lb plus pike. This was probably because spawning areas are much more numerous and consequentially there are more pike. Lough Conn, which is even less hospitable than Lough Mask would probably have been the ultimate pike water, had not the inept Irish fisheries boards kept up their gill netting for many years.

Stocked trout waters are of course where the bulk of the big pike are now being caught. This is hardly surprising because each of these waters is regularly stocked with rainbow and sometimes brown trout. This amounts to a substantial amount of extra food. Trout waters therefore tend to produce big pike and some quite a lot of big pike. Some trout waters are better than others. Big stocks of coarse fish can increase the potential for quality pike fishing, however adverse factors such as the netting of coarse fish and pike plus cormorants can all serve to reduce the potential of even the biggest trout water. As I write in 2002 we have just about run out of new trout waters in England. There may be the odd surprise here and there, but nearly all the big waters that have pike have been pike fished. Whether Scotland or Wales has anything to offer remains to be seen, but there are indications that there are a few waters in Scotland yet to be discovered.

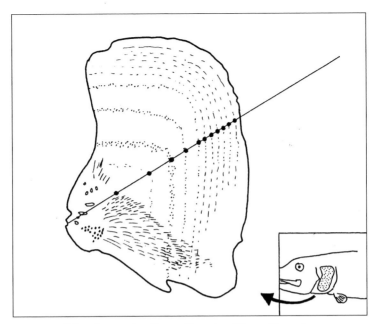

Pike Opercular Bone Showing Years Growth.
• Marks each annual winter/spring opague zone.

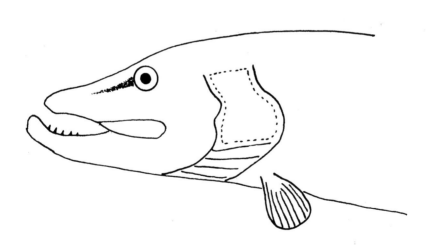

Location of Opercular Bone of Pike.
*Can only be removed when dead.

The age of pike interests most pike anglers though in reality it matters not a jot to most of us whether a pike takes 8 years or 18 years to get to 30lbs. To age a pike fisheries biologists use boney parts of a pike, such as scales, opercular bones, (gill covers) and cleithra or ear stones. The principle of aging is similar in each case. Each bone or scale grows more or less in proportion to the whole pike. Periods of winter growth appear differently to that of summer growth. For example with scales, a year's growth is laid down as concentric circles, which are known as annuli. In summer the annuli are wide spaced, in winter they are narrow spaced. Well that's the theory; needless to say it's not quite as simple as that. In order to be able to determine what constitutes a year's growth, great use is made of what are known as annual checks. Sexually mature fish quite obviously go through considerable stress at spawning time. Because of this the scale will frequently show some reabsorbtion of the annuli. This produces a check at the end of the winter prior to the new years growth in the spring. Now if it was a simple as this to read pike scales, we would all be doing it as a matter of course. Unfortunately it is not that straightforward. False checks can appear caused by factors other than spawning. For example poor water conditions in the summer, i.e. it is too warm or oxygen levels are low can result in growth stopping. People who work regularly with pike scales can spot such checks or pseudo annuli. The layman who attempts to read a pike scale may determine that it is 8 years old. Unfortunately if you are two years wrong either way, your scale reading does not really mean much. Such errors are all too easy to make and these days if I really had to know the age of a pike I would be inclined to get someone who works regularly with pike scales to do the job for me.

Another problem with scales is the fact that the older the pike the more difficult the scales are to read. The best scales are usually found on what we call the shoulder of the

Scale from a very old pike and because of this very difficult to read.

fish, behind the gill cover and below the lateral line. Even then some will be replacement scales. These will perhaps have been lost when the pike was older. Though the same size as the other scales nearby they lack the central details which indicate the age before the original scale was lost. There is also the problem that once a pike ceases to grow, no new annuli are added to the scales. A pike could therefore appear to be ten years old, yet have lived for 7 years longer. Readers will by now appreciate that telling how old a pike is from scales is not straightforward.

The accepted best method of aging pike is not very good for them. Opercular bones and cleithra have to be removed from the pike, the pike having to be killed first. Sometimes when you find a dead pike it is interesting to remove the opercular bone. To do this you need a sharp pair of scissors and simple cut along the lines shown in the diagram. Then boil it is water to remove the skin and then allow to dry. On a black background you will see the separate bands that denote winter and summer growth. The central part of the bone of old fish is frequently very dense, making estimating the early years growth difficult. Fishery biologists have a method by which they can estimate the early years growth, but for information on this you need to read a textbook on fisheries science.

There are a number of questions we as anglers can ask which are of interest to us. The first must be, how long can pike live? Because I do not have access to every piece of scientific research, it might be possible for someone to contradict me here. To the best of my knowledge the oldest pike recorded came from Lake Athabasca in Northern Saskatchewan in 1974. It weighed 14.2kg (nearly 31lb) and measured 110cm (44ins). The pike in this lake exist for much of the year under ice and are slow growing. Interestingly rapid growth is negatively correlated with maximum age. It would appear therefore that to reach a ripe old age as a pike you need to grow slowly. We are aware of this from the situation on trout waters where the pike grow extremely rapidly yet appear to suffer early mortality. On the Broads growth is probably slower, but a similar maximum size can be reached over a longer period. As a generally rule in this country a trout water pike can reach 20lb in six years. Thirty pounds is possible in 8 or 9 years. That these fish probably fail to reach more than 10 to 12 years is consistent with a maximum weight of 40 to 46lbs. Though in theory an 18-year trout water pike might weigh 70lb, we have no evidence that they ever live for much longer than 12 or 13 years. As far as I can remember every trout water 40 pounder has failed to reappear at 40lb the following season. Both of the Llandegfedd forties from the first year failed to reappear the next year. The Gareth Edwards 45 was almost certainly Paul Elbourne's 37 the next summer and Roy Lewis's 46 pounder was certainly not seen again. The two Bough Beech biggies the 40 and Nige Williams's 39 were not seen the next season. I would suggest that when a trout water pike gets to 40lb or thereabouts it is very close to the end of its life. The Roy Lewis 46 pounder certainly survived an earlier capture because Steve Gould had her at 29lb four years earlier. This to my mind suggests that capture by an angler is not fatal in itself.

So if you wish to catch a 40lb pike I'd suggest you find non-trout water where a 40 pounder has already been caught. The chance of a repeat capture is much greater;

witness my own Thurne 40 (at least 8 captures) and the Bluebell 40, at least 6 captures. Trout water 40s only appears to turn up twice in rapid succession, never with a years interval between captures. So if you want one, you'd be better being the first person to catch it, or fish the water non-stop for two weeks should it get caught again! It all smacks of desperation when you think about it. If you decide to make the capture of a 40lb pike your lifetimes work, you will almost certainly be disappointed. It is far better to set attainable targets, reach them and then set your target again.

Actually knowing how old a particular group of pike is, though interesting will not help you catch them. Neither will it help you catch a big one. It will not help you choose the right water because pike are very much individuals. Even in a group of fish, which are growing at only a moderate rate, there will be the odd individual that shows exceptional growth. Loch Lomond is a popular pike water. By any standards it would be defined as a good pike water. It is not the place to go to if you are seeking a 35lb plus pike. Its track record suggests that 30lb pike though a possibility are very rare. From a base where 30lb pike are rare you really are dealing with wishful thinking if you hope to catch a 35 pounder. The odds are astronomical!

Llandegfedd as was, had quite a large base of 30lb pike and clearly from the results there did have 35lb plus pike potential. Track records are important in pike fisheries and it is no good kidding yourself that a certain size of fish is there if no one has ever caught one before. Rutland water for example is a nice place to pike fish, can provide good sport with double figure pike and the odd twenty. However it has a poor track record as a producer of really big pike. Grafham has a better track record, but mainly as a water, which produces big fish in nets! It may well be that on some trout waters the methods we can use and the areas we fish do not give us much chance to catch the really big fish.

The reader should understand that I am writing from my point of view here. A viewpoint that relates to big pike differently from someone who is not so serious as I am. A 20lb pike is still a big pike and the day I become blasé about catching them will be the day I pack up fishing for pike.

It is a fact that pike will reach 20lb in many different types of water and because of this such fish are available to most anglers. It is only as we reach 25lb that they start to become rare and then we have to start to be selective as to where we fish. As I will show in later chapters it pays to consider lots of different waters in your quest for a big pike and learn to never say never!

Another question, which comes up from time to time, is how far do pike move? A lot of research has been carried out on pike using conventional tagging and more recently radio tags. A conventional tag is a device, which attaches to a pike and enables us to identify the individual fish. The tag will carry a number. Years ago tags were fairly primitive and chicken wing tags were popular, attached to the jaw or the gill cover. All these attachments were to some degree traumatic and may have inhibited feeding and therefore growth. Today we have the use of the Floy tag. This uses the same principle as those frustrating cloths tags you get when you buy a new shirt or jumper. The tag is attached using a needle gun, which leaves the T bar of the tag embedded in the muscle below the dorsal fin. The tiny tube attached to the strap carries the number of the particular fish. Retention of the tag is pretty good though some are invariably lost in the landing net on capture. Tags are also shed at spawning time when the pike can be very frisky in the weed beds. A conventional tag tells you about movements of a pike between captures. It obviously tells you nothing about movements in between captures. Over the years I've carried out a number of tagging projects, the most comprehensive having been on zander as part of an MPhil study. Pike tagging has always been on a small scale and it has revealed that pike can certainly move 5 or 6 miles without difficulty. On large gravel pits of 60 acres plus, all parts of the pit will be visited at some time by each pike.

The PAC inspired tagging project on Loch Lomond showed that a handful of pike moved around a lot while most had limited home ranges. Since my little problem with the old Scottish PAC I've not been inclined to ask for further information, though I've had two or three tagged pike from Lomond.

Radio tagging studies show that individual pike can move around a lot in a day, but there will also be periods when pike do very little. Repeated studies have shown that pike activity is also greatest at dawn and dusk. I once spent a day out on Staunton Harold Reservoir while Ros Wright was carrying out her pike tracking. It wasn't very exciting that day, but later talks given by her supervisor Gerry White showed that an individual pike was capable of moving a couple of miles in a few hours. This is obviously interesting from our point of view because it gives us hope that a bad swim choice may not always be hopeless. A big pike could move in at any time.

There is plenty of evidence to suggest that pike can return to the same areas year in year out for a variety of reasons. On Lough Mask several individual pike were recaptured from the same areas, though where they were in between years is anyone's guess. On Lomond, pike have returned to the same areas to spawn, as have those from Windermere. Even on Fen drains pike that have moved around a lot during a year frequently end up in the same areas as they were caught the year before.

Repeat captures are a fact of life with almost all our coarse fish species. Pike because they are more fragile than carp are never likely to be caught 50 or 60 times over a 40 year period. However there are several examples of pike that have been caught 10 to 20 times. These are generally mid range fish of 10 to 15 pounds because as we have mentioned earlier fish which are nearer to the end of their lives do not get a chance to be recaptured many times. Any pike angler who has been around for a few years will know how it is possible to identify pike by their markings. For the benefit of those newer to the sport I'll explain here. As far as we know a pike's markings are unique to each individual fish. Certainly I have never come across any two fish, which resemble each other. Apart from individual pike markings being unique, there is also an interesting variation in markings between pike in different waters and sometimes even between pike in the same water. Years ago in a small scientific paper (FICKLING 1982) I attempted to classify these markings as well as demonstrate the evidence for being able to identify pike using their markings. Pike markings tend in juveniles to consist of longitudinal bars. These markings are clearly of great use to the young pike as it hides in vegetation. As the pike gets older this need to hide in vegetation is reduced and the bar makings gradually break up into a series of spots. These spots can vary in size and shape. Many Irish pike have spots that are elongated, almost horizontal bars. I have never seen a Scottish pike like this though I have seen some examples in one sandpit in Holland. There are odd pike in England which show the horizontal bar markings.

Most Scottish pike have relatively small spots and certainly Lomond pike clearly have lots of small spots giving them a very attractive look. Many big lake pike such as those from Windermere are similar. All the big lake pike appear very green in colour. Trent pike and those in some peaty waters look very brown. Frequently these brown looking fish have large vivid spots. Some fish have rounded spots, others oval. Irregular or star shaped spots are also seen.

The identification of an individual pike depends on the variation in spot shape or position along with the markings on the anal fin. To do a comparison between two photos of potentially the same pike I like to find three different areas of similarity. Good areas to compare are around the tail root, the anal fin itself, and the line of demarcation between the body side markings and the underside and the head. All these areas show up distinctive features, which can be useful for identification purposes. Sometimes unusual marks such as yellow blotches will be distinctive enough to recognise an individual fish, but beware of using just one reference point. There may be more than one pike in a water with a yellow mark on it's underside, so always follow the rule, look for three different features then you are unlikely to make a mistake.

Pike just like any other fish are subject to genetic abnormalities. Normally predation is enough to weed these freaks out. Sometimes one or two get through. Odd pike do not usually concern us but once in a while one makes it through as a giant. Eric Edwards's 38-10 Lough Mask pike was a pug nose and this deformity didn't seem to have done it much harm! Indeed the same fish is thought to have been caught by John Matthews earlier at 36lb. Pug nose pike are quite common in Ireland. They are quite distinctive, having a markedly shorter top jaw than the lower. The profile of the top jaw also appears convex rather than the normal concave. Pug nose pike also turn up from time to time in the UK, but rarely reach a significant size. Hunchbacks, pike with truncated tails, upturned jaws and missing fins all turn up from time to time. In America odd examples of blue pike turn up, fish with no spots and a strange blue colouration. There have been noted in this country the very odd cases of albino or very pale pike. Parasites such as eye flukes result in blind pike, usually in just the one eye. It is without a doubt a disadvantage for a pike to be blind in one eye and many of the pike at Weirwood in Sussex were afflicted with this problem. *Diplostomum* the eye fluke is present in the lens of most fish. When it reaches a very high level of infestation it causes a cataract. This results in blindness in one eye. It is a very unlucky pike, which has a heavy infestation in both eyes. I have only seen one pike that was totally blind; it was black in colour and obviously struggling to survive. I would suggest that a totally blind pike would be unable to compensate using its other senses.

Of course what we would all really like to catch is a perfectly normal, rather large pike! Hopefully later on in this book I'll be able to point you in the right direction! For years when I was a keen, but only modestly successful pike angler I was interested in pike lengths for weights. The Mona scale was often applied as the norm for comparisons of weight for length. Fred Buller showed quite clearly that Mona's scale was of little use when looking at the exceptional pike caught from around the world. While a 24lb pike may in many cases measure 43 inches, there will be many waters where such a fish goes 30lb. What exactly makes for this huge difference in weight at a given length? Inside a pike it is not as one might suspect a complex array of vital organs. Though everything vital for life will usually be where it's supposed to be, the main organs of a pike have little bearing on the weight of the fish. The liver, stomach and intestines are purely functional and do little to bulk out the weight of a pike. What does pile the weight on is an increase in thickness across the back. Trout water pike invariably appear to be very broad across the back the depth or fatness of these fish is usually caused by heavy fat deposits, which are carried around the gut. Many fish deposit fat around the gut and on the odd occasion I have had to dissect a pike it was clear that pike are no exception. Fat is a food reserve which all animals use to tide them over during periods of food shortage. Trout water pike are probably so well fed that fat reserves are never needed. These pike are in effect obese and this may have a bearing on the longevity of individual fish.

In the case of female fish, spawn obviously has a bearing on the weight it attains. Spawn production does not get under way until the autumn, though the ovaries are always present. I have followed weight changes of quite a few pike from the period September (before the ovaries develop) to the end of February. (I have not managed to catch any known fish during March). Weight changes of 21 to 28lb can be attributed mainly to spawn and though this is exceptional it shows how significant spawn can be when looking at the maximum weight of a pike. When that spawn is shed, the pike obviously drops to its minimum weight. It is rare to catch pike immediately after spawning, though sometimes on waters such as Loch Lomond where fishing pressure around the spawning areas is intense, it does happen. A favorite remark on landing a 28 pounder in April is " It would have weighed 30lb before it spawned" Well this might well be true, however as each week follows spawning you have to realise that a pike is now growing and also replacing lost weight. I do not believe the 38-08 I had from Lough Mask in early May would have weighed significantly more if caught in March. There's no way to tell anyway because it is rare to catch these fish just before they spawn and presumably at peak weight.

Another influence on the weight of a pike is what it has just eaten. A thirty-pound pike can easily eat a 5lb fish. If you catch that pike just after the meal you have a 35lb pike! Unfortunately the probability of catching it after such a big meal is low. Catching it when the meal is half digested is much more likely, but then you are down to 32-08. If you are like me you specialize in catching other peoples 30lb pike after they have not fed for a week. They then weigh 29-08! Dick Walker was seldom right when it came to commenting on pike, but one of his remarks about angling in general referred to the influence a few ounces of "shit" could have on the weight of a fish. Crude, but very true.Fluctuating weights are a fact of life when fishing for any species, which are subject to recapture. I caught a 32-14 pike a few years ago which later in the season reached 35lb plus. Did I cry about it? Don't bother to ask daft questions!

CHAPTER 2
THE TACKLE

In carp fishing we have seen the evolution of a new creature. They call them "Tackle Tarts." Personally I cannot see the connection between fishing tackle and pastry confectioneries, but I suppose it takes all sorts. The TT is the angler who spends a lot of time acquiring the latest fishing tackle, polishing it and making sure that everything is just right. There is nothing wrong with taking pride in your tackle and keeping it clean and well maintained. I however find that the desire to actually use the tackle means that I do not get time to keep it spotless! Neglect is probably my middle name and it always comes as a great relief when I manage to find the time to do some simple tidying. I prefer my rods neatly hung up in the garage rather than propped up all over the place. If I had to model my garage on anyone's it would have to be Pete Haywood's because of the immaculate red floor. For sheer number of boxes full of useful tackle it would have to be Mick Brown's. You can always spot the people with the really good jobs, they have tidy garages!

Like many of the better known anglers I have a sponsorship deal or two. I've been with Daiwa for over 15 years, worked with Partridge for a similar length of time and advise Middy on pike tackle. I have a minor association with Garmin sonar and GPS and get free Polaris floats! There that has got the sponsorship out of the way. Those of us who have sponsorship deals have to try and promote the company's products. The degree of effort that goes into this depends on who you work for. You do see quite a bit of deliberate product placement in the fishing weeklies in particular, however those consultants who get paid the most also have to give their sponsors a return. My sponsors are happy with my name on the rods and some packaging, plus the hats with the company logo on. When I mention specific items of tackle it is up to you the reader to decide whether I am being sincere or not!

Rods have changed a lot since I started pike fishing. As luck would have it in 1966 I acquired an Anon Shaw Leger Pike rod. I say, as luck would have it because it was the best 5 guineas work of strawberry picking money that I ever spent. That rod is retired and sits in my loft. It was a surprisingly good 9ft glass fibre rod that was capable of casting a half mackerel 60 yards with ease. That was a great help to me in my formative years as a pike angler. I may not have had much idea as to what I was doing, but at least the rod wasn't a handicap. Meeting other anglers on the Relief Channel in the late sixties and early seventies showed me that though my humble rod could manage most aspects of pike fishing a longer rod would be better. Also everyone fished with more than one rod so I needed another. It is hard to remember the exact progression at the time, but I know I had a Tag Barnes rod of 10 foot and I eventually won a Hardy's MkIV carp rod. All were on the light side and I still lacked a rod, which could handle big baits. I even borrowed someone's light beach rod! I eventually obtained an Auger Sabre Carp rod, which was quite a powerful rod. None of my rods however were quite good enough. I cast envious eyes on people like Bill Chillingworth and Barrie Rickards. They were using 2¾lb Olivers rods and some of them were 11ft long! I eventually bought a slow action 11ft 2¾, which was ideal for casting half mackerel and followed this with a fast taper version for casting smaller, baits and big leads. We were beginning to be influenced by events at Abberton even though most of us would never see the place. Glass fibre rods seemed wonderful in those days and I'm sure that if carbon fibre rods had not been invented we would still be fishing quite happily with glass rods. Still progress was on its way and needless to say I wasn't changing whatever happened. Then in the early eighties Andy Barker brought out a range of fishing tackle and amongst this gear was two rods. Both of carbon composite they had my name on them and both were improvements on the glass rods that had come before. After that I worked with Daiwa and today we have a multipurpose pike rod, the Dictator that is 3lb test and 12ft long. Will it catch you any more pike? Probably not, but it is nice to use, casts well, can handle a wide range of bait sizes and does not splinter into a million shards of carbon if you only look at it! There are other makes of rod that will do a similar job, but I would always be careful to make sure they are made out of quality carbon. I've seen some good looking "carbon" rods which ought to be brilliant for less than thirty pounds, but their durability has to be suspect.

Very few through action rods are made these days. The Dictator has most of its action in the tip, which is something I might not have approved of once for a general-purpose pike rod. Yet it works fine and I use mine for my zander fishing, Canadian carping and my pike fishing boat or bank. Recently there has been a trend for some anglers to use shorter rods for boat fishing. The reasoning being that you do not need to cast vast distances from a boat and long rods tend to get in the way more. I'm not sure I agree with this reasoning. I certainly like to do a long chuck when I'm fishing on the broads and a longer rod is a definite advantage when you are moored up against a reed bed. My rods when they are on boat rests are out of the boat most of the time and when folded 5ft against 6ft is not much of a difference. Why buy an extra 3 or 4 rods just for boat fishing? Having said that one of my customers who is rather particular about his tackle uses the Daiwa boat catfish rods, which are shorter than conventional pike rods. So some pike anglers do find the shorter rods useful. Just as an aside, any two-piece pike rod should when folded end up as two equal sections. This applies when you are keeping everything made up, reels, hooks, floats and traces in place. A rod that folds into equal sections has to have the rings positioned correctly. Then when you wish to carry your rods you do not have to put up with one section being longer than the other. I've not seen a carp rod ringed up like this for ages and assume all carp anglers use rod holdalls! For lure fishing I use mainly the more powerful of the Daiwa jerkbait rods. This is a nice rod, which does the job without being over gunned. Some jerkbait rods are so stiff you could reasonably expect to grow beans up them. Tip stiffness is important in a jerkbait rod for giving action to the lure and also as a point of strong resistance for hooking the pike when it hits the lure. However a rod can be too stiff! Rods designed for muskie fishing with 8oz lures are not required for most of our pike fishing.

A good reel is of course essential. I've used my share of good and bad ones. My first reels were Intrepids made by a company called K.P.Morrit. They were British made and

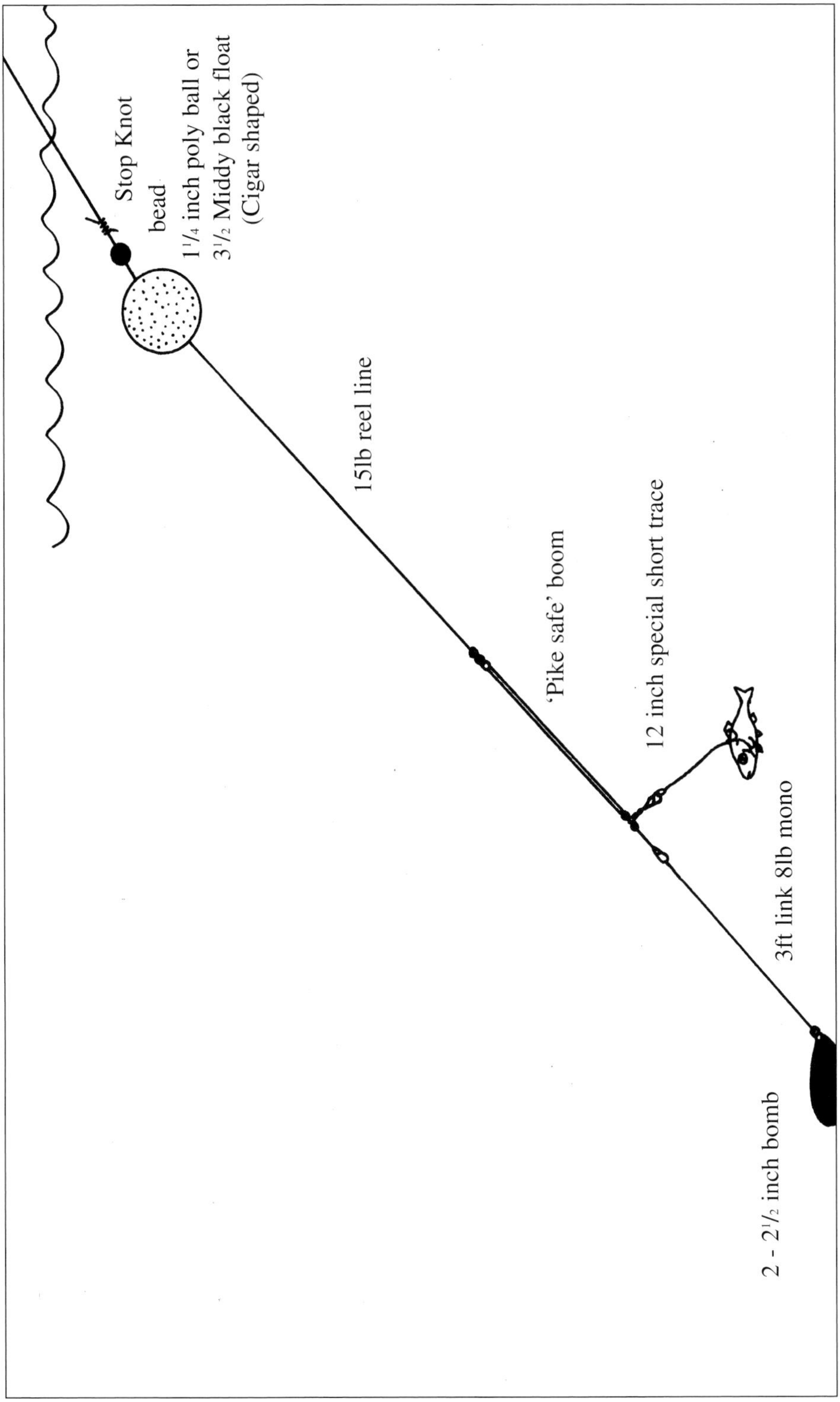

Stop Knot

bead

1¼ inch poly ball or
3½ Middy black float
(Cigar shaped)

15lb reel line

'Pike safe' boom

12 inch special short trace

3ft link 8lb mono

2 - 2½ inch bomb

Sunken Float Paternoster

fairly reliable as long as you didn't have the top of the range Elite. My father passed his on to me, but because it has nylon gears it was prone to the gears slipping when playing a heavy fish. I added a Daiwa fixed spool reel to my collection in about 1968 for writing a letter to the Anglers Mail. It was a comparatively cheap reel (value about 5 pounds), but it was well made and had a deep spool with a decent line lay. Reels came and went after that including one of the first reels with a stern rag the Abu 444A. Eventually Mitchell 300s and 410s were acquired s well as a couple of Cardinals, one a 54, the other a 55. The 55 had an interesting fault, the bale arm snapped over on the cast! Bait runner reels are comparatively new, but before them we used to slacken off the rear drag of the reel when fishing rivers or from a boat. The advantage of the bait runner type reel is that you can in effect engage a slack clutch instantly. Shimnano were first to have a bait runner reel on the market with a reel that was really designed for predator fishing in warmer countries than ours. They were good reels and those that followed had good line lays. Then things got silly with reels having twin handles, a rather pointless exercise! Daiwa entered the market a bit later with their "Bite n run" reel. This had the free spool lever the right way around (i.e. when up the reel is in free spool.). I'm still using some of the original models, which came out about 10 years ago. The free spool function is a definite advantage for pike fishing. You can use it for bite indication when boat fishing. If you are river fishing you can float leger a bait on the bite n run with the rod tip well up. When trolling a pike can take line. I certainly would not be without this type of reel. Whichever make of reel you choose you should make sure that the knob on the reel handle is a nice big one. You'd be amazed how difficult it is to hold a small one with frozen fingers.

While the standard bite' n run type of reel is a good casting tool, there are reels, which can add yards to your cast. Several companies sell really big spooled casting reels. These have a huge tapered spool; will take enough line to go around Loch Lomond twice (OK I exaggerate!) You can also get them as bait runners. I use the long cast reels for some of my bank fishing and if I ever have a major requirement for long casting from the bank the reels are waiting there ready to be used. Multiplier reels are essential for lure fishing and many anglers continue to use the Abu Ambassador. Daiwa do a couple of nice left hand wind reels. Note that if you are right handed you need left-handed reels! (And vice-versa). The reason for this is the strongest hand should hold the rod. If you are right handed your strongest arm will be your right. Until my left-handed reel arrived I was fishing with a right-handed reel and changing hands on each cast. It seemed OK then, but now I could never go back to that approach.

A few of our most experienced pike anglers use multiplier reels for their general pike fishing. It should be noted that they almost exclusively fish from boats. The ratchet mechanism of the Ambassador reels produces a "You cannot ignore it" sound much louder than any of the bite n runs. Personally because I do a lot of bank fishing I feel the fixed spool reel offers me a casting advantage when using smaller baits so the multiplier option is not for me.

Possibly the most important item of fishing tackle is your line. When I first started pike

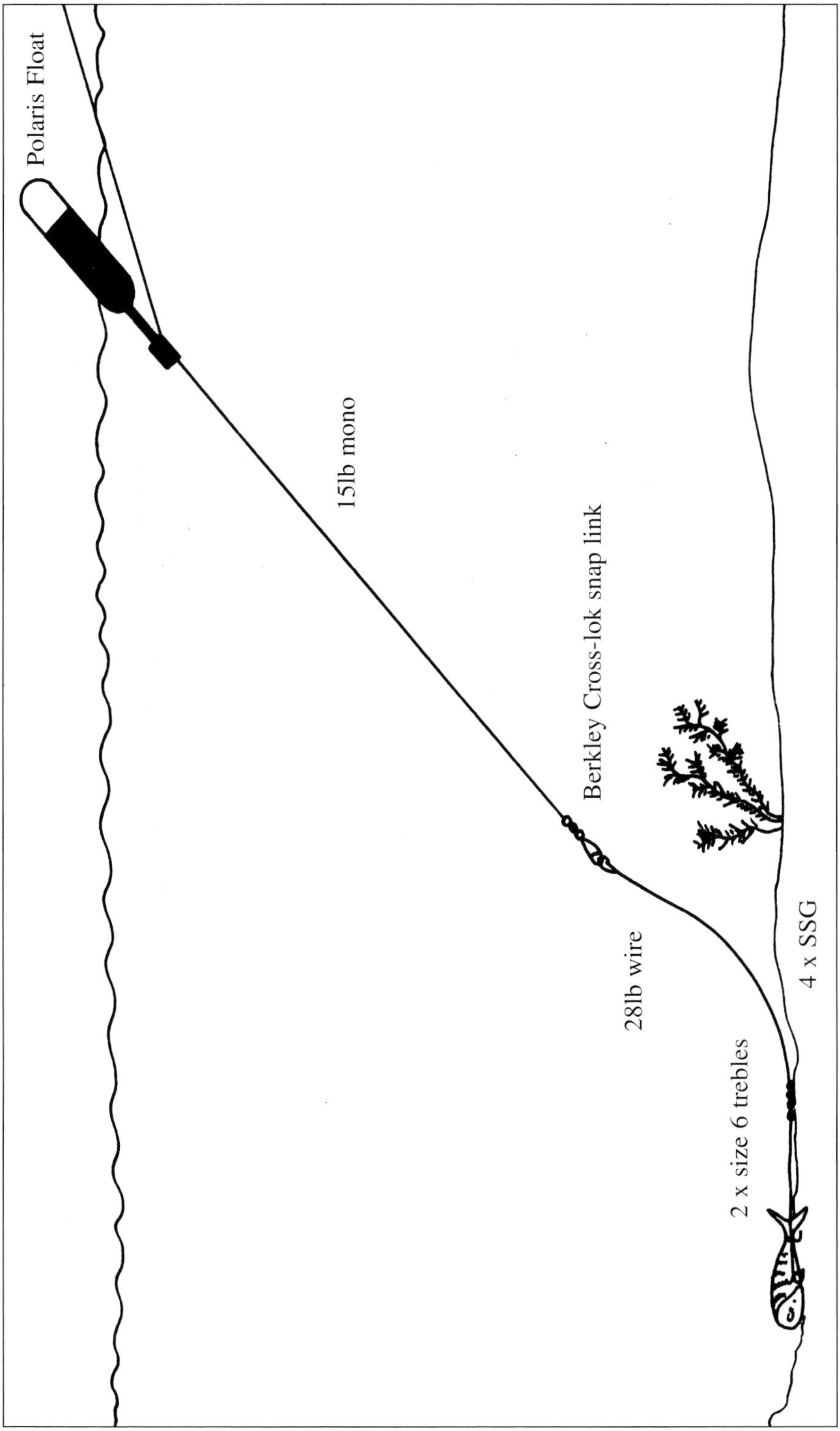

Polaris Float

15lb mono

Berkley Cross-lok snap link

28lb wire

2 x size 6 trebles

4 x SSG

Polaris Float Ledger

fishing we used bulk pools of 9lb Gantel line. As time has gone by the breaking strain of the line has increased simply because pike anglers in general have accepted that lost fish may be dead fish. Today as far as monos are concerned I used Daiwa Sensor. This is a cheap reliable line available on spools of around 900 metres for around 7 pounds. At that price you really can afford to change your line regularly. Sensor is not one of your ultra fine lines, but serves me well for 90% of my pike fishing. If you were into long casting you would have once considered some of the low diameter lines that are now available. Though I have used them I always worry about the abrasion resistance of a thin line. Because we have a whole host of modern braids available now the day of the ultra thin nylon mono has now probably passed. Braid offers no stretch and a lower diameter for any given breaking strain. It is a bit more temperamental to use and you should never over fill a fixed spool reel unless you want trouble!

Daiwa imported some multicolored braid from Japan and I've been using this for about 5 years now. It is marked off in 10m lengths, each ten metres being a different colour. It is quite useful for trolling. Unfortunately it is not available in the UK, but Newtech Power Cable can be bought and it is very similar. I've had no trouble with either for lure fishing and have even used the 30kg braid on my float trolling or free-swimming float rig. For lighter work Shakespeare Bionic Dynacord in 52lb gives you the diameter of 15lb line for a 52lb breaking strain. I've used Spiderwire fushion for paternostered live-bait work in 30lb strain and you certainly get extra distance with the finer line. Fraying of the fused coat does occur so you do have to discard a length every so often. Life is too short to have tried all the other braids, but I will be trying out a few others as time goes by. The only reason one should consider using braid is because of improved casting and greater strength for a given diameter. The lack of stretch is only really of marginal use because we do not strike home the hooks when live or deadbaiting. The hooks are pulled home because the angler applies maximum pressure as the pike tries to eject the bait. The hooks go home under direct tension on a non-stretch braid or via an elastic band effect on a stretched mono. I've noticed no difference in hooking efficiency using braid or mono.

Trace wire is also a very important link in a pike anglers tackle. There are dozens of different type of wire available and though I've tried a few of them, I am not inclined to experiment for the sake of it when the wires I use now have proven to be satisfactory. When I first started pike fishing we didn't have much choice, it was single strand alastacum, which worked after a fashion though once kinked was a bit of a pike deathtrap. Then braided alastacum arrived and it served us well for a number of years. I think it was 15lb-breaking strain and because it was a soft wire it was easily straightened if it became a bit wrinkled. Its only snag was its limited breaking strain. In the late seventies the trolling wires such as Berkley steelstrand became available. These were stiffer, but of a higher breaking strain. They caught a lot of pike in the 30lb breaking strain, but were not that easy for a hardened alastacum user to get used to. You had to learn to twist the wire or use crimps. I myself have never been a user of crimps, preferring to use my forceps to twist the wire. I'll describe making a trace at the end of this section. We have also seen various wire substitutes none of which to my mind have been worth taking a chance with. Wire is the only material that I have come across which is consistently proof against a pikes teeth. A pikes teeth do not cut through wire on a direct cut, the effect is the same as pulling a piece of line over a saw blade. It takes a couple of pulls back and forward to cut the line, but sooner or later cut it does.

Kevlar coated wires do have a use, but there are good ones and bad ones. Some of the ones I have used are very supple, in fact so supple that livebaits tangle them up and tangles occur on the cast with deadbaits. Now we need these problems like the proverbial hole in the head. I've used Middy Tech Core, which was first introduced to me under another brand name by Duncan Kay. I've used it for about 15 years and I find it very useful for livebaiting. It is now available in 28lb breaking strain, but for many years 20lb or 15lb was it. I make traces up exactly the same as with any other wire, except that one end will have a loop rather than a swivel. The swivel is not really required because I use a Berkley cross-lok to attach to the line. The Tec Core does not tend to kink because the coating of Kevlar helps stop the wire from getting itself into knots. During use the Kevlar coating does tend to get a shredding from the pike's teeth, but the trace seldom has to be discarded because of any failure in it's strength, rather because it looks terrible.

For my deadbaiting work I go for an indestructible wire. I do not go for fine or super supple wires because they lack the durability of the Middy 28lb seven strand (Drennan does a similar wire). The Middy wire is fairly thick and it is quite stiff, it is black in colour. During one week in I think 1999 I caught 16 double figure pike on one trace. I only had to discard that trace because hooks and pike were stuck in the landing net! When you are catching pike one after another (yes it does happen!) the last thing you want to do is change the trace every fish. What you want to do is catch the next one, the big might be next. The secret of making any trace by twisting is to obey a couple of simple rules. First cut about 2 feet of wire. Make a loop and push through the eye of the treble then pull loop over the hook. Pull tight and then grip the loose end of the wire with forceps. The twisting bit takes a bit of a knack, but all you do is spin the forceps around an around so you get a neat twist. Cut off the loose end and then slide your

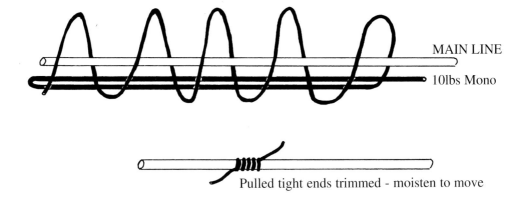

MAIN LINE

10lbs Mono

Pulled tight ends trimmed - moisten to move

Sliding Float Knot

25

second treble onto the trace. This can be fixed by twisting the wire around the hook. For those who must have a swivel on the end of the trace, make another loop, push through swivel and pull over it and then twist again. I prefer to make a simple loop knot and then twist. The twists are best covered with silicon tubing to avoid any loose ends that may cause tangles. One little mean dodge I employ is to make a trace of 3 feet in length. The bit that gets damaged is always near the hooks, so to remake the trace all you do is cut off the offending 6 inches and fix the hooks as specified before. Mean, but effective!

Hook choice is always a personal one. Years ago when I was talking to Partridge of Redditch I asked to see their range of trebles. One of the models was a salmon treble; I think the name on the packet was Jock Wilson. Well whoever Jock Wilson was he had good taste in treble hooks! These hooks were made out of a heavier gauge of wire compared to other trebles and because of this were incredibly strong. Having straightened a few trebles in my time I was impressed. Eventually my name ended up on the packet and I've been using them for at least ten years. Apart from not bending you can also stick them straight into frozen baits without the hooks snapping. They do not come in a semi barbless form, but that is very quickly rectified with the use of forceps. I crush the barbs down on two of the three hooks. I generally use sizes six to twos, eights being more suitable for zander fishing with small baits. I have realized over the years that you can be much more confident about a quick strike using larger hooks. That does not mean going straight to size twos! You use the smallest treble you can use with effective hooking.

There are quite a few small bits and pieces we all use to complete our pike rigs. I use Berkley Cross-Loks for trace attachment and cheap Mustad snap links for running legers. Bombs are as cheap as possible, sometimes home made if someone else is willing to make them! Floats are Polaris self-locking floats, used for most of my deadbaiting and sunken paternostering is carried out using some slim black balsa floats Middy has produced for a number of years. Any nice big "shark" float that will support 1 to 2 ounces does the trick for float trolling and free-swimming livebaits. If I need a drifter I use a Middy drifter. In the old days drifter floats were fished with a detachable tip ring so that you could wind them in easily. Today they have a stem with a float attached. This keeps the line on the surface and means that the float is in effect fished end ring only so the retrieve is quite straightforward. A spool of 8lb mono serves as paternoster link material. Beads are small bore from I cannot remember where, but they should be big enough to not pass through the hole in your float and the hole should be small enough to stop a knot made from 12lb mono.

Rod rests are preferably stainless yet they are all cursed with one problem, the screw which controls the height of the adjustable type always falls off! I choose stainless because the thin diameter ones are the only rod rests I have used which can be used effectively on big lakes with stony shores. For back rod rests there is only one choice, the John Roberts butt grip. Such a simple piece of kit yet so good! The soft rubber grips the rod allowing rods to be fished at all sorts of interesting angles and of course they stop the wind blowing the rods out of the rests. Because I use Delkim TXi's as bite indication I do not need front rests. The Delkims are expensive, but you do get a remote system for the price, which is a big advantage for night fishing, and wave washed shorelines where many buzzers are drowned out. They are also great for telling you, that you have a run (in your top pocket) without everyone else hearing what's going on. It is not often that it matters, but there are some waters where the competition is intense and it does not pay to needlessly identify a good swim. The Delkim also has a considerable degree of sensitivity adjustment. This enables the angler to adjust them to suit particular conditions and techniques. They work best on a tight line, something that is not always easy to manage when float legering. I personally am prepared to trade a few stray bleeps for information on how my bait is working, i.e. the bait will set the alarm off from time to time. You also tend to get a pre warning of a run when float or straight legering. The chances of a pike swallowing bait when using Delkims is reduced which must be good news for the pike.

If you are not up to spending on a set of Delkims then Ghettoblasters are the best economy drop offs. They use the same cam system that was the basis of the original ET Backbiter. The Ghettoblaster has a simple baffle type volume control which is less prone to go wrong than rheostat controlled volume control.

When using a Delkim type head indicator you need a drop off bobbin. This is because pike sometimes give slack line runs when they run towards the bank. A drop off bobbin is something we used to have to make for ourselves and the old favourite was a red painted $1^1/_2$ inch poly ball, a Gardner line clip a metal rod and a terry clip. Lots of different companies make them these days. I use a Middy one and though they have additional weight I generally double this to make the bobbin drop back more readily. The better drop offs have adjustable clips, which enables the angler to counter various flow or wind conditions. One of the funniest things I came across was years ago on Lough Corrib when I was running one of my earliest guided trips. Duncan Pritchard and his nephew Ben were fishing from an island with a castle. The castle was neither here nor there, but the number of false alarms the pair were getting was worrying me. On investigation I found that both of them were clipping their bobbins up with the line held by the very end of the clip, not exactly how it was designed to work properly. Duncan is still embarrassed when I mention this to him over ten years later. These drop offs work best fished with the bail arm of the reel open. I see so many people fishing using them with the baitrunner that I wonder if they have given real thought to what they are doing. You should always where you can use an open bale arm to allow a pike to take line unimpeded. Using the baitrunner when you do not have to causes more resistance than needed and also kinks the line more than necessary. The resistance is probably of little importance in most circumstances, though when fishing weedy water the resistance from the baitrunner plus the weed can spook the pike. You'll know when this happens because you will get a storming run followed by the pike leaping out of the water usually throwing the bait out as it leaps! At least using an open bale arm you will still have a fairly quick run, but you'll usually get to the rod in time to strike before the pike panics.

To survive the experience of being on the bank you'll need a few more bits of gear. I have a plain JRC chair that has lasted now for over 10 years. From a manufacturers point of view this always seems a bad move. After all in an ideal world the chair should wear out after 4 years encouraging the owner to buy another, thus keeping all chair makers in business. Still it's good news for me! I do not generally night fish for pike these days and if I do it is usually with the campervan. I do have a JRC defender bed chair and a Kevin Nash Titan bivvy that has served me well for the odd carp and zander trip. However this sort of fishing, i.e. the sit and wait approach is not really what pike fishing is about. Half a day in one swim is usually my absolute limit. I carry my rods in one hand, my chair in the other. I can carry a small livebait bucket with the same hand I use for the chair. An Umbrella, 42ins triangular landing net, bank sticks and rod rests are all carried in a quiver type holdall. A 50 inch umbrella is vital for winter fishing in the fens though it is quite heavy. I sometimes settle for a 45-inch model to lighten the load.

I carry all the bits and pieces in a Daiwa rucksack, which has such comfortable straps that it is easy to walk good distances. In the rucksack is a Fox box with all the small bits of terminal tackle and another cheaper box with floats and the like. I still have an original ET weigh sling that lives in one of the outside pockets. Reuben Heaton 60lb scales live in another pocket, with a compact pair of Nikon binoculars tucked in yet another pocket. I carry two cameras a standard Canon SLR and an Olympus with an infrared remote control. I did have a mini tripod, but I seem to have lost it somewhere. So for the moment I have resorted to keeping a full size tripod in the van and going back for it. I must buy another mini tripod as soon as possible, they really are useful. I usually balance it on top of the freezer box, which in turn stands on the livebait bucket! Talking of the freezer box, forget cool bags and the like, they are useless compared with the small Coleman cool box. I get enough deadbaits in mine for a day along with a freezer block. This goes inside the rucksack. A few lures usually lurk in another pocket and a Gardner rig bin has ready-made traces in it. If I need to take more lures I have a cheap flat lure box which I do not have enough arms to carry. This is usually carried in the boat or the van. I'm not a fan of the really big lure boxes simply because so far I've never felt the need to take the whole shop with me. Everyone has or should have a good quality pair of long straight forceps. Mine were found when we moved the Tackle Shop to it's new building about 12 years ago. They are proper heavy-duty forceps, not like some of the ones you get these days. When I'm boat fishing I carry all my tackle in one of those Daiwa seat boxes. OK so they are standard gear for match anglers, but that should not put any of us off. Their big advantage is that they are waterproof and they provide a nice extra seat in boats with a remarkable lack of seats! I'll deal with boat fishing itself a little later as it is a specialized subject all of it's own.

Pike anglers cloths have improved a lot over the years. I dare not mention what I used to wear except that an army surplus shop wouldn't have been prepared to sell them. I personally do not suffer from a cold body. I think this is related to the blubber I have the misfortune to carry around with me. I do however suffer from cold feet and cold hands. So far I've never found a complete answer to this problem. Any make of moon boot such as the SkeeTex ones will keep my feet warm in most situations. Unfortunately when boat fishing in very cold weather I still suffer from cold feet. My only solution is to go to shore and run up and down. Roll on the day when electrically heated boots are readily available. You get them if you go to the moon and they are probably available to deep-sea divers as well. Leggings present me with constant problems because I invariably rip a hole in the crutch!   The Goretex outfit I have at the moment is the most waterproof outfit I've had so far, but when you are heading into the wind in a boat and spray is covering you, water seems to find a way inside any outfit unless you are really well wrapped up. In the last year I have discovered what useful things neoprene chest waders are. Not only are they warm, but also they are obviously waterproof. With neoprene socks they keep your feet warm and also ensure you can walk long distances in them. This is the one snag with moon boots; they tend to be very uncomfortable to walk long distances in. If you wear neoprene's all the time like me you cannot expect them to last for more than a year, but at about 60 pounds I think they are well worth paying this for once a year. As an under garment I have one of those one-piece fleece lined suits which is something I end up wearing all through the winter. I am not prepared to make any comments about any special underwear I might wear...

CHAPTER 3
BOAT FISHING

This is the one aspect of pike fishing, which is certain to reduce the bank balance without a doubt. There is no real upper limit as to the amount of money you can spend. If you wish to import one of those flash American aluminum boats from the States, equip it with a good sized engine and a state of the art trailer, 11,000 pounds might just about cover it! However for those who wish to start at the beginning… First how many boats have I got? Well this is a sore point with the wife who cannot understand why I have so many, but honestly there is a reasonable explanation. Smallest is an 8 foot inflatable. This does not get used much for pike fishing though I have landed pike to 21 pounds while using it. I've often quipped that when you get a big pike in the boat I have to get out. It actually gets used more for carp fishing these days, but if I had a need to row baits out on say a gravel pit I would have a boat I, which was easily transportable. The next boat is an 8ft Sniper, which is easily roof, topped and a boat I have used a lot on the Trent. It is a good boat for getting in and out of situations where there are absolutely no launching facilities. It is a one-man boat and with a 4hp engine it wallows along so it is not a boat for speed. Snipers are made from a thin plastic coating over a foam inside. While fairly strong they will not tolerate abuse. The plastic is easily cracked and do not try pulling them out of a river with your car! I pulled the front off mine! My 8 ft Sniper is at present serving as a workboat on the carp lake.

Trolling Outfit 1988 - little changed today
- Minn Kota Electric Motor, sonar, aerator

A couple of years ago Nige Williams owed me a couple of hundred pounds and happened to mention he had a 10 foot Sniper for sale. We did the swap, his boat for the money owed. Now I've only used the boat a couple of times so far, but I'm sure it will be useful. With a 5hp motor it planes and will do 13mph, which is fairly quick. Alastair Rawlings puts a 15hp Honda on the back of his and it goes like the wind. Whether the boat implodes one day is another issue! The 10-foot Sniper can still be handled by one person and has more space. It can be roof topped. You could fish two people in it, but you'd have to be really good friends! If you are going for a boat that is easy to get in and out of the water you might opt for a 12ft aluminum boat. I've never owned one, but you do get a larger boat for the same weight as a smaller glass boat. This makes fishing two in a boat a lot easier. About 15 years ago I was passing a boat yard in Mountsorrel and saw an Orkney Spinner for sale. It was priced at 275 pounds. I quickly returned with the trailer. It was a good buy because I still have it. I've used it on Loch Awe, the broads and Lough Corrib. At 13 foot it is just about big enough to use on a big water. Two people can fish from it easily and I can launch and recover it without a launching ramp single-handed. Mind you it needs a bit of traction from the van to get it out at Horsey Mill on Horsey Mere. I've since bought a folding cuddy for it, which makes for very comfortable fishing on wet and windy days. Call me soft, but I definitely appreciate protection when boat fishing. My Spinner has a straight transom, which means that it needs a long shaft engine, but the advantage with a straight transom is that you can mount an electric motor next to the petrol engine. Because it is a displacement hull there is virtually no way you can make it plane and go fast. I use a 5 or a 15hp engine on it, and with either it is a pedestrian rate of progress. Today a Spinner plus a good trailer will cost you well over 1000 pounds so buying secondhand is worth giving serious consideration. Things to look for when buying secondhand start with the trailer. These days any reasonably new Spinner will be on a galvanized trailer. Make sure everything works including the winch, jockey wheel, and roller adjustment nuts. Mudguards should be in good condition. As far as the boat itself is concerned ensure that the rubbing strip is intact. Watch out for poor repair jobs. The winching ring should be well attached and the rowlocks mountings solid. How much you pay for a secondhand boat depends on how many of the above items are in good condition.

Another of my boats is a bit of an embarrassment! It was the first boat with a cabin I purchased. It was bought from someone on Lough Mask. It was for a while ideal for what I wanted, a boat with a cabin so I could static deadbait in the depths of winter. I also needed to have my own mini fleet of boats so that I could bring small groups of anglers to Mask and Corrib. I felt at the time that boats with cabins were a selling point because in winter though not as cold as the UK it could still get pretty chilly. Unfortunately this boat was not really designed for big water fishing. It had no rubbing strip on the keel and the hull was very thin. The boat was really a day boat for trips out on a canal or the Norfolk Broads. Putting a 15hp engine on the back and progress was slow to say the least. I tried a 30hp engine and with the weight forward it planed. However the back of the boat had a nasty look about it! It was exhilarating motoring at about 20mph, but probably totally unsafe. Despite this for a couple of years I went tearing around on Lough Mask in an orange boat supposedly called Seaspray, but soon renamed by all who saw her as Tango!

I was then offered another boat with a cabin, a 16ft Bonwitcho. I added that to my fleet, but not before some nasty experiences. It was May and Nige Williams, Gary Banks, Kev Shore, Neil Hodgetts and Duncan Pritchard had come on my last trip of the spring. Unfortunately it was to prove to be a disaster. We had gale force winds almost all the week and Nige's Isuzu conked out costing 500 pounds to mend. We had managed to get out early in the week and decided to head again for upper Mask from Maamtrasna. Now upper Mask is a good hours run from our base with 15hp engines. Before we set out I asked Gary Banks how much fuel he had. He had a full tank so there would be no problem getting back. Unfortunately and unknown to me Gary rather than having the standard 20 litre tank had a horrible little 10 litre effort. Duncan and I returned early because the weather didn't look too clever. We decided to pull the boat well up onto the shore, a good 10 yards from the water's edge. Sure enough a gale was blowing up. Meanwhile on Upper Mask Gary and Nige in two separate boats were working their way back. The problem with Upper Mask and the main lake is that they tend to have their own microclimate. You can be in Upper Mask and the weather seems a bit windy, but not too bad. Come through the Ferry Bridge and if the wind is from the North or North East then all hell let's loose. Getting back to Maamtrasna can be a very hairy experience. Well Nige and Gary were about to get a taste of a hairy experience! Gary with his small fuel tank ran out of petrol right in the middle of the worst bit. In Anglers Mail the story said 12-foot waves, but because I wasn't there I'm not in the position to argue about it. Whatever the state of the waves Nige had to take them under tow and affect a rescue. They arrived back OK, but suitably chastened. It taught me a lesson when dealing with paying customers. Never make assumptions and always check the fuel yourself. The next day when we went to check Tango she had been moved about 20 yards along the bank. Because I had left the back anchor inside the boat it had given the inside of the boat a right pounding. The windows were almost knocked out and there was a crack in the roof and a hole in the floor. Rolling over had removed the navigation lights. All in all the boat had been messed up and it took some time to do the basic repairs. When you leave a boat on the shore or if you are trailering it never leave heavy weights such as anchors inside. The Irish roads will soon see the heavy weight trying to work is way through the bottom of your boat. If you decide to trailer with the engine on make sure the engine is well attached. I had an engine leap into the boat once and break a rod! Yes it was Tango again!

The purchase of the Bonwitcho from Gary Banks was not entirely straightforward. The cabin was not attached very well… We had pulled it up at the Ferry Bridge and put it on the trailer. I pulled the trailer out while we sorted the next boat. The boat was facing stern to the wind when there was a sudden gust. The cabin was torn off the boat and went about 25 feet up in the air, blew horizontally another 20 yards before realizing that it was of a poor aerodynamic design dropping like a brick the other side of the bridge. I was horrified because it could have dropped on a passing car or even decapitated someone. I also thought I had lost it in Mask. Luckily it was stuck in some trees and we fetched it with no obvious signs of damage. The boat disasters did not end there, but rather than go through all of them here quickly are two of them! I had bought a tiller extension so I could get a better view as I was motoring with the Bonwitcho and the 30hp motor. I was motoring into Maamtrasna bay at full speed, but noticed that the tiller seemed under a lot of strain. I slowed down to half throttle as a precaution. Suddenly the tiller extension broke; the engine lurched to the right. I was thrown into the bottom of the boat, but luckily the engine throttle was not locked so the engine returned to idle. I gathered myself together and continued back to base again suitably chastened! The least lethal, but funniest (and most expensive) was on Lough Allen a few years ago. Now I know the Lough like the back of my hand and we were motoring back with the 30 from the North to O'Dwyers. The Lough was quite low so near the end of our journey I slowed down. All of a sudden there was a loud bang and then we carried on as if nothing had happened. When I tilted the engine on dry land there was a huge bite out of one of the blades of the prop. Either the pike were very hungry or I'd hit a rock. It cost sixty pounds to repair.

That readers covers my fleet of boats except to say that the Bonwitcho is the fastest boat I have, but it sits very low in the water and the cabin is also very low. This means that you can only really sit inside the cabin on a low chair or an unhooking matt. If and when I buy a boat to replace Tango (which will probably be given a Viking funeral) I'll go for a 16 to 17ft boat with a non-displacement hull. I shall have my 30hp Mariner converted to remote operation so I can steer from the cabin of the boat. I will also have one of those break back trailers, which means I'll be able to recover from poor ramps. It will also have a cabin you can sit in comfortably. At the moment I need to save up about 6000 pounds, so please everyone buy this book (twice!).

One basic good piece of advice, do tie your engine to the boat with either a chain or strong piece of rope. When you do hit something at speed the engine will be less inclined to jump over the side. It has never happened to me, but I know a man who has… Big engines should be bolted to the back of the boat, that way they cannot come off. My multitude of boats work for their living, but they also give me a lot of flexibility. Having the best boat in the world is no use unless you can launch it. In certain situations it is better to rough it on a 10 foot boat because at least with one this size you can get it on the water without having to employ a crane! Having said that a really good boat is a joy to use and one day I hope to be sufficiently wealthy and organized to own one myself. Most of what I have written above would amuse your average Canadian or US boat angler. For a start boat ownership amongst anglers in these countries is much greater than here. The size of their fisheries gives them little choice. With even a small water fifty miles long you are not going to get very far bank fishing. The size of these waters means that boats have to be seaworthy and the distances involved require big engines. I've fished on some big Canadian waters quite a few times and seen how the locals carry out their boating activities. For example on Last Mountain Lake in Saskatchewan Robert Shulz runs a guiding service. His hire boats have 40 hp engines! His own boat is a 19ft aluminum job fitted with a 125hp Yamaha outboard. This combo will with two up go at an amazing 50mph! Of course if it is rough or fully loaded speed is reduced, but the boat has the capability of high speed making transit times on big lakes bearable. Robert's boat has a bow mounted Minn Kota electric. This is not the type of motor we use. This one has remote control and an autopilot. For trolling lures for long periods there is an auxiliary petrol motor on the

FLOATING TROLLING

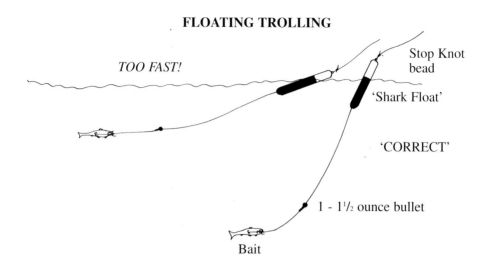

TOO FAST!

Stop Knot
bead

'Shark Float'

'CORRECT'

1 - 1½ ounce bullet

Bait

SLOW TROLLING

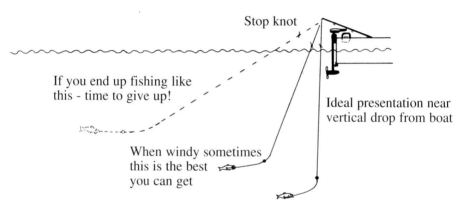

Stop knot

If you end up fishing like
this - time to give up!

Ideal presentation near
vertical drop from boat

When windy sometimes
this is the best
you can get

FRONT ANCHORING - Boat with cabin

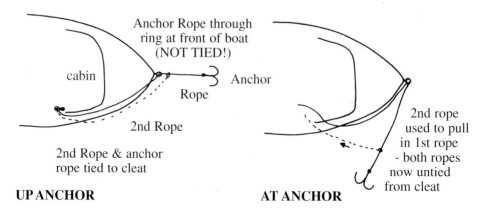

Anchor Rope through
ring at front of boat
(NOT TIED!)

cabin

Anchor

Rope

2nd Rope

2nd Rope & anchor
rope tied to cleat

2nd rope
used to pull
in 1st rope
- both ropes
now untied
from cleat

UP ANCHOR

AT ANCHOR

back, which also serves, as back up should the main engine fail. You do not row these boats! Inside the boat is a live well where you can allow your catch to recover. There are various stowage compartments and padded adjustable seats. You sit behind a windscreen and it's rather like being in an open top sports car. The boat has it's own inbuilt battery power and the sonar unit is permanently mounted in the boat. To recharge the batteries Robert plugs in to a powerpoint coming from his house.

The trailer is a sight to behold. Twin axels and enough rollers to satisfy anyone. Launching ramps in Canada tend to be steep which allows for easy launching and recovery without having to get the car wet. Robert had a 6-litre four-wheel drive wagon so launching and recovering the boat is simplicity itself. Robert does not need to use a winch to get the boat on the trailer, he simply motors onto it! It really beats trying to drag your boat out on a rope. Not all Canadians are as organized as Robert. At Port Credit on Lake Ontario I had an amusing experience as I watched someone who obviously didn't have too much idea try to recover his boat. He had a Transit sized van and the ramp was steep. The ramp was obviously a bit slimy because he struggled to get up the ramp because his wheels were slipping. Rather than use a bit of thought he obviously lost his temper and gunned the throttle, spinning the wheels even more. The result was spectacular; the friction set fire to his tyres! The state of the art US style boats are a joy to fish from, but they do not offer any shelter in wet and cold weather. US and Canadian anglers do not do that much lake fishing in really cold weather simply because many of their lakes freeze solid! They fish in huts that they slide out onto the ice. They do not do much static fishing from boats, which would tend to make cabins superfluous. My preference remains with the glass boat with a planeing hull and cabin. Interestingly glass boats are very rare in the areas of North America I have visited.

If you have the time you can rig a boat up to be highly functional. I've never had the chance to do this, but look forward to doing this one-day. Most boat anglers tend to use a fair proportion of hire boats even if they have their own. Boat rod rests are useful items and I've used a variety over the years. We sell some adjustable models at the shop, which are fine for static fishing. You can also troll with them though if I have my back to one rod I attach it with a lanyard, just as a precaution. If you have your own boat permanently mounted boat rod rests are better. Roberts and Berkley do models that can be permanently attached. A good anchor is essential and while it is true that you can anchor any boat with a big enough anchor, pulling it up is a different ball game. I use a homemade effort made by Gary Banks. This design with 4 grips, weight on the shank and an extra bar of iron to make it grip works well in most situations. I have mine on about 50 feet of good quality climbing rope. The reason I use this is because it is kind on the hands and softer on line if a pike goes around the anchor rope. I have had varied luck with anchor ropes over the years. Pike which are still fresh and not played out are the dangerous ones. Though we do not want to exhaust a fish, having a strong fish close to the boat too soon is risky. Generally if a pike goes around an anchor rope you open the bale arm and in so doing give the pike slack line. You then pull the offending anchor rope up and hopefully clear the line. This worked for me on Weirwood with a 28-08, but that was a fairly docile fish. An unseen fish on Loch Awe was sorted out and I was back in touch with the pike only to find that it had swum into a sunken tree. I lost that fish. Even worse was a powerful fish on the Lake of Menteith that I had pulled up to near the surface of the water. I didn't see it as it plunged back down. Neither did I realize as it swam under the boat that it was going to catch the back anchor. I try to pull it back, but this fish was too powerful. I suspect it turned on the back anchor rope and the combined friction and pull was sufficient to break the line. It was one of the few pike I have ever hooked that felt big. I had ten fish that day, the best 20-02. Only a 13 pounder felt like a big fish so you cannot always tell how big the fish you lose are.

Front anchors work OK on flat calm days with the rope straight own. However how many flat calms do you get these days? As the wind increase you will have to put more rope out. In a really strong wind you may need twice the depth of rope that you are fishing over to hold position. A back anchor is essential to stabilize the back of the boat if you are static deadbaiting. If you are lure fishing you can get away without a back anchor. I use quite a light back anchor weighing about 25lb maximum. The back anchor goes straight down and this is the one that tends to cause problems with pike going around it. The reason for the light back anchor is you need to be able to pull it up in a hurry sometimes. Anchored on a long rope you always have a certain amount of sway, which can to the uninitiated look like a run every five minutes. Fortunately you soon get used to this and the movement of a float because of pike activity is very obvious if you are paying attention to your gear. Generally the amount of sway you get in the wind is never enough to see the boat-sitting broadside to the wind, unless your anchor has dragged. If your anchor has dragged you have to be careful, particularly if you are being pushed out into deep water where the anchor rope will eventually not touch the bottom. The boat may also do a neat 360 degree turn which will see lines under the boat, caught around the engine and so on. This should be avoided at all costs! If your anchor is dragging all you can really do is let out more rope. If it still does not hold it is probably too rough to be fishing anyway! You should move to a more sheltered area or go home.

Open boats are easy to anchor because you simply tie off the anchor to the retaining ring at the end of the boat. Never tie to a seat, because there is a possibility that you might pull the seat out. People do from time to time fail to tie anchor ropes on properly. Nige Williams did it to me on Rutland Water, but fortunately by casting around he managed to hook the anchor rope and my best anchor and rope were saved. It is a good idea to put a small buoy or float on the end of the anchor rope as this will float should your rope come untied. Not attaching the anchor itself is a rare problem, but while fishing with Mick Rouse on the Erne he pulled up, er nothing! The rope had slipped! I have lost one anchor and that was in about 6 feet of shallow peaty water on Lough Mask. I suspect it was a sunken tree. I tried everything to shift that anchor. Full throttle with the engine pulling one way then the other. Eventually I had to cut the rope. It is possible to have a safety release anchor, but this entails having an extra eye at the opposite end to the normal attachment. You then use a weak link (often wire) to attach the rope to the normal attachment point. If you get snagged the wire should snap and then the anchor is reversed. I've not used this system because it does not work very well with the anchor I use.

Boats with cabins are more complicated when it comes to recovering the anchor. I have had to resort to climbing on the roof of Tango in the past and this really is not advisable. The sensible solution if you do not have a door in the front of the cabin or a roof hatch is to use a rope on a shackle or a spring clip. You then run the anchor rope through your retaining ring on the front of the boat, keeping the loose end in the boat. Clip your second rope, which only needs to be 6 feet long, or at least the length of the enclosed part of your boat to the anchor rope in front of the retaining ring. You then let out the anchor and when settled tie the second rope to a cleat. When you need to up anchor you release both ropes from their respective cleats and pull on the second rope. You will then find that you can bring the anchor rope to hand without having to move from the safety of the cockpit. The diagram, hopefully explains everything.

Anchoring on shallow waters such as the Broads can usually be carried out effectively using mudweights. These will be weights of around 25 to 30lbs which when dropped over the side get well and truly stuck in the mud. You can also give yourself a hernia pulling one up! I prefer to use my grip anchor wherever I fish. That way I hope to not succumb to any repetitive strain injury! The best way to anchor in shallow water is to use mooring poles. These give you a very stable boat. Unfortunately poles only work if supplied with the boat. Most of us would struggle to get 10ft poles in the back of the car!

Oars are usually the last resort of the pike angler. Using them usually suggests that some other form of power has conked out. Rowlocks are not that easy to come to terms with for some people. Oars tend to jump out after you give a particularly hard pull on them. You can get rowlocks with a bar across them that prevents this. When rowing, short sharp pulls are better than trying to dig in too hard or too deep. The alternative to rowlocks are thole pins. These consist of a pin onto which the oar fits. It is impossible to pull the oar off of the pin and makes for easier rowing in difficult conditions.

Pike anglers have various opinions as to the effect of petrol engines on pike. As a matter of respect to other anglers I try to avoid using a petrol engine near to them. Personally I do not think it matters a jot on most waters. You will without a doubt move a pike if you get too near it using a petrol engine, but in my experience moving a pike is just as likely to encourage a pike to feed as put it off. It is easier to use an electric motor to move around when fishing on say the broads. It avoids having to start a petrol motor, which is only easy if you have a decent engine! It also means you will get closer to a pike before you spook it and you might just see it. This in turn gives you the confidence to fish the area you have chosen if you know there is a pike about. People who are paranoid about noise are a pain, but why be noisy when you can be quiet? It's just as easy!

On a lot of waters locating the pike requires mobility and drifting on a drogue is a great way to find the fish. A drogue is simply an underwater parachute, which you tie to the side of the boat near the middle. You then drift slowly sideways usually casting lures downwind with if you choose a float fished deadbait dragged behind the boat. At the end of a drift you pull the drogue in and motor upwind again repeating the process. Remember to tie the drogue on properly, because yes I lost one myself on Bough Beech years ago! Bob Hopwood specializes in catching other peoples lost drogues and Duncan Pritchard runs him a close second. The score at the time of writing is two one respectively.

Quite a few pike anglers who have boats permanently moored at a fishery deck them out with carpet or carpet underlay. This is good if you put your pike down in the boat and it also helps deaden sounds. The snag with carpet is that if permanently in the boat it is always wet. Even if you take your boat home you have to dry the carpet out. I tend to opt out of the carpeting caper and take a decent unhooking mat with me. Unhooking mats are generally easy to get dry. The reason I am fussy about this is because my van is used to transport fresh fish as part of my business. My van is smelly enough without adding to the problem! Because I rarely put a pike down in a boat the unhooking mat is only there, as protection should the pike slip out of my hands. The degree of effort you put into your pike fishing normally reflects in your results.

Quite a few pike anglers spare no expense to fish for pike. By this I do not mean people who spend a fortune on the latest fishing tackle. . Personally it is up to the angler, but I'd rather use my money to help me to directly catch pike. One such item of tackle I should have is a bait boat. I will get one eventually, it's just that at the moment as I write I've had rather a lot of van, camper and cold store bills! Bait boats are very useful on large waters particularly those that are featureless and where the pike could be anywhere. Several friends of mine have made great use of bait boats over the years, including catching pike over 30lbs. I first saw a bait boat in action on Sywell reservoir in the 80s. Andy Barker was the owner and this certainly helped him to catch some good fish. Bait boats as well as allowing you to drop deadbaits off beyond casting range also enables livebaits to be placed at long range without the risk of casting them off. You can even put a free-swimming livebait out against the wind and allow it to drift back towards you. Brian Ingrams even uses a bait boat to put out paternostered baits on Lomond. He reckons it saves knocking his baits out with long casts. Prebaiting can also be carried out of the way of anglers casting from the bank. One of the gravel pits I used to fish was full of bars and islands and luckily I had it to myself. If I had been competing with other anglers, using a bait boat I could easily have prebaited well away from the bank and reduced the chance of other anglers benefiting from my prebaiting.

All the tackle in the world will not help you catch pike if the fish are not here. The most important single factor for success is finding the right water. Having the right tackle and the application of the right method be it lure fishing, deadbaiting or livebaiting are obviously vital once you have found the fish.

CHAPTER 4
CAR, VAN OR LIMOUSINE

I do a lot of driving associated with work and fishing, sometimes nearly 30,000 miles. Because of this I've had quite a few different cars and vans. All have advantages, most have snags. I started my motorized pike fishing on a Honda C50 motorbike. This was a bit of a death trap so once I'd passed my motorcycle test I decided to buy a three-wheeler, which you could at the time (and probably now) drive on a motorcycle licence. The Reliant Supervan I started with lasted less than a day before I rolled it over putting the van and myself plus 4 passengers into a ditch. (Overloaded I think!) I bought another one and then another, driving one from about 1972 until 1978. Though not much fun to drive they at least gave me true mobility and my Supervan reached as far north as Loch Lomond. Eventually I passed my test and bought a brand new Bedford Chevanne. This was the van that featured in my first solo book, Pike Fishing in the 80s. Now it was a nice van, but it suffered the problem of all vans in the 80s, it was noisy. It was long enough in the back to lay full length so it could be used for trips away. After 3 years I had decided I wanted a bit more comfort so I bought a new Astra Estate. This had a 1600 engine and seemed very quick compared with the van. I used to enjoy trying to beat the clock in the estate, always trying to shave minutes off the 140-mile trip to the Thurne. I shaved a little too much once when a speed cop clocked me going a little too fast in Narborough. For the next 15 years or so I had various estates, plus a brief fling with a Calibra (heated leather seats and so on, you grow out of these things eventually). Ultimately I had my dream car a 2-litre Astra Estate a car that went very well. Unfortunately we had now entered the period when speed cameras were everywhere and racing around was no longer a practical proposition. As my career took a different direction and I found myself dealing with large amounts of fresh fish and ice, it became clear that a nice estate car would end up as a smelly estate car. So in the end it was back to a van. Now modern vans are much nicer to drive, quieter and surprisingly economical. I bought a Vauxhall Combo van and at the time of writing I'm still driving it. It's a bit pedestrian, but you can get a lot in it. The only snag with it is that the load floor is just a little too short to lie out flat. The next van I get will have to be just a little bit bigger, probably one of the Scudo or Expert type vans with a side door and three front seats.

I know it's greedy, but I've also had a Volkswagen camper for 11 years. Now I always promised myself a Camper and in 1990 I took a chance seeing as I had just left the water authority and spent 16,000 pounds on a brand new camper. My only regret is that I bought petrol rather than a diesel one. At 22mpg it is a very expensive vehicle to run! At least compared to in 1990! The beauty of a camper is that you have a sink, cooker, fridge and heater plus plenty of space. It makes a 2 or three-day trip bearable. In fact several times I've used it for a weeks holiday and provided it doesn't pour with rain it's been good fun. It gets used less for long trips these days because of the cost of fuel, however it is great for night fishing. I seldom need to use a bivvy now. Sadly I'll probably never be able to buy another new camper. A comparable model costs 28,000 pounds. I would suggest that for far less you could equip a new van with the essentials. After all pike anglers do not need curtains! My only criticism of any of the vehicles I have driven is their lack of 4-wheel drive. Now I've been on the Land Rover training course at Solihull and have no wish to take a van down that sort of terrain. However I could sometimes use a bit of go anywhere. Nige Williams has had 4 wheel drive vehicles for at least ten years and it does make getting boats in easy. Unfortunately I cannot justify buying a 4-wheel drive van because I'd only use it 4 or 5 times a year. Once in a while then I have to pay someone a fiver to pull me out of the mud!

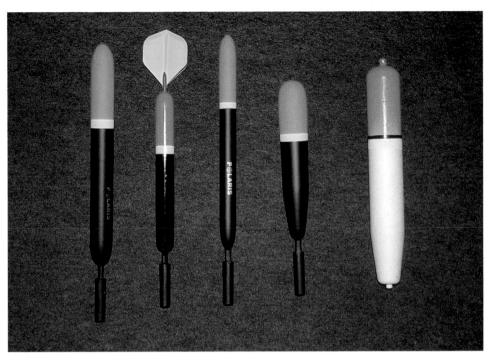

My favoured floats. A selection of Polaris floats, plus one 'shark float'

Middy drop off indicator with adjustable weight.

38-08 from Lough Mask

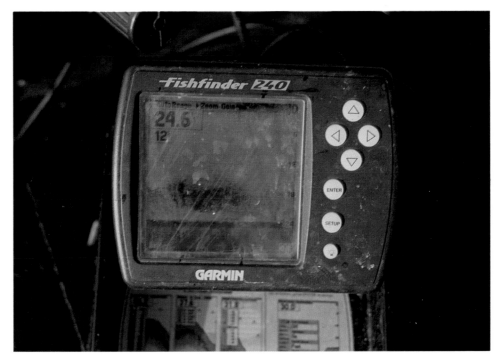

Garmin 240 sonar showing weed.

The 8ft Sniper is easily roof topped.

Boat fishing

Home made and effective anchor.

Jason Davis home made pork chop jenkbait which accounted for his 37.

37-00 to Jason Davis from Blithfield

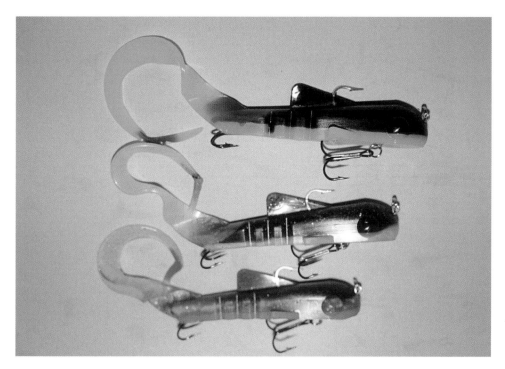

Essential Lures Bulldawg

Small mackerel mounted for trolling

28-08 pike from Weirwood on half mackerel

32-14 prebaited from a large stillwater.

My biggest Canadian pike of 14lbs - beautiful markings

CHAPTER 5

LURE FISHING

Years ago when I wrote Pike Fishing in the 80s and Pike Fishing, I did my best to cover lure fishing. The problem of course was that I'd done relatively little of it! Things are different now, but I still cannot claim to be one of the nations leading exponents of lure fishing. I've done enough lure fishing now to give the reader enough pointers to help him or her catch pike using this exciting method. One plea before I go on, don't become a lure fishing nut! I refer to people who give up bait fishing entirely and then try to catch pike using lures when other approaches might be better. Doing the opposite and failing to come to terms with lure fishing is also a bad idea. I'm a great one for moderation in my fishing and totally believe in the concept of being flexible.

The main difference between lure fishing and most forms of bait fishing is the fact that you have to keep fishing if you are going to catch. Deads and lives will to some extent fish themselves. Lures have this terrible disadvantage of being totally useless if legered. Mind you having said that I've had pike try to pick Springdawgs off the bottom though of course I had been winding them in before!

Lure fishing then is harder work than bait fishing unless you are an advocate of float fished free-swimming livebaits. Hard work though is not always bad for you and nothing keeps you bubbling with enthusiasm more than an exciting day with lots of follows and hits. You do have to have confidence to lure fish effectively and that confidence can only be obtained by catching a few fish. Going to Llandegfedd for a first trip and expecting to have success   lure fishing is rather like expecting to get onto Millionaire first time. You need to fish waters where the pike respond to lures and that knowledge can either be obtained from fellow pike anglers or by fishing yourself. Once you start to catch on lures then your confidence will increase. With that increase in confidence you will start to catch more pike and so things will get better and better. Whatever you do, do not be discouraged by a few bad days. We all have them and even if you had a tremendous day the week before there is no reason to expect to repeat the performance.

I' m going to write here from the beginner's point of view, because to my mind this is the best way to get the basics across. I guess that all of us started lure fishing as a first step in trying to catch pike. My first pike ever of 1-04 came from a Fen drain in 1963 on a copper no 6 Mepps spinner. A couple of years later I had graduated to fish of 4-08 on a homemade silver spoon. Then of course I became convinced that live and deadbaits were *the method to* catch the larger fish. Though in many situations this has proved to be correct, in recent years with the advent of some of the modern lures it has become clear that lures can actually out fish live and deadbaits. If you had told me two years ago that livebaits would be totally out fished by lures, I'd have laughed at you. I'm not laughing now.

It is possible to lure fish using the same gear as you would for deadbaiting. A 3lb test 12ft pike rod and standard fixed spool reel loaded with 15lb mono or 50lb braid can be used to good effect on most waters. This outfit is best suited to spoons and the smaller rubber lures. Do not try it for chucking the larger jerkbaits unless you are into weight training. I've tried and to be honest I'm not up to it. The fixed spool outfit can outdistance multiplier/ jerkbait rod combos and is useful for bank fishing applications. However I'm a convert to the multiplier/jerkbait rod setup. How did this come about? Well I had organized one of my trips to Lough Mask after the first test nettings for pike had started. One of the anglers on the trip was Derek McDonald. Now I try to keep an open mind though our results on Mask had been reasonable. However they had started to decline in the past couple of years. With this came the Dutch pike anglers with their modern lure fishing techniques. Derek turned up just in time to give me a bit of a nudge towards the new lure fishing approach. I fished with him for a couple of days and he was good enough to lend me one of his lure outfits. We did not pull up any trees that week though Derek managed three doubles to 19lb. My first on a Jerkbait was 9lb though I did drop off a larger fish later in the week. The outcome was that I enjoyed the method and it felt right, so the slow progress towards achieving some level of proficiency in lure fishing or should I say the new lure fishing started.

Because I work as a consultant for Daiwa it is my job to keep them informed of any new developments in pike fishing. Now for all of you out there who were using jerkbaits and rubber baits 10 years ago it might seem that my advice was a little bit late. However you should remember that new methods only become apparent once more than a few people start to publicise their successes. You cannot become aware until someone spills the beans! A big step forward in my own understanding of how good the soft rubber baits could be came again via Derek McDonald. An exhibition on Llandegfedd, which led to his catching a 34 plus a 20, led me to investigate further. The writings of Dave Lumb and Dave Kelbrick indicated that there was definitely something in this lure fishing. As usual I'm not very good at taking advice from articles, so I started a short journey to what was to become a degree of success using lures.

Initially I did a fair bit of jerkbait fishing, using a variety of lures including some home made flipper/dolphin type lures. I caught a few fish including a 17 from Rutland and did *not* catch a brownie of about 7lb that promptly threw the hooks! The technique of jerkbait fishing depends on the angler jerking the rod tip between winding with the reel. The lure then makes a series of lazy swoops through the water. You can make the action more erratic or even lazier depending on what you think the pike will respond to. There is a whole host of jerkbaits all with different actions. Lures made by Cobbs, which have a wonderful gliding action, look really good in the water and catch pike too. The Loz Harrop darter is another, which simply looks good in the water and catches. At the other extreme are the homemade jobs, which look like pork chops, and cast like bricks. These too catch pike sometimes rather big ones! I was thrown out of woodwork after 3 terms (It took me a term to saw through one piece of wood) so there really is little chance of me making my own. Yet many lure anglers do make their own and enjoy doing so. Because of my inability in the do it yourself department I'll not describe how to make these lures, however it is a simple job for Pikelines or Pike and Predators readers to look up some back issues. The Lure Society almost certainly has some detailed contributions from it's members on this subject.

My renewed interest in lures has come about because of the soft lures. The first soft lure I had to play with was the Profi lure, which simply consisted of a shad, mounted on a snap tackle. I chucked them around a fair bit and caught fish to 14lb. The secret of this lure is its flat-faced tail. This vibrates and wriggles as it moves through the water. Now we know that food fish as they swim have a rhythmic beat as the tail propels them through the water. It seems as if these shad type lures exaggerate the beat of a food fishes tail. I would not say that a pike finds this irresistible, but on some days it certainly works. Being slow on the uptake I didn't start using the larger soft lures such as the Bulldawg until about 3 years ago. Mick Brown showed me how effective the Springdawg was on Rutland water. A rather nice pike in the 20lb class followed Mick's lure right to the boat, munched it, but came off! That together with Derek Macs demonstration on Llandegfedd saw me start to try them.

I started with the Bulldawg itself, which is a fairly meaty lure and toddled off to Grafham water. Results were not immediate, but when I eventually found some fish I actually had five takes on a rainbow trout pattern Bulldawg. The three I landed were all low doubles to 12lb, but they did wonders for my confidence. Chances to use this lure didn't really arise again until the following autumn when I arranged a contest in Pike and Predators. The winner and myself got a preview day before the start on Grafham. My first take on the Bulldawg was 21-04 and I was now a convert. Actually fishing the lures seemed simplicity in itself. All you did was cast out, let it sink and wind in as slowly as possible. The need for variety came later.

I hadn't really given much thought to the Springdawg, the Bulldawg's little brother. As I said earlier Mick Brown gave me a push towards thinking about using them. They are smaller and lighter than the larger model, but still have the key feature the wriggly tail. Yes we are back to wriggly tails! I do not know what it is about any of the wriggly tails you see on soft lures. All of them seem to do something to pike, which makes them respond in an aggressive manner. So from my point of view where you can get away with the smaller lure, it is more pike friendly because the hooks are smaller. It is also a lot less hard work casting it all day. The Bulldawg is the better lure for fishing on the deeper reservoirs because of its heavier weight. It stays down near the bottom if required. On faster flowing rivers the same applies. The Springdawg comes into it's own when you are fishing shallow waters. My first positive experience with the Springdawg came in the fens about four years ago. The deadbaiting had been deadly slow and wasn't improved over much when a pike took a swipe at a herring reeled in backwards! I managed to catch one decent pike on a wobbled deadbait, but suddenly remember that the lure rod was in the van. A few minutes later I was giving the Springdawg a try and not much longer afterwards caught several pike up to around 16 pounds. Now this was a bit of a revelation, the normally effective deadbaits having to be supplanted by lures!

A week later when I returned the drain had been pumped down about 3 feet. There was a nasty mud shelf, which if I were to land anything would have to be negotiated. The deadbaits were a dead loss again as was a paternostered livebait. The lure however was chomped several times, the big surprise being a 22-08, my first twenty on a lure from the Fens. More pike followed despite the water clarity being poor. I'm still not experienced enough on a wide enough range of waters to say that the wriggly tailed lures work well in coloured water. The results though have so far have been promising, as I'll show later in this book.

The seismic shift in my lure fishing career came about when I managed to gain access to a water I call Mason's lake. In the first year that we fished it, the initial results on lures were poor. As time went on though I started to pick up a few fish on Bulldawgs and Springdawgs. Once again it was a case of building up confidence in the method. That is strange really after having already built up the confidence elsewhere. You shouldn't have to do it on every new water, but that is what happens sometimes. Now Mason's is a very special water with some very big pike. Competition from other anglers is non-existent. It is the ideal place to have success with a lure fishing technique. Anglers reading this cannot expect to have my good fortune because sometimes it is not a case of what you know, but where you know!

The most memorable day so far on Masons came about without any premonition or warning. Nige Williams and I started fishing at what we call the lagoon. We chucked everything at the pike, livebaits and lures, but with only a small return. I picked up a double on a Springdawg, but nothing else seemed to be interested. We decided to split up and try some different swims. I headed for a point, which looked promising. After about an hour and a half I had the distinct feeling that the nearest pike was about 300 miles away. Nige meanwhile had passed by heading for the grassy bank swim. Not having the option of trying that spot it was time to try a totally new area. By now the frost had returned, the sun was setting and it was cold. I opened the back doors of the van and thought, "The full set up or can't be bothered!" Can't be bothered won hands down! One lure rod and a rucksack accompanied me down the bank to the likely looking swim. I fished a fire Springdawg and worked along the bank casting a few times in each spot, always moving along. I reached some trees, which prevented me from going any further so I retraced my steps. I've probably said this before, but lure fishing consists mainly of casting and winding in. You have a fish on when you cannot wind in anymore!

My example of not being able to wind in came a few minutes later and didn't feel exceptional. The pike (at this stage I was still not sure it was a pike) must have stood on it's nose and simply attempted to swim downwards as I tried to wind it in. This resulted in some very large boils coming to the surface. Now in ten feet of water you have to have a fairly big tail to cause that sort of disturbance. None of this registered at the time, but what happened next did register big time. Suddenly this sullen fish sprinted 15 yards very quickly tearing line off of the clutch of the multiplier. If I had been confused at the time, my confusion soon turned to astonishment. I turned the fish and pumped it up to the surface. About 10 yards from the bank a rather large pike surfaced. Now the absence of a landing net might cause weaker souls to panic. In my case though I'm probably a weaker soul, the hours spent wasted not catching big pike give you a certain determination to land a big pike regardless of the obstacles around you. As soon as I saw the pike I was determined to dive in and rugby tackle it if required. There was no way this one was getting away. Luckily there was no need for drama as I managed to hand land it without much fuss. Thirty pounds was not in question, but how big a 30 was in doubt. Weighed it went 37-08, eight ounces more than what I had thought was going to be the biggest pike I was to see that season. (Jason Davies 37-00 from Blithfield.). I set out to find Nige, but bumped into him on the way around. He came and helped me photograph the fish and within a few minutes back she went. We were both bubbling with speculation after that. How big do the pike grow in here? It was not a mega fat fish so obviously another fish the same length, but a lot fatter would press the 40lb barrier. At the time it was the biggest UK pike on a soft lure and at the time of writing remains the best on a Springdawg.

The story as reported in the papers suggested that I had wandered away from my kit when I caught the fish. I then had to suffer an idiot who wrote in to complain about this. The above account should make it clear that you should never believe what you read in the papers. The capture of a single fish does not teach you very much about lure fishing techniques, but little bits of information are added. In this case I found out that a repaired Springdawg would still catch fish. The lure in question, a much used fire pattern had lost its tail in some mishap. A grub tail had been welded on using a soldering iron. The resulting abortion still had a wriggling tail and obviously worked well enough. Quick repairs are something you can easily do with these lures. The aforementioned soldering iron is very much a master botchers tool. Yet it's use can transform an obviously useless piece of rubber into an effective lure. One or two people complain about the price of these lures, yet when you have caught twenty fish on one, this compares very favourably with the price of deadbaits.

At the risk of sounding like a one lure angler, I should explain that I have caught a few on lures other than Springdawgs. My early experiences on Blithfield for example showed that naïve pike were not that fussy about what they took. A wide range of cheap and cheerful lures caught a large number of pike and all I did was follow suite. My best two fell to Toby type spoons, a 29-15 on a 1oz Toby and a 31 on a slightly smaller Daiwa Crusader Spoon. There was nothing revolutionary about any of this, the key advantage of these small spoons being that they cast well enabling a lot of water to be covered when the deep water is a long way out. Today on Blithfield some anglers are trying to replicate this casting performance using very dense and hence heavy jerkbaits. The approach works, but one has to wonder if the humble Toby might have it's day once again.

Blithfield was also famous as the place where the Shakespeare Big S had its finest hour. This perfectly adequate lure caught some good fish on the basis of a wriggle and an internal rattle. I've been in boats when other people have had 25lb plus pike on Big S lures, but my best so far has been 18-11. Lures suffer from fashions and today both the Big S and the Toby are unfashionable. I think it is fair to say that there are better lures than these two available to the pike angler, however the unfashionable lures will still catch pike on many waters and should not be ignored.

It is an oft-quoted jest that lures catch more anglers than pike. I'm sure this is true because while there are a handful of full time lure anglers who can make use of the vast collections they carry around with them, the rest of us cannot. I restrict my lure range to ones which I know work because either I've had fish on them or I know how good they are from talking to other people. Spinnerbaits for example work well and I've had a lot of pike on them, best fish so far a 19 from Corrib. You must have a few of them in your collection. I stick to mainly twin blade models with half to three quarters of an ounce of weight. Skirt colours are generally orange or yellow. Zalts have a good reputation, but I've not used them enough to have caught anything on them yet. The same applies to the shallow and deep Invader lures. I've had a few hits on the Deep Invader, but have yet to hook a pike on one. Any decent sized spoon is worth having in your collection. Kilty do some nice weighty spoons, which cast well while the Shakespeare Stouraen Spoon is a proven pike catcher. Old antique lures like the Guiderbro Sniper catch pike. I once went to interview Ken Latham of Potter Heigham. Ken had been the first person to import large quantities of American lures. He showed me his huge lure boxes and offered me one, a Sniper. I gratefully accepted it and went on to catch a Blithfield 27 pounder many years later. There are also dozens of different soft lures, twin tails, shads and big grubs with wriggly tails. A lure, which Dave Lumb and Nige Grassby seem to use a lot, is the Squirrelly Burt. Now the name is bad, but the actual lure seems to combine the traits of jerkbaits and the soft plastics. You could safely fill a very large lure box with all the lures available but you can bet you'd probably never get around to using most of them. Some lure anglers I have met have buckets of lovely homemade jerkbaits. They all catch fish at one stage or another and part of the satisfaction they get is from catching on home made lures. The danger with lure fishing is getting carried away with buying them! I have not even mentioned surface lures here simply because my experience is very limited. I've had odd fish to 8lb on lures such as Crazy Crawlers, but generally I've done better using a spinnerbait sub surface.

One aspect of lure fishing, which has me totally baffled, is when other anglers catch and I do not. Please do not join in a chorus " It's because you are crap". It's not as simple as that. While I accept that there are lure anglers out there who because of their long-term experience are likely to have an edge on the rest of us, the fact remains that if you are on water with them it is better to watch and learn rather than to pass their success off as pure luck. Bob Hopwood and I were lucky enough to come up in the draw for fishing The Lake of Menteith. My good friend Mark Ackerley was good enough to supply me with the information on the best areas. Needless to say on coming out of the boatyard I was already lost and we wandered around aimlessly while I suffered from a case of map reading dyslexia. Eventually I got my bearings and arrived where we were supposed to be. Final confirmation of it being the right area was the presence of Dave Lumb and Nige Grassby. We proceeded to troll Bulldawgs in order to get to know where we were fishing. I had a take off of a small fish, which came off straight away, which was enough to convince me that the approach was worth sticking with. Three hours later with nothing to show I had changed my mind! In the meantime Nige and Lumby were drifting on the drogue and then motoring back upwind using the electric motor. We saw Dave get an 18 on the drift and then Nige hooked a superb 31-12 while running back upwind. By the end of the day Nige had added three more twenties. Whatever they were doing resulted in lots of big pike, while we caught nothing. Plenty of other people had the same problem, so my view afterwards was that, next time I have to try and adapt or improve my lure fishing. Our way around the failure to catch was a case of quick adaptation. I saw Tony Cookney land a 26 pounder on a bait so the decision as to what to do next was simple. We anchored up and fished deadbaits, lure fishing in between the baits We ended up with ten fish to 20-02, 8 of them doubles. We had nothing on lures at all. Please explain to me how our lure fishing efficiency could have been 100% inferior to those around us? There is no short explanation, so I simply accept that sometimes something's are not meant to be. I will not be fazed by any of this, but I will try and work out how I can be more successful at my lure fishing. If I should fail I'm not going to go out and shoot myself! Please note that Dave Lumb was fishing with Nige Grassby and compared to Nige he had a poor day, so there is room to accept that if it can happen to him…

Trolling lures could merit a whole chapter in itself, but because my experience with the method is not that extensive all I can do is refer to it in passing. Elsewhere in the book I cover deadbait trolling on the petrol engine. The basics for both lure and deadbait trolling are very similar. The choice of lures is such that I might need another chapter to describe these! Most lures that I've trolled have a diving vane and the size of this influences how deep they will go. On the tackle I use, none of the diving lures I have will go below 20 feet. Most only fish 10 feet, which is OK in the situation I have encountered to far. If you end up fishing water such as Windermere which has a reputation for producing pike deep down you need to take the advice of people like Tony Cookney, Dave Kelbrick, Dave Lumb or even the dreaded Gord. Unfortunately only a couple of them write regularly and I cannot recall them covering deep water trolling. (I may be mistaken here.) I have trolled Super Shads, which sometimes hit 10 feet, Big Ss (the same), Depth Raiders that just once in a blue moon touch at 20 feet, Cisco Kids (which I lost my example of trolling for Ferox on lead core on Lough Mask!). Of course I have trolled Bulldawgs and Springdawgs with some success. The Bulldawg will fish down to about 10 feet while the Springdawg manages 8 feet. You can put lead on either of these and they still work. Nige Williams had a lead on a paternoster attached above the trace on his Bulldawg when he caught his Blithfield 32. So far I've not caught anything on a leaded Bulldawg, but expect to give the method more effort next winter. The other soft lures such as the Invader look good and fish down to 12 to 15 feet, but so far all I've had on them are nibbles!

The way we troll lures in the UK is of course primitive with how they set about it in the USA or Canada. You only have to look at the set ups used to see how seriously they take trolling. A lot of this is carried out fishing for Chinook salmon, but the techniques could be applied to pike as well. Downriggers are used to fish lures at constant depths. The method employs a heavy steel cable on a reel preferably graduated in feet so you can see how deep you are. On the steel cable you will have a weight of at least 6lb. On the cable or the weight will be attached a release clip. Into this goes the line say 10 yards up line from the lure. You then lower everything to the desired depth, set the rod in a tube holder and tighten up until the rod is bent. When you get a take the line is pulled out of the release clip and the rod springs straight. The most well-known downrigger manufacturer is Canon and on some boats on the Great Lakes you will see a dozen downriggers and rods in use! As a precision trolling tool you cannot beat the downrigger and I'm still trying to figure out why I've never used one!

A poor second choice to the downrigger for deep trolling is lead core line. My limited experience of using it was somewhat traumatic. I had decided to try trolling 40 to 50 feet of water on Lough Mask in the hope of contacting a Ferox or of finding where the pike went to when we couldn't find them in shallower water. The first time I snagged up the lead core helped get the Cisco Kid lure stuck even more than it had been when I started! I lost that lure. I tried a Big S and lost that. I tried something expendable, but didn't lose that one! This lead core fishing is obviously not as simple as it looks and I've a bit more to learn here.

Most newcomers to lure fishing will struggle when it comes to lure choice. You cannot substitute experience for a huge box of lures. The best approach is to buy a small selection of lures with known fish catching abilities. You can choose these lures based on what you read here, or you can glean as much as you can from magazine articles. I'm in the trade so I ought to be telling you, that five hundred pounds worth of lures is essential to get started, but in reality this is not the case. You can start lures fishing with less than one hundred pounds worth of lures and catch pike. Colour permutations can be a problem as having one of each colour of most of the popular lures can lead to imminent foreclosure on your bank borrowing! My advice is to buy two totally different patterns of each model. Then you will have a contrast in colours, one of which will hopefully work on the day. If you fail it's no good going out and buying a couple more patterns. Instead pay attention to other pike anglers and ask them which pattern of lure they were catching on. If you've not got one of those then possibly it would be a good idea to put one into your lure collection. You do not need to have binoculars on other anglers all day long to get an idea of which colour is catching the fish. From a hundred yards it is easy to see if it's a red tailed bulldawg or a Cisco pattern. I am really not the person to give you chapter and verse on lure colours. Certain trends do develop on every water and sometimes these are self-fulfilling. If someone says a yellow lure is a good catcher on a particular water, more fish are going to be caught on yellow lures, simply because more people are using yellow lures. I keep and open mind and stick to using a small range of colours. You do have strange things happen for example on the Bann; I'd fished with a Cisco coloured Springdawg all morning with nothing to show for my efforts and decided on a change. (OK this does not show quickness of wit, but when you are deadbaiting as well you do not concentrate on your lure fishing as much as when you are only lure fishing.) I put on a yellow and black Springdawg and had a follow and a take straight away. Coincidence? Possibly, but it pays not to believe in coincidence when you are pike fishing! You get so few clues as to what is going on underwater it pays to take note of any little clues you might come across. Even if they are of no consequence, it can hardly have a deleterious affect on your fishing.

There is of course a lot more to lure fishing than I've written about here. However I'm not in the position to do more than skim the surface here. I'm building up my experience as I go along. I have a nice big collection of lures, most of which I never use. Many I use, but I never catch on them. Only a handful work at the moment for me. This would be different if I lure fished all the time, then I would quickly obtain the experience of catching on a wider range of lures. However I do not wish to dedicate my life to lure fishing and neglect other methods. This I am sure is how most of you will look at lure fishing. Any pike angler can obtain a certain level of success, but like most things practice makes perfect.

To lure fish properly with the larger lures you definitely need a lure fishing outfit. I for obvious reasons use Daiwa gear (i.e. I'm a consultant and it's good tackle anyway!) The specialized 6ft or 6ft 6ins lure rods are much nicer to use than longer rods. Together with a decent multiplier reel, the outfit just feels right. Load your reel with about 10 yards of 15lb mono and then connect to your 80 to 100lb braid using a shock leader knot. The mono prevents the braid slipping on your reel. A solid steel leader or a home made trace using 80lb wire and a duolock completes the outfit. For smaller lures there is a lighter Jerkbait rod available from Daiwa. Coupled with a small multiplier reel and 40 to 50lb braid you should enjoy effortless casting all day with 1 to 2oz lures. You can of course scale down your rods and use a fixed spool for even smaller lures though this probably reduces the effectiveness of the lure fishing approach for really big pike.

Landing pike with a mouthful of lure with big hooks attached can be a dangerous affair for both pike and pike angler. I like hand-landing fish, but I'm very careful about how I do it. Hand landing saves lures getting caught in the net mesh. Whatever you do, do not use a conventional landing net. A couple of years ago while trolling Bulldawgs on Masons I had a take, which came totally out of the blue. Such surprises tend to unnerve even the most experienced pike anglers and this one felt a good one. The net was not set up so Dave Moore quickly put it together. As the pike came to the surface it looked bigger than it was so I elected for Dave to net it. This he did first time, however the tangle that resulted was horrific. The pike luckily unhooked itself, but the Bulldawg was totally lost in the mesh of the net. I had to cut the lure out to be able to use it again. Needless to say the net was now useless not that we intended to use it again anyway! The pike by the way weighed 20-06. Though large mesh landing nets have the potential to split the pike's fins, they are much easier to extract the pike plus hooks from. There are a variety of mesh types about, the best one I've seen was on Derek McDonalds round frame. It is the same knotless material that my 100-metre seine net is made from. Now I'm not about to cut my seine net up so for the time being I'm making do with a net and frame I bought secondhand from a friend. It is pike friendly, but snags on absolutely everything in the boat! I will get a better net made up as soon as I find someone willing to do the stitching.

Flying trebles do tend to catch in the gills and this can lead to bleeding. All my experience with recognizable pike and tagged zander suggests that bleeding looks bad, but clotting soon stems the flow and these fish are caught again. Hooks well inside the mouth can usually be removed using forceps or pliers. Cutters are not much help simply because you do not want to leave bits of hook in pike. The only hookhold, which is very dangerous, is the one that ends up at the back of the throat in the roof of the mouth. This could in extreme circumstances penetrate the heart with fatal consequences. Luckily this is no reason to expect this to happen and touch wood it has never happened to me. Bad hookholds can happen when you are live or deadbaiting so there is no reason to condem lure fishing as particularly dangerous to a pike. The size of the hooks however does give rise to more cases of external mouth damage. In the end you have to decide whether to go pike fishing or not. The only way to not harm them is to not fish for them.

Once you get into lure fishing you will start to learn more each time you fish. Most lure fishing in the UK is carried out by casting from the bank or boat. Boat lure fishing involves anchoring and casting and then moving. Drift fishing using a drogue allows the angler to cast covering a little bit more water each cast. There's nothing technical about either approach, you simply keep casting! The deeper the water you are fishing the less efficient the cast and retrieve approach is. This is simply because most lures tend to spend much of their time climbing through the water and not fishing near the bottom. (If that's what you want.) The longer your cast the longer the lure spends at the required depth. Some lures such as Bulldawgs and heavy jerkbaits can be made to crawl along the bottom, but obviously still have to climb up to the surface. If you wish to fish a lure at a set depth, trolling is the best option. Again there's nothing over technical about this, simply pay out 40 yards of line with the lure attached and drag behind an electric or petrol motor on tick over.

I've done a lot of trolling with lures and everything from copper spoons to Bulldawgs has caught good pike. One useful rule that will generally reap a reward is to avoid trolling too deep. Now there are bound to be situations where a lure needs to go down 30 or 40 feet. However on most waters a lure which fishes ten feet deep will catch a heck of a lot of fish. The reason for this is simple; pike have good eyes and a well-developed sensory system. A lure passing ten or even fifteen feet over a pike's head is easily detected and if the pike is interested it will move through the water body to intercept it. Because of this you only need to consider trolling deep if the shallower option fails.

Trolling works because you cover a lot of water and because of this a lot of pike. You make the valid assumption that somewhere out there, a pike is willing to have a go at a lure provided you can put a lure past it. In the last year at Blithfield the anglers fishing there have had to decide whether to cast from the bank, cast from a boat or to troll. At the moment honours are fairly even, but the option of trolling has made a big difference to the pike fishing. Many trout waters notably those of Anglian Water do not allow trolling and this makes the fishing on these waters much more difficult. As I write you still cannot troll on Grafham, Rutland and Pitsford. This policy means that none of these waters can be pike fished effectively. It is time that the management there decided whether or not they really want us to catch pike there.

On Blithfield I have been a lure trolling failure though I live in hope. As I write we have just had the February 2002 sessions. Nige Williams and I headed off to where we thought we would have a chance casting lures. After about an hour and a half in the top section of the reservoir we retreated to the bottom half where the water clarity was much better. We started trolling with a variety of lures and soon noted a congregation of boats on the west side of the reservoir. This always means that someone has had one. So it proved, a 33 pounder for starters! This encouraged us so we carried on trolling. I hooked a one-pound rainbow on a depth raider; otherwise nothing disturbed our steady trolling up and down. Meanwhile another thirty pounder had been landed along with a 25 pounder. It was one of those days when the big fish were feeding. I think another big one came out which rather than inspiring me had my hopes gradually fall to rock bottom. By the middle of the day we had stared to get a bit silly. I was on the engine as usual (Nige tends to break them). When I spotted ET trying to " Be alone " in the SE corner of the reservoir. He was trolling with his back to us. I managed to get right alongside of him without him realizing, close enough for Nige to tap him on his shoulder with his rod. It took three taps and a good clout to get his attention. When we got through to him he nearly jumped out of his boat! We fell about laughing as we motored away only to see him get his line around the prop!

An hour later we found him trying to be alone at the end of Ten Acre bay. I decided that a troll in was in order just to show him that he couldn't get away from us. Nige was trolling a Cisco pattern Bulldawg, while I had changed over to a Guiderbro Sniper. Nige had a paternoster and a 2oz bomb up the line to get his lure down. As I motored in the depth changed from 20 to 12 feet and it was clear that if we went too close to him we'd spook any fish, which happened to be, near him. I turned the boat, but the space available was insufficient to keep the lures clear of the bottom. I increased the speed as we hurtled around and out of the bay. Nige shouted I've got one. Now Nige is forever saying "I'm in", "It's a big one" and so on so I ignored him and continued to motor out of the bay. I think by now a rather large pike must have been surfing behind the boat. Again Nige said he had one, again we motored on. Finally at the third time of asking I looked over my shoulder to see a bent rod and Nige hanging on. I put the engine into reverse and we proceeded to try and land whatever it was. The drama wasn't over then because I was loath to keep us in reverse because of the risk of the line coming into contact with the prop. My second chance to net it was made in haste because it looked as it the lure was going to pull out. Normally I always go for a pike tail first when netting a lure caught fish. However this pike presented itself headfirst so I had to decide whether to wait or chance it. I decided to chance it and needless to say the pike came to be half with its head stuck in the side of the net and with its body half out. If at this stage it had thrashed it would have escaped, luckily I managed to bundle the rest of the pike into the net. She weighed in at 32-06, Nige's 14th over 30lb and the end of an 18 year quest on and off at Blithfield. Poor old ET, he'd have probably have caught that fish if we had not been bored and playing silly games. The next day John Davey had a 37-12 trolling while Jason Davis had a 35 casting from the bank. A big fish weekend indeed.

Before we move on to the next chapter I ought to ask the question, "Why do lures work"? Well the obvious answer is that a lure looks in some way like a prey fish and pike being predators try to eat them. This is all well and good on many natural waters, but on trout waters where the pike are really well fed, hunger is probably something a lot of pike do not experience! I have lost count the number of times an area which probably holds big pike (a classic example the rolling pike on the North bank at Llandegfedd.) has taken several hours to produce any fish. It seems as if something triggers those pike to change from not interested to interested. We know that pike have feeding periods, but it is more complex than that because we also have periods when the pike are following lures rather than taking them. You would think that any sensible pike would either sit tight or attack the lure if it really thought that it was edible. I would suggest that pike are to some extent curious. I have certainly watched pike in clear water investigating objects, which I can see, are not edible. There are obviously visual cues that pike respond to and the lures we use obviously provide some of these cues. Can a pike be annoyed into taking a lure? The only way to answer this would be to ask a pike. Clearly this is impossible and you can also be sure that you cannot annoy a pike in the same way that you annoy me! Fish though do exhibit aggressive behaviour. When I did my zander research at Aston University one particular zander we kept in a large aquarium (we called him or her "A") was terribly aggressive towards any other fish put in the tank with it. This aggression ran to attacking models of fish as well. I never did figure out what the cause of this behaviour was, but it shows that it is possible for a predator to attack something, which it either cannot eat (too big) or does not wish to eat.

It might well be that the superb paint finishs that people put on some home made lures are a waste of time. While I can accept that a bright orange lure will be seen differently to a black or green lure, it is questionable whether eyes or scale finishs have any bearing on the lures effectiveness. It doesn't matter at all because if you enjoy painting lures to shop bought standard, then do it. Just do not convince yourself that you are going to outwit the pike on the basis of paintjob alone! I at the moment struggle with lure colour choice. I try and have a bit of variation in my box, but have discerned few patterns other than that mentiond earlier where a change in lure colour did produce a take. The reader should read the material written by people like Dave Lumb and Dave Kelbrick in Pike and Predators if they wish to think more about their lure fishing. Gordie can sometimes be informative when he is not too busy telling us he is the worlds greatest lure angler or spinning one of his yarns! In the end simply believe that lures work, but also understand that other methods can work better. Be adaptable and keep catching.

CHAPTER 6
DEADBAITING

More pike are caught on deadbaits than anything else in this country. Strange really when you consider it was only in the 50s that the Taylor brothers publicised deadbaiting. (I think it was Dame Juliana Berners who mentioned it first!) You only have to look at carp fishing to see how the blatantly obvious gets ignored for years and years, the hair rig for example (I had no idea either!) Either way deadbaiting came from behind in the 60s and 70s to overtake livebaiting as the most popular method of pike fishing. We have always associated pike with eating live prey fish, yet with most coarse fish surviving for only 5 to 15 years they have to die sometimes. Our friend the pike obviously clears up the corpses, but probably also nobbles them before they die. On the other hand we have people who should know better telling us that big pike are lazy and are suckers for an easy meal that cannot escape. I do not think any wild animal can be described as lazy otherwise they will as a species have died out years ago. Lions, leopards and cheetahs look lazy when at rest, but the physical effort it sometimes takes to catch prey when they are hunting is anything other than lazy. The pike is the same; it conserves energy when conditions are unsuitable for hunting yet when everything is right pike are very mobile and obviously very successful.

The basic method of deadbaiting involves sticking a bait onto the hooks, casting out and waiting. There are variations of this theme, which I'll cover in due course. What though do we use for bait? Any old dead fish? Well not quite. I've been involved in selling deadbaits for over 15 years now. It always seemed a bit of a comedown to be a bait packer after obtaining two degrees, but very few of us can plan our lives with total precision. Pike bait should have the following properties. It should be a sensible size, 2 to 6oz, be easy to obtain, smelly and bright in colour. It ought to be fresh. If it's cheap so much the better. If pike like to eat them, then we have a winner. You hear a fair amount of twaddle written by people who are so poorly informed that I'm amazed they have the intelligence to get dressed in the morning. As I write today there is a piece in Angling Times where the writer claims that he always uses mackerel off of a fishmongers slab because it is fresher! This does not take into account the fact that many of the mackerel I sell are frozen on board the ship. You cannot get much fresher than that. Anything that has been on a fishmongers slab will be less fresh than anything we buy simply because we freeze it a day before your average fishmonger gets hold of it. I've seen some terribly tired looking sardines, herrings and mackerel on fishmonger's slabs and though these will catch pike lets not kid ourselves here. If you are obsessed by fresh bait at least make sure you actually use it! Here I'll run through the baits I use and of course sell via my company Lucebaits. First I like to classify deadbaits as the true oily baits such as mackerel, herrings, sprats, sardines, horse mackerel and anchovy and all the others which obviously include eel, lamprey, coarse fish, sandeels, pollan, smelt, trout and capelin. It is a classification that works for me though some of the latter group are sea fish while others live in freshwater. I suppose you could group

63

deadbaits as natural baits and unnatural baits, but that doesn't work very well because species such as sprats and herrings though sea fish do colonise brackish water where they may encounter pike (i.e. the Baltic). I'll stick to my system with its limitations. My pike fishing experience has shown me that pike can discriminate between the oily baits and the others. Discrimination between the fish in the groups is something I've not come across.

HERRING

The original deadbait! The herring is still fairly common in the North Sea and around our coasts. Getting hold of suitable sized herrings is therefore not that difficult. Obtaining small ones invariably means sifting through boxes and boxes of larger fish. Herrings vary considerably in freshness and the nice ones are those that still have their scales on. With handling the scales are soon removed. Local estuary caught herrings are because of the short distances involved the really fresh ones. I get a lot of mine from the East Coast, but when needs must they can come from Ireland or as far away as Denmark or Norway. I like small herring of around   8 inches. Anything bigger than that I will use as half bait. They do not cast very well once thawed so I always put them on the hooks frozen. The herring continues to catch big pike and probably always will. It accepts colourings quite readily (except when fully scaled), is inexpensive, but is a bit fragile and certainly does not stand more than a few casts. They troll quite well and because they are soft you'll not miss many runs. Generally a couple of size 6 trebles will give you a good run to pike conversion.

MACKEREL

I would say that the mackerel is the most popular pike bait of all. We buy them by the tonne! You can use the mini mackerel of around 6 to 7 inches or you can use a larger fish and cut it in half. Personally I do not use the mini mackerel that much, but they are incredibly popular bait. They are rather soft and again best cast frozen. They tend to explode after several casts! My preference is to use larger mackerel and cut them in half. This gives you two highly aerodynamic baits that can withstand casting several times. I use heads just as readily as tails. There are few waters where mackerel will not catch pike, but several times I have seen them out fished by non-oily baits. I talked to quite an experienced pike angler once who didn't believe this could happen. All I can say is it happened once during a week on Corrib and once during a week on the River Bann. The reverse has also happened with the mackerel cleaning up while other baits did little. Mackerel can be coloured easily and though tough skinned do not present hooking problems provided your striking technique is good. I'd use two size 6s or 4s if the bait is a big half section. I would never fish a whole mackerel larger than 8 inches long. The bigger the bait the more difficult it is to hook the pike. Mini mackerel are very good trolling baits and I've had quite a few good fish up to38-08 on them.

Just as an aside there are in fact two species of mackerel, the one most of us are familiar with and the Spanish or Chubb mackerel. The Chubb mackerel is a little more portly, has a bigger eye, more spots than bars and has a swim bladder. I bet you didn't know that! Our native mackerel has no swim bladder; one of life's mysteries why one species should have one while the other does not. It matters not a jot, which you use, they both catch pike. Another piece of nonsense you sometimes hear is that " The pike need to get used to a particular type of deadbait because they've never seen it before". This is clearly not the case because on waters where deadbaits work, alien baits such as mackerel usually work straight off. The only situations where something like mackerel does not catch right from the off is the situation I've described earlier. Then for reasons better known to the pike they can show preferences that can alter the next time you fish the venue.

HORSE MACKEREL OR SCAD

This relative of the mackerel is not used that much for pike fishing, though my business gets through a fair number every year. In size they range from about 4 inches up to about a foot long. They are tough baits silver in colour and not as oily as mackerel. They are cheap and a useful change bait. I keep meaning to give them a more serious try, but always end up forgetting to take them with me!

SARDINES/PILCHARDS

A large sardine is a pilchard! One, species different names so to avoid confusion I'll use sardine in the context of this book. Sardines are generally a product of Spain or Portugal and are easily obtained via larger supermarkets or from tackle shops. Large amounts are also landed in the UK particularly from the Cornish Ports. A really fresh sardine is a creature of beauty, a solid bar of silver. The ones you frequently see on a wet fish counter are frequently falling to bits with the guts out. Sardines are a soft fish already so hanging around on ice for several days does little to improve them. The best ones are frozen on board a factory ship and though you tend to get minor blemishs due to the machinery that handles them, they are good baits. Size wise sardines are usually 4 to 8 inches, though once in a while I have picked up some whoppers a good ten inches long. Recently I have been able to import some beauties from California. These chunky sardines cast like missiles provided they are kept frozen. When thawed big sardines do not cast at all well so I usually cut the lower quarter of the fish off. It then casts rather like a mackerel head. All sardines are best-hooked head up the trace using the top bait holding hook stuck into the skull to take the force of casting. Only when frozen and preferably with some thread to hold the hooks in the tail root do I mount them differently. Head down the trace casts much better than head up. The big thing about sardines is their oil content. I do not know how much of the oil from deadbaits becomes suspended in solution in the water, but you have to believe that an oily bait is a good bait! Sardines have been in use a long time, I remember seeing Hugh Reynolds fishing with some on the Relief Channel in the early seventies. He bought his from Mac Fisheries in Cambridge. I of course couldn't buy them in my hometown of King's Lynn! Mac Fisheries, those were the days! Later Bill Chillingworth was to catch some fine fish up to 28lb from the Delph on them.

SPRATS

I reckon we sell about 50 stone of these every year, God knows who uses them.

They catch pike without a doubt, but to my mind are a bit small. I spend ages checking boxes of sprats to try and make sure that I have decent sized fish to sell. Sprats are at the biggest 4 to 5 inches in length and you get a lot to a pound. This is why they are still a popular bait. I've had pike to 22lbs on them, but have not used a sprat for 15 years! Some anglers like to use them for sink and draw; others use them frozen hooked through the eyes with a big single for distance fishing using a big lead. I've had quite a few pike fishing them suspended under a float on a paternoster. Sprats were probably responsible for more pike deaths fished under a bung on two size 4 barbed trebles than any other bait or method. If you have to use sprats remember they are in season from about August until March. The larger run of sprats gives way to very small fish by about January so it pays to stock up before Christmas and freeze some down. Tackle shops will usually have decent sized sprats all the year around.

ANCHOVIES
Not many people have ever used these. They tend to turn up in sprats and are another oily bait. They seldom grow bigger than 5 or 6 inches and deteriorate faster than anything I've ever come across in the way of deadbaits. They catch pike, but in reality are a novelty bait. You can of course put them on your Pizza.

SMELT
Probably the second most popular bait after the mackerel. I may not have discovered smelt as a pike bait, but I certainly popularized it's use, the first mention being in the Anglers Mail in the early to mid seventies First shown to me in 1966 by Mr. Harry Nelson while pike fishing on the Relief Channel at Magdalen, his first pike in front of me weighed 18lb. I then had a big fish follow a smelt to the surface while I was bridge fishing. Time makes the image less sharp but it still seems like a big pike to me. In those days you got your smelt by fishing for them in the tidal Ouse the day before. Because I had school on Saturday mornings and was restricted to one days fishing a week I did not have time to catch smelt. Instead I would be constantly watching our local fishmonger hoping and praying that some smelt would turn up. One February some did and I bought the lot. I caught my first twenty on a smelt that weekend, I think it weighed 21-10.

Since then a lot of water has flowed through Denver sluice and getting hold of smelts remains a constant problem. Why they are such good pike bait is unclear. They are a nice size, generally around 6 to 10 inches. They are firm and have a wonderful cucumber smell. I've always felt that pike have a number of instinctive behaviour patterns imprinted into their genes. Smelt run up into freshwater to spawn and many of them die after reproducing. Is it so unlikely that pike simply know that a smelt is an easy meal?

Anyway that's my story and I'm sticking to it. The only snag with smelt is that the supply of this fish is limited and the really good places for getting them are or should I say were closely guarded secrets. That is changing fast and with over exploitation I suspect that we are going to have to learn to use alternative baits such as pollan instead.

It was fine while the smelts were being harvested at a low level, now looks as if thy may be fished until it will no longer be worth fishing for them. No one thought the Newfoundland cod stocks would collapse, but they did and they've never recovered. So before anyone blames me if smelt become scarcer than they are now, I've been taking roughly the same amount for 15 years and they still keep coming. However if because of other netsmen, the take increases to double the smelt fishery may decline. Smelt work on almost every water I have fished though they can be very slow on the very heavily stocked trout waters. On these waters it is almost all livebaiting or lures. Smelt catch big pike and small pike alike, whereas the oily fish tend to be a little more selective. Two size six trebles suit the size of smelt I prefer i.e. around 8 inches.

POLLAN

I've already mentioned this as an alternative to smelt as non-oily type bait. They are an interesting fish, a form of whitefish that exists in a number of forms in several waters around the country. Names such as Powan (Loch Lomond), Vendace and Schelley (Lakes district) and Gwyniad (Llyn Tegid or Bala) are no doubt familiar. Pollan come from Ireland and are found in a number of waters notably Lough Neagh where there is a commercial fishery. They are generally around 8 to 10 inches in length; silvery with a smell I cannot quite place. They are nice firm fish that because they are netted at some depth still have their swim bladder intact. They tend therefore to be self-popping up which is handy for those keen on that particular approach. I've used them a lot and so far I think about 19lb is the best I've had on one fished static on the bottom. I'm sure though as time goes on that I'll catch some good fish on them. Unfortunately the last couple of seasons have seen more pike on lures and lives because of the nature of the waters fished. Lomond trips where you'd expect pollan to out fish everything else have seen mackerel doing the business! Funny things pike. I fish pollan on a couple of size 6s and always put SSG shot on the trace rather than a running lead Otherwise they can end up on the surface.

TROUT

Because trout are farmed and because feed prices keep going up trout are the most expensive bait we commonly use. While in certain parts of the country, i.e. Scotland you can catch your own, generally if you want them you have to buy them. Almost certainly the best trout are wild brownies and luckily my business has an occasional supply of these. They are firm baits, which sometimes (note I said sometimes) have an edge on other baits. Whether or not they could possibly be better baits than farmed trout I do not know. Rainbow trout are fine as baits, but should really be starved before use; otherwise the digestive juices quickly eat through the stomach wall causing the fish to split. It is sometimes possible to buy salmon smolts, a by-product of the caged salmon rearing industry. These make fine baits, however they are not going to give you any sort of edge simply because I doubt if a pike can distinguish between a salmon and a brown trout. It would be nice to sell char and brook trout as bait, just for the variety. Indeed years ago on Loch Awe I had my biggest pike of the week a 17 pounder on half a brookie. The fact that, that was the only brookie I had for bait was probably why I didn't place too much significance on the capture. No point in getting worked up about it if that was the last of that particular bait.

Because trout can be tough skinned you have to be sensible with your hook sizes. An 8 to 10 inch trout is going to need a couple of size 4 hooks if you are to connect with any takes you may get.

COARSE BAITS

There are an awful lot of different coarse baits you can use and all will catch pike. For static deadbaiting favourites have to be roach, rudd, bream and perch. I've had pike to 27 on dead rudd, 27-14 on dead perch and an unknown number of twenties on the others. Wobbled roach has accounted for fish to 26lbs while plenty of pike have fallen to trolled roach and perch. Getting hold of most of these baits is not difficult, however in these days of cormorant ravaged fisheries I think it is ill advised to go and help yourself to an angling clubs stockfish. I may have a vested interest in selling baits, but the truth is that it is better for everyone to buy them rather than help yourself. Our coarse fish come from sources where the fish are not fished for and therefore removing them has no impact on anyone's sport. For wobbling fresh baits are the best because they withstand casting better. Generally though most of us have to make do with frozen fish and because of this wobbling requires regular bait changing. I use size 6s for most of the coarse fish I use. Small pike are also good baits and though very hard to get hold of are worth giving a try. My first Lomond pike of 20-01 fell to a half pike deadbait. Recently someone phoned me to say that he was going to propagate small pike for bait. It will be interesting to see if this come off and even more interesting to see if the resulting pikelets are affordable. At certain times of the year there is good reason to feel that a bait that mimics what is most readily available works best. I would certainly continue to use perch deadbaits if I was spring fishing in Ireland. Perch after they have spawned are completely clapped out and I'm sure lots of them die to be mopped up by waiting pike.

EELS

I use eels mainly for zander fishing, but lots of pike anglers have great confidence in them. Pike in some waters eat lot of eels. They also probably dig the odd ones out of the mud when they are hibernating. The only problem with eels is that they are horrible and slimy. Well most are, but ours are not. We have ours de-slimed which makes for a much more socially acceptable bait! When using eels I use half of a 12 or 14-inch example and always use good-sized hooks, for example size 4s to ensure good hookholds on a quick strike. I very much prefer to avoid using or selling eels over a pound as bait. We have to remember here that fellow anglers would consider a 2lb eel to be a specimen; therefore chopping one up for bait is hardly likely to go down well with an eel angler!

LAMPREY

This is our most primitive fish species, in-fact it is so primitive that the lamprey was around before our more familiar fish developed jaws. The lamprey uses its circular sucker with its rasping teeth to make a hole in a fish's side. By doing this it extracts blood and bits of flesh from the unlucky host. A thoroughly loveable lifestyle! Luckily the lamprey does all this at sea. When it arrives in freshwater in October it is purely to find a mate and reproduce. They ascend many of our rivers in numbers and must at certain times be a staple part of the pike's diet. I've seen lamprey sticking out of a pike's throat several times. Many die after spawning so again dead lamprey may seem like natural food to pike in many rivers. I first started using them in the late eighties when odd fish turned up in the smelts. Then a local eel fisherman working on the Trent got some for me and I started fishing with them regularly and was able to sell some to the public for the first time. Unknown to me though, my local eel fisherman had decided to start up his own bait business and on the back of the lamprey got off to a very good start. All that's in the past now and both bait companies are doing fine. I've had a lot of pike on lamprey and while a few people who have probably been pike fishing for about two years are trying to tell us that lamprey are not a wonder bait, it leaves me to ask. "Who said they were a wonder bait anyway?" Certainly not me! They are a perfectly good pike bait that work on many waters. In the Fens they certainly catch as much as smelt and zander love them as well! The lamprey's big attraction is the sheer volume of blood that leaks out of a bait. I cannot understand where it comes from, but it one of life's mysteries that lamprey never stop bleeding. This blood is water-soluble and must provide a scent trail for a pike to home in on. I use half baits when fishing with lamprey and have had success on both the head and tail halves. The head section is probably the most attractive from our point of view in that it seems to bleed longer. They are tough baits, but use two size 6 hooks and you should hook most takes. Usually you get the bait back as well which means the one bait can go a long way. Just as a matter of interest my best Fenland pike of 30-08 fell to lamprey.

CAPELIN

This is a small relative of the smelt, which spends all it's life in the sea. I obtained a supply a few years ago, but this has now dried up. They catch pike without a doubt; my best while I was using them was 15lb. Two size 8 trebles are more than enough hooks for this small bait.

SANDEELS

Commercial fishing for fishmeal has made serious inroads into sandeel stocks. The large ones I used to sell are very difficult to obtain. I have used them quite a lot and they do catch pike particularly well on the Fen drains. My best two weighed 21 and 23lbs. I'm not sure that they offer any advantage over lamprey or eel deadbaits so not having them does not worry me in the slightest. The much larger snake launce is usually fished as a half bait and was a popular bait when it was available. Some pike anglers actually catch their own and I had one in Western Ireland a few years ago on a spinnerbait of all things!

OTHER BAITS

I've tried all sorts of alternative baits, but really nothing stands out as a better bait than those we already use. I've had pike to 17lbs on garfish sections. They cast well and are tough, but they are not something I bother with now. Various small sea fish species turn up as food or as waste fish. Red mullet, red snapper and gurnard are different and if you desire a change bait these are worth a look. Some pike angler's rate small whiting and pouting. These members of the cod family are fairly soft baits, so cast best frozen. One small fish with a very pretty dorsal fin the dragonett actually smells like a smelt. Unfortunately they only turn up once in a blue moon.

The best market for interesting baits would be North America and Canada. They have their own landlocked smelt that has a black stripe along its lateral line. Unfortunately they tend to be small and do not smell of cucumber. I imported a sample from the Great Lakes in the hope that this would solve the smelt problem. It wasn't to be though, the baits being too small. There are a host of members of the carp family, suckers, and chub like fish and pretty looking shiners, which would I, am sure catch pike. In the end any species of dead fish will catch pike.

FLAVOURED BAITS
The best known must be the kipper. Quite a few pike anglers have experimented with this bait. I tried it quite a bit in the early 80s and had fish to the upper teens. To fish one you need to tie it back together using cotton thread (biodegradable). I cut the head off and tie the tail half to the hooks. They are too expensive to catch only one pike on them. Generally the most favoured   flavoured bait option is to use oils or artificial flavours. Natural fish oils include mackerel, herring, sardine and capelin. These generally become very viscous in cold weather. One option is to mix them 50 ; 50 with corn oil. Another is to buy a winterised fish oil. Pilchard oil is the most readily available. I always struggle a bit to understand how non water-soluble oils can be attractive to pike. Also they tend to float! I have no scientific evidence to support the following supposition, but this is what I feel happens. There is probably a minute fraction in any fish oil which is either water-soluble or becomes emulsified when it leaks from your bait. Fish have a very good sense of smell, indeed salmon and eels use smell to find their home river. If we could extract any such water-soluble fraction we could of course avoid all that nasty smelly oil. As it is we cannot so most of us will continue to inject oils into deadbaits. There are water-soluble flavours, which can be used, none of which are nature natural. They are synthetic flavours made in a factory and the nearest they have been to a fish is when you inject it into a bait!

Smelt, grayling, tuna and many of the now defunct ET flavours may not have any pike attracting properties as such. Where they have value is in the modification of the smell of the bait. When pike have been fished for a lot they still want to eat a deadbait, but unfortunately become very difficult to tempt. Now it is stretching one's imagination to believe that pike are sufficiently intelligent to be able to discriminate between a bait which it has been caught on several times and one it has no unpleasant experiences with. Yet it does happen on some waters. Certain baits cease to be effective and change baits give a new lease of life to deadbaiting. It is a logical progression to flavour your baits to make them smell differently. While to us it seems logical to flavour baits using fish flavours in reality if you are using a synthetic flavour I fail to see how a pike can discriminate between synthetic smelt and synthetic strawberry. I've messed about using various non-fishy flavours and have caught using smokey bacon or spicy liver flavours. There is plenty of scope for experimentation here and those people fishing very pressurized waters could do worse that to give this approach a try.

VERY BASIC TWO HOOK RIGS

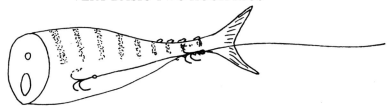

Half Mackerel

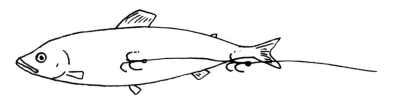

Smelt ot Trout
Generally 2nd hook about halfway along flank of bait

WOBBLED DEADBAIT

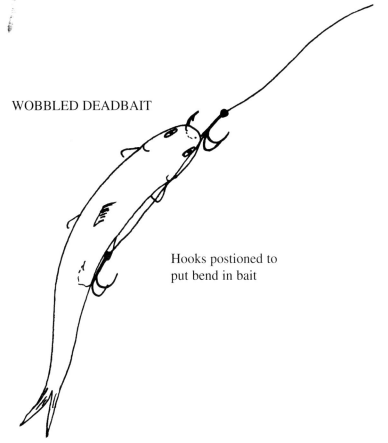

Hooks postioned to
put bend in bait

One thing does concern me about pike oils and flavours and that is those, which purport to be something that they are probably not! Lamprey oil for example does not convince me for a minute that it has any lamprey in it at all. When giving lamprey a sniff I cannot discern any unique or special smell. Certainly nothing that can be duplicated by the flavour industry.

Using oils and flavours is quite straightforward. I use a large bore needle (the fine needles get clogged by oils) and simply inject 5ml of oil or flavour into the bait. You can also spray the baits with a flavour prior to freezing and wrapping and let the flavour soak in. Spraying before casting out probably makes little difference because contact with the bait is not long enough to allow the flavour to impregnate the bait. You can also use a separate flavour or oil source near to the bait. A very small feeder can be attached to an up trace above your hook bait trace, filled with foam, which in turn is steeped in the desired flavour or oil. The reason for attaching the feeder to an uptrace is just incase a pike decides to take the feeder.

It is also possible to build up a scent trail to your swim particularly if you are fishing on a river or drain with a flow. I would make up a 50:50 mix of white crumb and fishmeal, add 5ml of a desired flavour or 50ml of fish oil. Then make into balls much as if you were fishing for roach or bream. Hopefully the scent trail will help attract pike and if that does not work the groundbait might assist in getting some food fish activity in your swim. These are not revolutionary ideas, but if you enjoy messing about and trying new things they cannot do any harm. It never ceases to amaze me how quickly a pike can find a bait particularly on large waters. No-one can convince me that every time you catch a pike within 15 minutes of casting out you just happened to drop your bait on it's head. I'm sure that a scent trail spreads though the water and pike detect it. What the distance limit is I do not know, obviously there must be a limit otherwise you'd never need to move. All pike would be catchable from one swim. I certainly try to move 100 to 200 yards away from an earlier spot and fish usually respond within the hour. This suggests that the influence of scent is limited. It may be that at a certain range, say 100 yards the scent trail is so diffuse that a pike cannot follow it, or it becomes undetectable. Whether increasing the smell of your bait helps or not, I'm not sure. As I said earlier I cannot see why a pike should respond to an artificial flavour and suspect that there is only a tiny fraction in fish oil that a pike can detect. This tiny amount is probably undetectable at 100 yards. It would probably be better to use fish juices to attract pike. The term fish juices is vague, but would basically cover any water-soluble fluids, which seep out of fish. Fish blood being the most obvious. In reality we have enough pressure on certain of our fish stocks not to want to liquidize vast amounts to make a commercial additive. On a small scale the individual pike angler could always make up his own liquidized lamprey for example. Be careful though because lamprey blood and certainly eel blood is said to be toxic to vertebrates. Once cooked the poison is denatured.

COLOURED BAITS

Now the idea of using coloured baits is an old one. Salmon anglers have been colouring sprats and prawns for years, but for the purposes of pike fishing I think the jury is still out. I have fished coloured baits and I have caught pike on them, but I'd be hard pressed to prove that the colouring had made any difference to my catch rate. It hardly matters what my personal results have been. Other anglers rate coloured baits so I have to describe how to colour them here. The easiest way to obtain a coloured bait is to use a spray colour. The bait has to be defrosted first and comparatively free of scales otherwise the colour will not take. The best fish to colour are herrings, sprats, mackerel and smelts. Sardines and dark fish such as eels and lamprey are not worth trying to colour. I cannot see much point in using dull colours such as blue and green. Red, orange and yellow seem sensible if you wish to make the bait stand out better. Colouring baits cannot do any harm, but that is as much as I can say about them!

DEADBAIT TACTICS
These can be divided into static and mobile methods.

STATIC METHODS
The majority of the pike I catch fall for static deadbaiting. In it's simplest form this means float legering a bait in a swim you fancy and leaving it there for a couple of hours. I always try to float leger rather than straight leger a bait. This is because much of my fishing is carried out on weedy waters where it is much easier to get a pike to the surface when using a float or on waters where snags on the bottom are more easily avoided if the line is kept out of them. If you are going to static fish a deadbait then the aim should be to keep it where you cast it. Weight is the answer and I always use sufficient to keep a bait in position. Sometimes three or four SSG shot on the trace is enough. At other times a 1oz bullet running on the line may be required. Fox do some egg shaped sinkers which I've still not tried, but I think I will have to change that soon because they seem very popular. A 2oz bomb might be required on a fast moving river, but by the time you've had to resort to that much lead the float is probably ineffective anyway. Only then do I give up and straight leger. Float legering baits can be carried out using two basic designs of float. We have the Polaris type float, which incorporates a "Frixion" device, which does away with stopknots and beads. The float locks itself on the line at just over the required depth. Provided you tighten up well and use a drop off bobbin, the Polaris will stay put. It is only in strong headwinds that it has the tendency to creep up the line. If you cannot cope with not having to use stop knots and beads you can use end ring slider floats. The one's I use are Middy ones and the self-cockers are useful for boat fishing because they stand out well. Non-self cockers are best for bank fishing because you cock them yourself when you tighten to them. Traditionalists can of course carry on using the painted poly ball or cork ball. They still work well enough and the half red half black float is still effective when boat fishing because you can easily spot when a pike has picked up a bait because the black bottom of the float shows. Stopknots remain the same Billy Lane knot designed by the great match angler years ago. Some people like to use power gum for these knots, but I've always found nylon of about 12lb breaking strain to work for me. Always remember though when moving a stop knot to wet the line around the knot to avoid friction damage. Using a stop knot and bead requires a little more effort that the Polaris float and it does make you learn the features of the swim you are fishing. Even with a Polaris float though you

will have some understanding of the contours in front of you because you can count down how long it takes for the float to settle. Generally as a bait sinks the Polaris will sit low in the water as the weight and bait try to drag it under. Once the bait and the weight have hit bottom, the float will sit much higher in the water or even lay flat. A simple countdown will tell you a lot.

Static deadbaiting without artificial aids can be carried out up to about 80 yards range with a float. Possibly these days with the advent of braid you might be able to add another twenty yards to this. A slight increase in range can be obtained by removing the float, but to get range the bait and weight must travel together. This is why I favour SSG on the trace; it simply makes a reasonably aerodynamic combination. The alternative is to employ a very big lead up to four ounces and a small bait. Various combos of frozen bait and even a bit of PVA string can help the serious caster to get increased distance. I must admit however that many pike anglers now employ a radio-controlled boat for long distance work. Though at the moment I do not own one I have to give serious thought to buying one because there are waters where they are essential.

Some baits are better for distance work than others. The half mackerel must be the most useful bait and I certainly use them as my first choice if distance is required. An eel section and a big lead goes a long, long way. My first experiments with braid while zander fishing on the Relief Channel saw me have to stop the cast because the end tackle was going to hit the bank! A hundred yard cast. Unfortunately the next cast resulted in a birds nest, I had overfilled the spool... Frozen baits work better than thawed ones and I keep everything frozen in a small cool box. Baits thaw very quickly once in the water.

A lot of pike anglers swear by popped up baits, I probably swear at them! Seriously I've never seen much point in doing it. I am convinced that a pike's sense of smell is such that it can detect a bait long before it is in visual range. So why make it stand up off the bottom? Well it is a natural presentation, just as a dead fish on the lake or riverbed is. Roach in particular suspend off the bottom hanging head down and motionless. I have no idea why they do this, but it is a fact. If a pike has the intelligence to look at a popped up deadbait and accept that it's really a suspended roach instead of ignoring a deadbait on the bottom because it's been caught that way several times before I'd be surprised. Yet just the suspicion on our part that this might happen is worth considering. Experience has taught me one or two things about pike fishing. One of these is to never discount anything. Fish are funny creatures and sometimes we have enough going against us so that ignoring any little helping pointers is foolish. An awful lot of pike anglers swear by popped up baits so who am I to tell you they are a waste of time. Then again in the Middle Ages a hell of a lot of people thought the earth was flat! I simply do not deliberately use the method. Even in dense weed I firmly believe that pike will seek out a bait by smell. I do accidentally pop baits up. Pollan because they are netted from deep water have an intact swim bladder which mean that they pop themselves up. I fish them as they are and certainly do not try to puncture the swim bladder. Pollan are a fine pike bait, but whether or not it is because they auto pop up remain to be seen.

One presentation I still use quite happily is the suspended deadbait. Whether I've caught because or inspite of the presentation is something I'll never know. Sunken paternostered deadbaits see the bait suspended 2 or 3 feet off of the bottom. Logic says that the bait ought to sit horizontally but of course this is nonsense. Baits can be fished head down, head up, horizontal, upside down or even more illogically as half baits. My last ever session on Martham South Broad, a night venture saw one pike landed on a float paternostered herring head. 34lb. There's no logic in that at all, but we are not dealing with an animal that can do a lot of reasoning. It sees or smells food and if it is hungry it eats it. Less than a year ago I was boat fishing a shallow swim on one of the larger loughs. Results to float legered deads had not been very good. The day before I had been fishing with Alastair Rawlings and he had picked up a twelve pounder on a dead roach fished just off the bottom. It had been a long time since I had tried the method, drifting a deadbait under a float around the swim.

I wouldn't have bothered either if something hadn't happened to buck me up. Both the first and second day of the trip had seen me casting lures around the swim from time to time. Not a lot happened until about 10am on day two when what looked like a large pike followed the Springdawg in. I did not need telling twice and a smelt was soon drifting around the swim. Fishing on the drift requires your attention and it makes a nice change to actually concentrate and then actually see the float go under. That is what happened and on winding down a very, very angry pike decided to put some distance between itself and my boat. In shallow water in late August a slim looking pike really can get up to a frightening speed. Lily pads floated up as my line cheese cut through them. Eventually I landed this very long projectile and quickly unhooked and weighed it. 25-04 pike cannot be sneezed at, at any time of year and certainly not in August. The tackle was checked and another smelt cast out. You do not always get repeat performances when you've just caught a big pike, but I did this time! The float went under, I wound down and this time it powered into a weed bed. Eventually she came out and proved to be nearly a perfect match to the other one. A 24 pounder just after a 25, you do not have that much good luck very often.

Another approach used by some pike anglers is twitching the bait back to the bank or boat. This approach doesn't work in weedy waters, but is effective at covering water when fishing weed free waters. I do not use it much myself because once again I am fairly sure that pike home in on the smell of a bait. Moving it every five minutes may make it more difficult for the pike to find it. A recast from time to time, say every hour is sometimes worthwhile if you are covering new water, but I'd not bother if my swim only had three places I could present a bait in. One thing you should always do when winding in a deadbait is watch to see if Mrs. pike is following it in. Sometimes a static bait is not quite enough to get a pike interested. That movement, sometimes totally unnatural (well how often do you see a half mackerel swimming…) can evoke a response so always be prepared. Clues like this can lead to extra fish and certainly on one Fen drain I fish a follow off of a pike was soon converted into a take once I had rehooked the bait right way around!

WOBBLED DEADBAITS

Fashions come and go in all forms of fishing and pike fishing is no exception. In the sixties and seventies there was a lot of deadbait wobbling going on. Before this going back to the Victorian era, many specialized rigs and spinning flights were devised to enable life to be put into a dead fish. I can remember myself using Archer flights to fish spun deadbaits. We do not tend to do as much deadbait wobbling as we used to. I certainly used the method a lot more in the eighties, but then I was fishing waters, which responded to the method. In recent years I've often given a swim a few casts at the end of a session just to see if a wobbled deadbait can evoke a response from any pike that might have ignored my static baits. That is hardly likely to reap great rewards!

The most basic wobbled bait is something like a freshly killed dead roach mounted on two trebles, one through the top and bottom lips, and the other in the flank. The positioning of the flank treble can give the bait a certain amount of bend, which in turn causes it to rotate when drawn through the water. This is the classic wobbled deadbait as used to considerable effect by the great Broadland anglers such as Frank Wright. The bait should be fresh because frozen roach tend to be much softer and do not withstand much casting. If you have no choice other than frozen baits, fish such as pollen and wild brown trout tend to be tougher and can be fished for longer than delicate baits such as small mackerel and herring. My preferred bait size is up to about 4oz, but I remember Fred Wagstaffe fishing on Sywell with whacking great big herrings or mackerel wobbling them using a beach-casting rod! At the other end of the scale a lot of anglers used to use sprats for wobbling though you would have to make sure you had got hold of some larger samples because sometimes they were the size of whitebait.

The beauty of wobbled baits is their neutral buoyancy. With no lead on the trace they can easily be worked just over the surface of the weed. Pike without doubt sit in weed and a wobbled bait passing over their head will frequently see them crash out of the weed to investigate. To fish deeper simply add SSG shot to the trace. When I get a take I usually give it about five seconds before winding down. Always pay special attention at the end of the retrieve because follows can be converted into takes. I've had twenty pounders follow wobbled baits in and because I'm just about to run out of line I just let the bait sink. Usually a pike will follow it down and stare at it. You have one chance in this situation, a quick 12-inch pull. Often the pike pounces on the bait, and then it's up to the angler!

TROLLED DEADBAITS

Elsewhere I have given a detailed description of trolling with livebaits. I have also done a lot of deadbait trolling over the years. Generally I have had most success using baits of 2 to 4oz. Bigger baits do make for presentational and hooking problems and it just doesn't seem sensible trying to troll a 1lb dead roach behind the boat when a smaller bait will do. I might be wrong there because I was only the other day reading about Bob Church's fabulous catch of wild brownies from Lough Corrib. (fish to 17lb). These fell to 12oz roach deadbaits! My own best day trolling deads also came in Ireland, but was on Lough Mask rather than Corrib. I had made my first attempts at fishing Lough Mask in the late 80s, but to be honest it was so different from any water I had ever fished before that I was forced to retreat to Corrib, which was a bit, more like Loch Lomond and Lough Allen. It was Mark Ackerley who made me rethink my fishing strategy. He caught a fish of 32lb odd from Maamtrasna Bay on Lough Mask in May. Himself and Peter Robinson caught some good fish from that bay in that month and it became clear that Mask was well worth some attention. Now at the time none of us were aware of how effective the modern Musky type lures could be. It was clear that the usual selection of plugs and spoons did not catch well on Mask. Too many had been dragged past the pike by trout anglers. It was a simple fact that if the pike took any of those types of lures it was already dead! A form of natural selection where long life comes with not responding to Rapalas and Toby spoons!

Mark had found that float trolled deads sorted out the big fish. It was after all a mobile method, which presented a largish bait in a manner which caused the pike to respond favorably. It had little similarity to how the trout anglers fished. Indeed during all the time I trolled deads on Mask I never once caught a big brown trout! I did have a small mackerel hit hard and cleanly cut in two by what I think was a trout, but that was the nearest I came! So the trolled deadbait was clearly a selective method.

Now some might question the logic behind how I planned things, but to my mind it was a sensible approach. I felt that to catch a big pike from Mask I would have to fish it a lot. Indeed Mark had fished a whole year on the water (see his account in the big water section.) Now being recently self employed and not with the joy of a monthly direct payment into my bank account I had to figure a way of getting to Mask regularly at the lowest possible cost. The obvious answer was to take an organized trip. I would then get to fish and hopeful gain a week's wages at the same time. The first trip was in February and really we spent more time on the smaller waters near Galway. It wasn't until May that we determined to hit Mask properly. We spent the first day on Ballyquirke Lake, as time was short. Everything was then organized for the 50-mile trip to Maamtrasna Bay. There were six of us altogether. Martin Nelson, Steve Makin, Carl Barber, Ken Messeter and Dave Grover. We had three boats so we teamed up, Carl with me, Martin and Steve, Dave and Ken. Now readers should realize that I try not to pump my friends for information. If I had asked Mark about Maamtrasna I had either not asked much or I'd already forgotten what he had told me! So really we were all starting from scratch. It was a typical day in the west of Ireland, decidedly damp! Carl and I started to float troll using the electric motor and using experience gained elsewhere it seemed logical to start on the drop off outside he bay. This we did, but it wasn't long before I had snagged and duly had to pull for a break. A great start! Because I was on the electric motor we had to drift while I retackled. Carl just kept his float fished dead roach hung over the side while we drifted and as so often happens when you are not expecting it he had a take. I remember nothing of what followed except the weight of the pike, 20-12! I was amazed. I was also a bit miffed because I had really hoped to get a 20 from Mask and my boat partner had pinched one already. We'd probably not get another look at a similar fish all week.

Life was obviously good for Carl, but soon it was to get worse for me. My electric motor that has served me well for at least 5 years started to expire. By mid morning it was completely knackered. Now I have a tradition when I'm boat fishing with another angler. I generally look after the motor; the other chap manages the oars. Age before beauty or something like that! So quite rightly I set Carl to work on the oars. Now Carl is not stupid and did a reasonable job rowing around until we got into the bay properly. Now the depths change rapidly in the bay and Carl was struggling to troll the line I wanted. It was rather like trying to direct someone to your house while they are on a mobile phone. In the end I said I'd do some rowing, after all you must not wear out your paying customers… The precise details of other fish caught that day are unclear, but I think I had an eleven pounder and hooked something that went tearing off before the hooks pulled. I think I had rowed in and out of the bay at least once and we were now working down the north side of the bay. In one are the depth changed from 4 feet to 20 feet so I had my float set at about ten feet hoping that I'd sweep in and sweep out of the shallow water without snagging. The bait a small mackerel of about 8 inches was being trolled behind a suitably large red topped "shark float" The track I wanted to take prove to be correct as I didn't get snagged as the bait worked very close to the really shallow water before we moved out again. In about 8 feet of water the float dragged under, so I stopped rowing, reversed a bit and watched the float pop up. It could have been weed except the float was clearly moving away from us. Some things stay in your mind forever and that day the float appearing to wobble, as it moved away was the one thing that stuck!

It was obviously a run so I did the next obvious thing I wound down. I think I live to be a hundred I will still never hook a big fish and know it was a big fish straight away. I do not mean the ones you hook and then lose. You never do find out about those ones. What I mean is that none of my biggest pike actually felt that big on hooking them. All of them got bigger as they neared the net! This fish did not take that long to get close to the boat, but I had a problem. Carl could not figure out how to put the net together. Now many triangular nets are of the tensioned arm type and Carl had obviously never come across the concept before. In the end I suggested he forget the handle and just use the arms of the net. This he did and a rather larger pike was soon giving me a malice filled look from beside the boat. Now I always take the following steps when boat fishing for pike. When a pike is landed it is allowed to rest in the net while unhooking gear, scales and cameras are readied. Care has to be taken that it does not bang its head against the side of the boat. I try not to lay a pike down in a boat because the best way to control a pike is to keep it off the deck. It was drizzling gently as I unhooked what was clearly a 30lb plus pike. I took my Rueben Heaton scales out to weigh the pike and the hook promptly pulled out of the bottom of the scales. The fish looked as if 32lb Avon's would not do it justice, but luckily Carl had a set of 40lb Avon's so we quickly tried again. It took the scales nicely past 35lb to settle on 38-08. Photographs were taken while our friend the pike proceeded to excrete some foul smelling gunk from its vent. I'm pretty certain that this fish had been feeding so hard that anything dead and not necessarily fresh had found it's way down this pike's throat. What I had on me was well-digested rotten fish! None of this was noticed of course and soon my prize was returned. She was caught again and returned two years later from nearby. The following year she most likely died in a gill net. A magnificent rare creature sacrificed at the alter of wishful thinking. That gill netting might improve the trout fishing and bring a few more punts (Euros!) into the local economy.

Trolled deadbaits can also be fished using the petrol outboard. This presentation involves going much faster than you would row or on an electric motor. I have a hand held GPS which allows me to calculate my speed on water. Trolling on a petrol motor will generally see speeds of 1 to 2mph. Electric motor or rowing sees speeds slower than this. To troll deadbaits on the petrol motor you need 1 to 2oz of lead and you have to pay out around 30 yards of line. The best advice I ever had regarding trolling deadbaits was from N.Ireland piker George Higgins. Now George has probably trolled baits more miles than I've traveled to get to waters! So when he says something I'm inclined to listen. His advice is to fish about 10 feet deep in most situations where there is 20 to 40 feet of water. The reasoning behind this is simple. In clear waters the pike can see or hear a trolled bait-passing overhead. If it is going to take it; it will move 10 foot up though the water column to grab it. While there are bound to be exceptions to this rule and waters where a deeper presentation works better, George's rule of thumb has proved useful in most of the situations I have encountered.

Favourite baits for trolling include herring, mackerel and trout. The aim is not to have them twirling madly though the water, but to gently rotate or slip gently through the water. I fish them with the baitrunner on, but suitably adjusted so that line is not taken on water resistance alone. You can rig baits up on a simple tandem hook rig or if the bait is over 7 inches long you can add a third hook. All sorts of instant strike rigs have been devised over the years most using something like one large single through the bait's mouth and two or three trebles. The mistake that we've all made is to rig things up with hooks, which are too small. Size 8s and 6s are just not big enough. You need 4s and 2s just as you would on a comparable sized lure. Using the right sized hooks means that you can usually hook a pike a few seconds after you have noted the take and given a few yards of line.

The weight you use depends on how fast you are going. You'll generally troll quicker with the wind rather than against it. Around one to one and a half ounces of lead is usually enough, preferably made from lead sheet and cut into a half moon. Folded over the line with a section of silicone to protect the line the half moon lead helps to prevent the reel line kinking really badly. I've not done a lot of deadbait trolling on the petrol motor recently so I've not had the chance to take advantage of the modern braids. We used to have to make do with mono, which is OK, but getting snagged up could be terminal unless you could reverse and jiggle the hooks off the snag.

When fishing on my own I've always tried to fish a lure as well as a deadbait when fishing two rods. There seems little point in duplication of baits when you have the option to fish a totally different offering on the second rod. Lures in the eighties consisted of home made copper spoons, Big S plugs and perhaps just to be really adventurous a Creek Chub Pikie. It's a lot different these days with a multitude of proven trolling lures.

PREBAITING

Prebaiting is a simple technique used to get pike to come to certain swims so you can catch them without all that nasty effort trying to find them! When it works, it can work brilliantly. When it doesn't it can be utterly useless! Generally the hungrier the pike are in the water the better prebaiting is likely to work. Do not bother tying it on your local heavily stocked trout water. The trout are more likely to take the prebait! I use prebaiting primarily on waters where I cannot fish the whole lake. My aim is to try and get the pike to come to me. It works sometimes, but there are periods when for reasons better known to   the pike they just disappear. People often ask me how much prebait they need to put in. Unfortunately there is no ready reckoner or formula that I can use to tell readers the answer. All I can do it give you some examples.

My first major experience with prebaiting came on some gravel pits near Lound. Here there were 4 main swims and by prebaiting you could get them to accumulate in any of those swims. They were almost tame at one stage, but they would not tolerate being caught too many times from the same swim. You could however catch them from another prebaited swim that they had moved to. This obviously leads to lots of repeat captures and the associated moral problem of how many times do you want to catch the same fish? I've always found that the big problem on some waters is that the pike get bigger as time goes by and you of course want to catch those bigger pike. When to stop fishing for them is the difficult one. Imagine a water where the biggest four pike are 21, 23, 25 and 26lb. A year later they weigh 25, 28, 29 and 30lb. It is difficult not wanting to go back and catch them again! I've never been lucky enough to prebait myself to a thirty pounder! The waters usually get emptied before that happens! Pike growth of course is something you do get with prebaiting.

Another water I fish only has a handful of swims. You can catch pike from one of the swims for a couple of weeks once you have prebaited for a couple of weeks. You cannot get them back there later in the season. I hope they turn up again this October! As a general rule I work on throwing in 2lb of prebait per pike over 10lb per week. If I think that there's 200lb of eligible pike in a water that means 40lb of prebait a week. Obviously this prebait gets unfairly distributed between the pike so that some get totally stuffed while others get little. However it does tend to cause them to stay in the area or at the very least give it a look sometime during the day. Sometimes coots and cormorants muck things up by eating your prebait and you can be pretty sure that eels do their worst. On one lake I used to fish otters may even have been helping themselves!

If you prebait regularly you need to find somewhere that will not be fished by other anglers. This is easier said than done, but long walks are sometimes the answer and sometimes a baitboat can bait an area 100 yards out of reach of other anglers. A tiny gap in a forest of trees, a swim that can only be fished with chest waders. They are all worthwhile tactics. Beware if someone does find your prebaited swim, because it is usually a disaster. Nige Williams did not catch a thirty out of his prebaited swim, but someone else did! The choice of prebait is fairly restricted. You may be able to go to your local fishmonger and get enough waste fish, but unless you live near to a fishing port you may have to buy it. My business generates a lot of mackerel heads and sprat waste. Most of this costs me more than the four pounds a stone I charge for it. However that is fine, I dispose of some unwanted fish, get some money back and the customer gets some reasonably cheap prebait. There is always the worry that prebait will not get eaten and I'm sure that this is sometimes the case. I have noticed that regular prebaiting of some swims increases the weed growth. This is because the breakdown products of dead fish will eventually fertilise the lakebed allowing more plants to grow. Pike will eat surprisingly fetid baits so I tend not to worry too much about baits remaining uneaten. That's no reason to use rotten baits though! Though prebaiting can work brilliantly it can also modify the feeding behaviour of the pike. Precise feeding periods can be dragged out to such an extent that all predictability goes out of the window. I suspect that this is because a pike that has been living on prebait loses the need to feed at optimum times. If it's in your swim it will eat as soon as it feels peckish which is in reality more dependent on how much prebait is left in the swim or when it finished the last of it off. For some strange reason prebait fed pike can also become very active at night. Whether this is because they are less likely to be hooked at night so they accidentally discover that feeding at night is safe I do not know. Either way it hardly matters because when you find that you are struggling in daylight you are bound to end up fishing at night anyway. Then you'll find out one way or another.

Prebaiting does not always work. I've tried it out on rivers, but no joy. Some customers have caught doing on Fen drains, but I've not managed to get very far with it. We all tend to carry out a mini prebaiting campaign simply by throwing used deadbaits in. I first noticed that this could get pike going on the Relief Channel in 1970. An 11 pounder was stuffed to the gills with herrings. It had really weighed about nine pounds!

Some waters I have prebaited have amazing pike, which clear off immediately you stop prebaiting. I have actually prebaited the day before with enough fish to kill the swim stone dead yet I've still caught! For you to be successful you really need to keep an open mind and play it by ear. You will by trial and error make the decision, which suits the individual pike on your water.

My best-prebaited pike came from a Yorkshire pit, which I knew held a big pike. I started fishing the pit a bit late as usual, but I had made progress by Christmas with a 24 pounder. I had been putting a little bit of prebait in, but really piled it in once the weather went very cold and it looked as if we were going to have a freeze up. The idea behind this was to prepare the chosen swim for a period under ice. The plan was to be there when it thawed out and that is exactly what happened. I had a jack that morning and the fish I was after at 32-14. As simple as that; which is of course so often the case. When you catch its easy. When you catch its easy when you do not it isn't! The prebait had been mackerel heads and the going bait that day? Yes a mackerel head! Unfortunately I had just bought a new auto focus camera with a manual auto release. I got one shot of the pike held properly and one shot of it struggling. The other three shots didn't come out because the auto release only pressed down on the button enough to auto focus. I mistook this sound for the camera shutter working! That was a pity because it was an impressive fish, however I try not to retain pike and I was happy to put it back thinking I had a few shots no matter how indifferent they might have been.

CHAPTER 7
LIVEBAITING

Who knows by the time this book is five years old, we might no longer be allowed to use livebaits to catch predatory fish. Another five years and we might not be allowed to fish full stop. Yes I know this is alarmist stuff and hopefully I'm going over the top here, but as I write this minute the House of Commons is voting on fox hunting and the vote is going to be overwhelmingly in favour of a ban. Hopefully the Lords will settle for the compromise solution of licensing and a total ban will be avoided. It is my opinion (and others have valid opposite ones) that the best line of defense is not to give an inch on any animal rights issue. It is sad that any of us have to adopt such extreme views and at another time I'd be keen to gain a greater insight into the pros and cons of hunting with hounds. As it is now, I'm only interested in putting up as strong a defense as possible against the antis. They seem to have only one aim, to ban everything that they consider cruel. The fact that a lot of people disagree with their ethics is neither here nor there, you cannot argue with fanatics. Therefore I have become an anti fanatic!

Though deadbaiting and lure fishing catch a heck of a lot of pike, it has to be accepted that live fish must constitute the bulk of a pike's food. So while we can catch pike on deadbaits and lures there are many situations where a livebait is the only option. For those who doubt this, just try catching pike consistently at one of our major trout reservoirs. You can have success with lures on waters such as Grafham, but the honest truth is that the large majority of the pike remain uncaught because lures are only 10 to 15% effective on any given day. Livebaits would probably enable you to catch 25 to 50% of the pike you present a bait to. It is quite possible that many pike on these waters remain uncaught and probably pass away before they can contribute to the pike fishery. On the other hand with the level of incompetence shown by some pike anglers it is just as well that the most effective method is not available on some waters otherwise the mortality rate would be even higher than it is. This gloomy synopsis does not have to apply in every situation and I'd like to think that with effective education and direction pike anglers could catch plenty of pike and get them back alive. At the moment the restrictions on some of our major trout fisheries are such that over exploitation of the pike stocks is the last thing that is likely to happen.

At the moment on many free waters, some club waters, most syndicates and a few trout waters we are allowed to livebait. This can make a big difference to the catch rate on waters that have very high densities of prey fish. It is only my opinion (but it is based on a bit of experience!) that the waters where livebaits are most essential are those where prey fish are so numerous that the pike have a very easy living. You only need to look at the pike in these waters to realize that they are well fed. Twenty pounders of only 36 inches long and thirties barely 40 inches. Indeed some of them might even be classed as being overweight! Tempting fish like this with a deadbait is a non-starter. Predatory fish, which are very well fed, need something extra to stimulate them to feed.

That stimulation can only be provided by a cue associated with a live fish. Often that cue has to be generated by a fish with an erratic movement. Now lures can in some situations provide that cue and surprisingly because of their exaggerated movement can actually out fish livebaits. However bring into the equation, less than ideal water conditions and lures can become ineffective. Coloured water for example can kill lure fishing stone dead, but livebaits can make a bad day an acceptable one. On waters where there has been a lot of lure fishing carried out, a decent sized livebait can make all the difference. Of course chucking a livebait out is not the simple solution to catching the pike of our dreams. Oh that any pike fishing problem could be resolved that easily. However the addition of an effective method to your range of techniques will in the long run make a difference. Trust me!

While deadbaiting and lure fishing does not have any legal implications for the participant, livebaiting does. In many areas such as Eire and Northern Ireland it is banned completely. I understand that the situation is the same in Holland and Germany. As I write a rearguard action is being fought in Scotland, the result of which is uncertain. The reasons for banning livebaiting are varied. In Eire it is banned because it is supposed to help prevent the spread of roach. Roach are not native to the Irish mainland, but you'd not think this now! The banning of livebaiting has served only to delay the spread of roach in Ireland. The problem in Ireland is the shambles their fisheries service is in. Enforcement is almost non-existent therefore the illegal movement of fish is difficult to prevent. I have seen ordinary local anglers fishing with roach livebaits by a main road bridge near Galway, not a small Irish city! (Only five miles from the headquarters of the Western Region Fisheries Board.) If you wanted to livebait in Ireland you'd probably get away with is for two or three years and then you'd have to be very unlucky to get caught.

It is a shame that certain activities which are legal in one country are illegal in another. Laws have to be enforced, but in these sorts of situation where the "crime" is not instantly recognizable as a crime, unlike theft and murder the individual has to make his or her decision whether or not to break the livebaiting laws where they exist. Where you decide to break a law you have to accept the consequences.

In the UK as I write, livebaiting is not generally banned though some angling clubs and fishery owners do not allow this option. Provided you catch the bait from the water you are fishing you may livebait on most waters. In recent years there has been a considerable amount of debate as to how far on a connected system you can move livebaits. It is generally felt that baits can be moved on foot from any one drain to another connected one. They cannot be moved using a motor vehicle. Though not totally logical it is probably the best compromise solution you can come to. In the old days of course we all kept a tank full of livebaits ready for the weekend. The tank would be stocked with roach, chub, crucian carp and so on and great care would be taken to ensure that all the fish in the tank were kept in tip top condition. Some of us still have a livebait tank in use, but the baits in it are of a much more limited variety. Farmed trout take precedence and in my case rudd from my own stock pond, which I use when, pike fishing on the waters I run. I cannot catch the rudd from my stock pond at Daiwa Manton carp fishery in winter. So I catch them in the summer and then use them in the winter having kept them at home. I realise that if checked by an Environment Agency inspector as I unload my van at my carp lakes I'll be unable to prove that they came from there originally. However he might struggle to prove otherwise. If we wish to get technical we could always submit samples for DNA analysis!

To livebait legally using baits such as rainbow trout caught from a trout farm requires a lot of effort. First you have to buy the trout, keep them alive and then get a section 30 consent to use them in a particular water. This consent is not easy to get, but here is how you do it. Write to the Environment Agency in your particular area (look on the back of your rod licence.) Ask for a section 30 consent form, then fill it in with the details of where the trout are to come from and which individual water you intend to use them on. Now if the water is a private stillwater with no designation as a Site of Special Scientific Interest and it is enclosed you will usually have little difficulty in getting consent. On some of our coarse fishing rivers such as the Thames you should not have problems getting consent. Indeed as a project I actually put in some applications to use rainbow trout on various rivers. I did not have a problem on the Thames, but came up against a brick wall on the River Yare and the Yorkshire Derwent. This is because both these rivers are in areas designated as of special interest as regards conservation. Now the fact that rainbow trout particularly small ones struggle to survive in the wild, do not breed (most rainbows are triploids and therefore sterile) and would have to be released in thousands to have any impact of a fishery, seems to have passed our fishery administrators by. You also have to realize that no one intends to release trout into a fishery. The odd trout might be cast off the hooks or slip out of your hands while baiting up, but almost without exception no mass release is going to occur. A lot depends on the particular fisheries officer you have to deal with. Some are fairly relaxed about trout livebaits, others must enjoy the limited power they have and wield it at every opportunity. I'm not going to say what I really feel here, but there's a lovely two-word expression that sums them up; jobs worth! I.e. it's more than my jobs worth mate to let you have consent. It is little wonder that there still exists a cavalier section of the pike angling community who have no scruples about using any type of bait anywhere. By being over restrictive the EA because of its inability to enforce its byelaws simply encourages the bad boys to be as bad as they like! One day all this will probably be used to encourage the total banning of livebaiting. Then it will be driven underground and there will then be no control over it at all.

Earlier I mentioned the livebait tank, an essential piece of equipment for many pike anglers. Over the years I have always had a livebait tank regardless of whether I lived in a flat or a detached house. Today I have two, both with a trickle of freshwater running through them. I also have aeration provided by a large double line aquarium pump with a pond pump as backup should the water supply go off or we have very hot weather. The two tanks are connected the water flowing in one and out of the other. Separate tanks are vital if you are to keep mixed species. Trout and other coarse fish do not co-exit well due to the trout nipping the tails of the coarse fish. Mix roach for

LIVEBAIT TANK SYSTEM

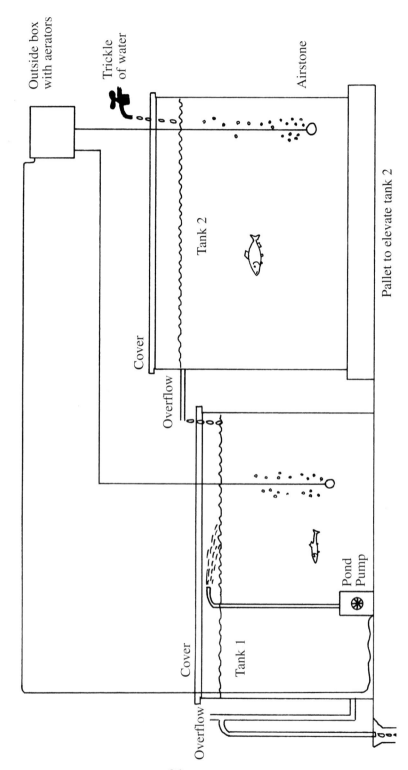

Outside box with aerators

Trickle of water

Airstone

Cover

Tank 2

Overflow

Pallet to elevate tank 2

Cover

Tank 1

Overflow

Pond Pump

example with trout and you will end up with a lot of dead roach. I have covers on each tank to stop the little beggars jumping out. The key to keeping any fish alive in a tank is to keep the water clean and to keep the oxygen levels up. You can feed trout if you are keeping them a long time with a few pellets a day. Roach and rudd will also respond to pellets. I find that once I've have stocked up with bait in the autumn they generally last me all winter simply because there's not a great need for livebaits each season. Keeping them long term is the reason for my feeding them. If you are into keeping Koi carp and the like you could set up a tank with filters which will keep baits effectively, but this is a major outlay. When the water is warm species such as roach, bream and chub are prone to catching a variety of bacterial diseases, none of which cause problems in the wild. Remember though that any fish kept in captivity is stressed to some degree and it is this stress that reduces any animal's immune response allowing diseases to take a toll.

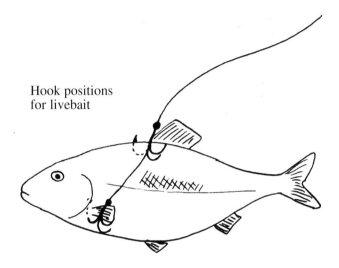

Hook positions
for livebait

I have mentioned trout as baits and generally these will be rainbows. Sometimes you end up with browns, but generally both are as effective as each other. I use them in the 2 to 4oz range for most of my pike fishing. They are a little more difficult to keep alive because all trout require at least twice as much oxygen as coarse fish. To get them from A to B you'll need a good quality bait pump such as an Airhead or a Power Bubbles. When you get to the water a bait cage or tube is essential and trout do keep surprisingly well in these. Less hardy species such as roach do not and these are better retained in the edge in a bucket with a perforated lid. Carp are wonderful baits, but sometimes you have to exercise great care. You do not want to roll up on any carp fishery armed with small carp. The risk to the resident carp is not worth any benefits you might obtain. Even health checked carp could carry diseases that can kill other carp. Where there are no carp in a water the same problems do not arise. The carp I have used from time to time have usually been the offspring of adult fish of known origin and used on my own waters thus reducing any health risk.

The size of livebait is also a matter for debate. In the good old days when 1lb roach were two a penny pike anglers would on some waters use these for bait. Two-pound chub were chucked around on the Relief Channel in the sixties. Things are different now. We have convinced the general angling public to put pike back and very few pike are killed these days in the British Isles. As a quid pro co we as pike anglers do not generally use baits which would be specimens for some anglers. Without a doubt a big livebait will get you a quicker response from a big pike. Experience has shown though that a smaller bait will get the response you want though it will take a bit longer. I do not expect that anything I can say here will alter the beliefs of the dyed in the wool big bait angler. However for the rest of you, believe me you can be successful as a pike angler without annoying the rest of the angling world. Take it from me if you tell anyone you are using 1lb baits you are likely to end up pilloried in the press and probably upside down in the nearest ditch with a livebait bucket on your head! My choice of livebait size is between 2 to 6oz with most baits 4oz and under. Smaller baits are more easily controlled, present less problems when it comes to hooking pike and of course you can get more small baits in the same bucket! The only situation where I would regret my choice of bait size would be if I was in a boat with Nige William and his baits were twice the size of mine. I get around this problem by not letting him in the boat with larger baits. No Nige, no! It is pointless trying to compete with another angler with big baits as I found out on Hollowel Reservoir in 1979 with Bryan Culley. His 8 to 10oz chub baits were taken quite freely while my 6 to 8oz crucians were ignored. You can imagine how this could escalate. I turn up with 1lb carp baits while next time Culley has 2lb bream in his bucket. Better to both have similar sensible sized baits and rely on watercraft and that element of luck we all have to contend with.

In the old days when we had a wide range of baits to choose from the swimming properties were important. Today you are generally going to fish with baits from the water you are fishing or with trout. I can only describe here the characteristics of the various livebaits based on past experience. Paternosters are designed to be tangled up by baitfish. The warmer the water the more they will tangle you. There is no such thing as the totally tangle free paternoster, though using the right baits at the right time of year will see problems reduced to a very, very low level. Perch, crucian carp and brown goldfish are examples of non-tangling livebaits. You can use them at any time of year without problems. Roach, chub, dace and common carp are well behaved in winter when low water temperatures restrict movement. In warm water they have to be watched, as they are prone to tangling most rigs. Rudd and silver bream can be a nightmare at any time of year. The problem with rudd in particular is it's desire to reach the surface. Specialised anti tangle rigs have to be used winter or summer. This tangling property is a shame because rudd are amongst the hardiest of baits. Where they occur in small ponds they can be caught at the rate of 2 a minute and they do not get diseased as roach do at high water temperatures. I'm amazed that rudd suffer from competition from roach because roach seem a far less hardy species.

Generally I catch relatively few pike on livebaits. Most fall to deadbaits and some to lures. I generally fish three rods when I am pike fishing, two with deads, one with lives unless I am on a water where deadbaits have long term proved to be miles better than lives. In rare situations I will fish two livebaits and one deadbait and on a water like Masons though I had a run on a deadbait once (!!!) I can end up fishing three livebaits. There are exponents of livebaiting such as Eddie Turner who without doubt show higher levels of effort with the method and this reflects in their results. ET has had quite a few thirty pounders on lives while I have only had the one. This is probably because I use deadbaits more than lives. My biggest pike on a livebait came while fishing the River Thurne in Norfolk. It was the day after the capture of the 41-06. I had moved further up river and had just repositioned my rods. One rod had a nice sized roach of about 6oz dropped in the edge on a sunken float paternoster. After catching a 40 pounder you do not really expect another big fish, so when the alarm sounded I was probably expecting something small. It was anything but small however and it wasn't helped when the handle of my Mitchell 410 broke off in my hand! With the help of Dave Plummer, reels were switched from another rod (you wouldn't believe that one reel handle had a male thread while the other was female and therefore not interchangeable.) Despite all this chaos the pike was landed and it went a pretty impressive 32-08. Since then I have come close with 29 pounders to mainly trolled livebaits on trout waters. The big, big fish have avoided me and to some extent because the waters I fish have changed in recent years, lures have become more useful to me than livebaits. I do not have a problem with this, however for many anglers on many waters, particularly the hard fished ones around the Home Counties, the banning of livebaiting would make catching pike almost impossible.

The techniques used to fish livebaits can be divided into the following groups;
Paternostered livebaits.
Free swimming livebaits.
Legered livebaits.
Trolled livebaits.

The paternostered livebait is still my favoured approach simply because it is economical on bait and very effective. The method falls down on very hard fished waters because the characterisic round and round movement of the livebait can in many situations signal danger to the pike. Sunken paternosters used in association with a buzzer are very popular and I must admit that I very rarely use a surface float. I've used lots of sunken floats over the years and though they look good the clear plastic ones end up getting chewed by pike! The Fox model is quite good. The Middy sunk float, which because it is black and streamlined tends not to attract attention from pike, which really should know better. All paternosters depend on a weight to restrict the movement of the bait. In the late sixties early seventies when I was first introduced to the paternoster it was commonly felt that the amount of lead to be used should be as small as possible. This was presumably because it was felt that a pike would not be prepared to tow a heavy weight around with it. Gradually over the years it has become clear that pike will happily tow up to 2oz of lead without dropping   a bait. So rather than have poor bite indication, due to failing to keep a tight line, we now use whatever lead it takes to keep the bait in place. To avoid tangles you also need some form of rotary rig. We used to use a three-way swivel, but this did nothing to prevent the bait tangling around the reel line. Then an uptrace was employed coupled with various devices designed to keep the hook trace away from the uptrace and the paternoster link. For a few years I had produced for me a purpose built paternoster boom that was actually made from strimmer line and some plastic mouldings. It actually worked quite well though the high visibility of the strimmer line might have put some pike off. When the chap who made these eventually lost interest in them I had consultations with Middy to try and come up with a less visible version of what had become known as the "Pike safe" paternoster boom. The end result was a fairly efficient combination of uptrace, protective plastic tube and a rotary rig. It works quite well though each boom only has a 20 fish or 10 session life due to wear and tear on the materials. The same would probably apply to any other uptrace system. The key thing with any paternoster system is to avoid any loose ends or bits that can cause tangles. Using silicon sleeve over all trace twists is essential. Nige Williams uses a John Roberts paternoster boom to keep bait trace and reel line separate. There is an alternative paternoster system, which reached its development stage at the hands of the late Colin Dyson. I've never felt the need to use it myself though it does offer a different presentation. For this reason alone it might be useful on hard fished waters.

Free-swimming livebaits offer the nearest you are going to get to a natural presentation. I have one rod set up permanently with heavy braid, nice big float and a one-ounce bullet. This I use for float trolling as well as free-swimming livebaits. The presentation is very simple and the only alteration one might make would be if you were fishing a shallow broad. Then the bullet might reasonably be disposed of. The idea of the free swimming set up is to allow the bait to explore a wide area. Pike will often respond to a relatively fast moving live fish, whereas a paternostered bait might be inspected for some time and ultimately rejected. Wherever possible with free-swimming baits you should make a gentle cast to keep the bait lively. Long hard casts though sometimes essential tend to see baits rapidly expire. With a floating braid it is easy to get a bait to drift considerable distances. The drifter float is a very useful tool for ultimate distance, but in many situations a plain float will do just as good a job. One big advantage of the free-swimming bait is that you can easily fish a wide depth range. This is something you will have difficulty doing with a paternoster. It does not happen often, but sometimes the pike will be high in the water and the only takes you are going to get will be if you put your baits just there. Fry feeding pike sometimes do this and certainly on some trout waters shallow fished baits are best.

Drifting floats have been with us quite a long time now since Eddie Turner and various other pike anglers publicized them. They are most useful on waters with a fairly uniform depth and where the pike are a long way out and you want to get a bait out to them quickly. They are also useful when boat fishing. You can drift a bait a long way downwind of your boat and in effect fish a totally new area. They are obviously limited to fishing with the wind, though using a radio controlled boat can enable you to do a reverse drift, thus enabling a lot of water to be covered. Obviously the bigger the livebait the more difficult it is to get a drift going because the bait can sometimes prove stronger than the drift!

LEGERED LIVEBAITS

It is strange to think that we used to do a lot of legered livebaiting, particularly in the 70s and 80s when this was a popular method for zander as well as pike. Unfortunately so many of our waters these days are weedy, which means that legered livebaits are a waste of time. The beauty of the legered livebait is that it presents a livebait in a more subtle manner than the float paternoster. Baits can be attached head up or head down and tend to sit on the bottom without moving that much. Adding a small poly ball to the trace will keep the bait off the bottom and make the bait work more vigourously. Legered livebaits sometimes produce suprises. I was zander fishing on the River Delph at night and nothing much had happened. At dawn I had a run on a legered livebait with a piece of polystyrene attached. Expecting a zander or a pike I was very surprised to see a carp swim past as I wound the fish in. In fact if I had been a user of Class B drugs I'd have thought I was on them! It was no drug-induced hallucination and soon I was looking at a 21lb carp in the bottom of my net, complete with one treble hook well inside its mouth. I've no idea whether it took the live roach or the polystyrene, the carp wouldn't tell me!

TROLLED LIVEBAITS

I am going to cover trolling in more detail elsewhere, but trolling livebaits is a well-established and highly effective method used on a wide variety of waters. There are two basic ways of doing it; Float trolling and float less, straight over the back of the boat trolling. To get either methods to work you need to fish slowly and the float less method really has to be used very slowly so I call it slow trolling. The second approach does more or less the same thing as what is known as bottom bouncing. Both techniques are boat methods and generally used in association with either electric motors or oars. I always try and fish a rod using each method because different waters usually respond better to one tactic on any given day. Establish trends also tend to reverse from time to time; therefore it pays never to put all your eggs in the one basket.

When trolling livebaits my first choice is always to use an electric motor. There is a school of thought that suggests that rowing produces a more erratic action from the bait though I personally have not noticed any difference myself. We all used to row in the days before electric motors were not widely available and I certainly did not catch more pike in those days! If you decide to use an electric motor you really need to choose one with step less control. The MinnKota range of motors are very good, but cursed with regular changes of spec and model number. Even those of us in the trade have difficulty keeping up! What I do know is that the models with a Maximiser and stepless control are much better for trolling than the cheaper models. Oh I said cheaper didn't I. That means the others are more expensive! To do the job properly you are going to have to spend around four hundred pounds. To provide the power for your motor you need a caravan or leisure battery (sometimes known as deep cycle). There are two ways of choosing the right batteries. If you do not have to walk and you do a bit of weight training, then one single 130-amp hour battery will provide enough power for a days fishing. However if you have to walk any distance and do not wish to get a repetitive strain injury, then two 80-amp hour batteries will do the job. Deep cycle batteries are a lot cheaper than they were with the larger of the two batteries costing around fifty pounds while the 80 amp hour units can be bought for a little as twenty-five pounds. You will need a good quality battery charger and somewhere set up permanently in and out building or garage to do your charging. Hydrogen gas is produced when a battery is charged so make sure you do this in a well-ventilated area. The curse of the battery user is leaking batteries. I try to be fairly careful about clearing up the odd drops of acid, which leak on charging, however you'll probably end up with a case of battery acid jeans due to carrying the batteries and the trouser leg rubbing against the battery.

The actual trolling process is worth describing here in detail because to be effective you do have to do it properly. It is a pity that so many of the really good trolling waters have ceased to be trout waters and in so doing the scope for this sort of fishing has been considerably reduced. Other trout waters such as Grafham and Rutland still have archaic non-trolling rules, which perhaps during the life of this book will be removed. One lives in hope!

Float trolling is a very simple process that can be made very complicated if you want to. The biggest single problem associated with float trolling is keeping the bait down. Now one solution is to use a self-locking float to avoid the bait running up the line too near the float. My solution is to use a larger float and a larger lead! Simple really. It is logical really, you can use as big a float as you like as long as you use enough lead to keep it 2/3rd submerged. The pike will not feel resistance from a very big float as long as you compensate with plenty of lead. I generally use a 6-inch polystyrene float, which will support about 1oz along with the bait. However if you are float trolling in difficult conditions, i.e. it is windy, you can use a bigger float and a bigger lead. I generally fish the float 10 to 15 yards behind the boat in 20 or more feet of water. In shallower water the float will be 20 to 30 yards behind the boat. The use of braid ensures that the line does not sink at any time. Sunken lines when float trolling result in chaos. The aim generally is to go at a speed that sees the float sitting at about 45 degrees. Faster and it lies flat, too slow and you do not move! You can never generalize too much about any technique so by all means concentrate on the slow as possible approach. Be prepared however to try going a bit faster particularly if you see someone else scooting along and catching pike.

Unless I am fishing in shallow water I try and fish a second rod with float less tackle. The reason for this that the float less tackle does tend to fish deeper and on some days pike really do want it right on their head. You cannot of course fish the float less tackle in shallow water so sometimes you might end up fishing two rods using the same method. I try not to complicate life by duplicating rods so would quite happily fish only the one rod using the one method. However when in deeper water it is daft not to try and fish the two different methods. Two baits in the water can sometimes be complimentary with one bait acting as the appetizer, the other following behind as the main course! The slow or float less trolling method works in the following manner. The rig is simplicity itself with just a wire trace and a bullet or bomb running on the line. The weight of bullets or bomb can depend on how difficult it is to troll slowly.

Generally the windier it is the more weight is needed or more effort with the electric motor is required to get the right presentation. I will use up to 2oz of lead and I watch the line to see at what angle it enters the water. Generally the angle will be from the vertical to about 45 degrees (see diagram). A stop knot on the line tells you how far from the bottom you should be if in an ideal world the line was vertical. Usually the line is angled and if I ever took the time to do the trigonometry I could work out at what depth the bait would be if the line were at such and such an angle. As it is you tend to do it all by dead reckoning and generally I lower and raise the bait to suit the particular angle of the line. I prefer to hold the rod using the baitrunner on the reel to allow a pike to take line. The second rod will be behind me on a boat rod rest again with the baitrunner set to allow a pike to take line. When there is two of you in a boat you can double up on the rods, but in this situation one person tends the rods while the other either rows or uses the electric motor. With 4 rods in a boat you'll probably be better off with rod rests for all the rods.

The only complication with multi rod set-ups is when you get a fish. Then the presence of too many lines can make life complicated. Two people who know what they are doing is essential and the last thing you want is a lost fish and two ex friends shouting at each other in the middle of a reservoir.

Several variations of the trolling described above can be carried out. One is usually described as bottom bouncing. Here a decent sized bomb of 1 to 2 ounces is attached to a running boom that is longer or the same length as the wire trace. The bomb is then allowed to bounce bottom, the bait trailing along behind. The problem I have found with the method is that it is a snag seeker! Now the people who advocate the method suggest the use of softish hooks, like the round bend fine wire Fox hooks. The reasoning being that with 30lb plus braid you straighten the hooks on the snags. Though you have to have a degree of respect for these people who have been very successful I prefer to stick with my approach using my usual Partridge extra strong trebles. Though the soft hooks will land any pike that swims I want to be confident that a big fish which comes up on the surface and which is difficult to land because of the wind pushing the boat along, is not going to thrash and straighten my hooks. I had this over 30 years ago with round bend trebles and know that a pike which is free to move in the air (on the surface a pike's head can be totally clear of the water) can place a terrible strain on the hooks. Hooks should therefore be as strong as you can get them!

You can also bottom bounce with a conventional sunken paternoster. The bait is mounted head up the trace and you simply troll with the paternoster touching bottom. This tactic was employed on Grafham Water by the bailiffs on the water in the seventies to take some nice pike. It was also coined "Trollernostering" on Bough Beech by the ever-inventive Eddie Turner.

Just before I close this section. Please remember one thing. As I write we still have the right to livebait. Only the Pike Anglers Club and the Specialist Anglers Alliance is going to fight to keep that right. If you want the freedom to fish without undue restrictions you have to be a member of these organizations.

CHAPTER 8
GETTING THE BEST
FROM WHAT'S LOCAL

While it makes interesting reading, the exploits of the go anywhere pike fishing community is not really relevant to the average pike angler. Many fish only once a week with extra days during holidays. Their radius of operation may only be 30 miles and in some parts of the country the pike fishing may not be very good. So much depends on where you live. If I had the artistic skills it might be possible to draw a map of the UK and colour it like a population map. For example red for the best pike fishing areas, yellow for the average and green for the don't live here if you want to catch pike areas! Unfortunately I do not have the artistic skills! Lets then run down the country from Scotland to Sussex and then from N.Ireland to the bottom of Eire.

The highlands of Scotland do have some pike fishing. I have dabbled as far north as Inverness, without particular success. There is still quite a bit of pike persecution up there though probably nothing like what they have suffered in Eire. The one advantage of the Highlands is that there are very few pike anglers up there! The one big problem with any upland fishery is the lack of productivity. Many of the Lochs are very barren and you can hardly expect them to support a big head of pike. You can always get the odd big pike even from a relatively poor upland water, but you are not going to get loads. As in many instances you may have to travel to improve your pike fishing. Further south in the central region of Scotland you have many fine waters. Open access waters such as Lomond, Awe and Venecar. Then there are the trout waters with limited access such as Menteith. If you live local to waters such as Lomond you are going to catch some good pike unless you are very unlucky. I'm not suggesting that Lomond is particularly easy, because it is not. This however is because of angling pressure. So many well-known spots are fished almost every day and this obviously reduces the chances of any one angler having consistent results. If Lomond had no pike anglers on it, any capable chap or chapess would have a field day!

The south of Scotland particularly the west offers lots of smaller waters as well as famous Lochs such as Loch Ken. Again if you lived in this area you would be able to find reasonable pike fishing. I'd not fancy my chances in Berwick on Tweed though! Now as we enter the north of England we have a contrast. If you live in Lancaster or Carlisle you have access to the Lake District, which does offer good, pike fishing. It is a terrible place to be in high summer because it is full of tourists, but in the winter I suspect it is a splendid area to frequent. You've not a great chance of a 30 pounder and very little hope of a 35, but almost all the regular anglers catch fish of 20 to 27lbs. The contrast comes if you look at a similar latitude, but to the east. There you have Newcastle down to Middlesborough. Now with apologies to the fine people who live in the area, why don't you move somewhere else? Anywhere else! The area is one of the worst I've ever come across for pike fishing. There are lots of pike anglers there, but nearly all travel north, south or west to catch pike. They have trout waters in the area that are supposed to have pike in them, but so far whenever I've fished any of them the indications are that there are no pike in them! That's not the fault of the pike anglers!

Moving down further to Lancashire proper, you have a big area of urban sprawl. Surprisingly there is some good pike fishing on lakes and canals in the area, but not enough to support all the pike anglers. Traveling into the Pennines does not help much. Lancashire anglers frequently end up on the Yorkshire Rivers such as the Ure, Ouse, Derwent and Swale. None of this of course helps our local anglers based in York who could probably do without the competition. Yorkshire though again very urban over much of its area does offer some good stillwater and river fishing. There are several anglers from the region who catch a lot of good pike in the area. Unfortunately as is so often the case you need to travel outside of the region for a chance of a really big fish.

As we proceed south we encounter the first of the big trout reservoirs, Blithfield near Rugeley in Staffordshire. Though exclusive fishing and limited to short periods of fishing it offers the best chance of a 30lb plus fish for miles around. Cheshire itself offers some mere fishing, but I think it would be fair to say that anyone who lives in that area would probably have to travel for really good pike fishing. If we wander into North Wales things get even more desperate. Other than Lyn Tegid (Bala) and a few smaller waters pike fishing is scarce. Over on my patch, the Isle of Axholme and north Lincolnshire and north Nottinghamshire offer much better pike fishing than was available in the 1980's. I can only speak from experience here, but pike killing held the pike prospects back for many years. Fish to 25 pounds are there to be caught, but bigger fish though they appear from time to time are generally scarce. I caught my only 30lb Fenland pike from north Lincs a few years ago, but that drain has not produced another since that fish died the following September after having been caught twice.

The rest of Lincolnshire offers some first class pike fishing. The large number of drains in the county means that there is always one capable of producing a really big pike. Unfortunately as I write the rivers really are in the doldrums. The Witham offers poor pike prospects, the Welland is a good doubles water, while little is heard of the Nene. Nottinghamshire has plenty of gravel pits and one or two of these have done fish to 35lb. It really is a case of keeping track of individual waters and being on the right one at the right time. A fair bit of the River Trent runs through Nottinghamshire and it is also my local river. It does produce 20lb plus pike, but as far as I know has not produced a confirmed thirty. One was reported without a photograph in Anglers Mail from Fiskerton a few years ago. Anyone who lives near the Trent should with some effort catch plenty of good pike and in so doing learn a lot which will stand him in good stead elsewhere.

The rest of Wales is a bit of a conundrum. Llandegfedd of course remain one of the best pike waters in the country. It will always have good years and probably several bad ones, yet it has the most incredible track record. The rest of Wales is a bit of an unknown quantity to me. While I worked at Bridgend in the late seventies there was a water nearby, Kenfig Pool, which had a big pike reputation. History sometimes repeats itself

I also feel that there might be the odd trout water in South or Central Wales that we still do not know about. One thing is certain; someone like me, 150 miles away isn't going to find it! Of course there is the River Wye, which does have a big pike reputation. I think if you live near it you will gradually amass a nice tally of big pike. The only snag with the Wye is the never-ending rain we seem to suffer from. Also there is the problem of it being a salmon river and much of it being exclusive, a fact one pike angler we will not mention by name nearly found out to his cost! The Wye unfortunately like most rivers in the UK does not have the salmon run it once had which must be a disadvantage if you are looking for it to produce that extra special fish.

Moving back east to the far extremities of the country we have east Norfolk. The Broads because of the sheer number of different waters continues o be a Mecca to the visiting pike angler. It is one of the few areas of the country that can support professional pike angling guides. You'd struggle to do that in Tyneside! The fishing really is so much better than most of the rest of the country it is no surprise that so many well known pike anglers have given it a lot of attention. You have such variety and even the gravel pits produce 30lb plus pike! A number of well-known pike anglers such as John Watson moved house to live in the middle of this wonderful area. I just wish I could move there! Back west you have the Cambridgeshire Fens and well-known names such as the Great Ouse, Sixteen Foot and the River Delph. None are as good as they were in the seventies, but they can still throw up some very big fish along with of course big zander. In the midlands we have the biggest of all trout reservoirs in the shape of Rutland water. It has never really lived up to expectations, but two or three days during the pike fishing weeks is always an enjoyable experience. Northamptonshire is the home of the smaller trout waters such as Ravensthorpe, Elinor and Ringstead. These water continue to produce 30lb plus pike though it is limited access pike fishing and you'll need a full chequebook if you are to make the most of the opportunities they produce. The county also boasts lots of gravel pits; some such as Bluebell lakes keep producing exceptional pike. Sywell reservoir the well-known tench water is always worth a look simply because tench make ideal fodder for big pike.

Life gets a bit more difficult if you live in the Birmingham area. Lots of pike anglers from here end up traveling, yet this is good pike fishing albeit not mega pike fishing on rivers such as the Severn. The late John Sidley caught a lot of big pike from this river, though he did spend a lot of time after them. Once you get down to Gloucestershire and Bristol you once again enter trout fishing territory. Chew when it opened in the autumn of 2001 opened a few eyes. Just a bit further east around Cirencester we have the Cotswold Water Park. A series of gravel pits almost too many to count offers generally slow pike fishing, but big pike always turn up from time to time.

Oxfordshire offers interesting gravel pit fishing while the Thames is a consistent producer of twenty pounders. Huntingdonshire has Grafham Water, which from time to time throws up the odd exceptional fish. I've never found it an easy water, but I keep going back in the hope of improving on my best from there of 24lbs. The Home Counties around Hertfordshire have alas become more and more carp dominated which is not good news for pike fishing. Pike like bream not 20lb carp! Yet the mega keen pike anglers who live in the area still managed to extract every last big pike that there is there on offer. Tring reservoirs though well fished still produce some good specimens, but you are now getting close enough to the capital to make competition from other anglers a serious problem. Suffolk is a county of gravel pits and further down in Essex we have the famous Abberton that still produces 20 and 25 pound pike every winter. Gravel pits such as the Warren continue to produce big pike and if you have a memory for facts it is interesting that some other Essex pits do keep producing thirty pound plus pike. There was a fine trout fishery in Essex, Ardleigh that did produce some very big pike. Unfortunately it is no longer a trout fishery so its future is uncertain.

That line that runs from the Thames estuary through central London out to Reading is not somewhere I'd long to fish. It is hard going, yet if you are willing to get into the right clubs or join an exclusive syndicate some good pike fishing can be found. I'm afraid you cannot just turn up and fish any old stretch of the River Kennet. You have to be prepared to join clubs or get on a waiting list. Living around London may not be good for your pike fishing career, but for someone like me who lives out in the sticks it has compensations. At least in London there is entertainment! Try finding a decent concert to go to in my part of the world. (Other than the Spilsby batter pudding throwing clubs annual regatta…)

Now we are nearly at the end of our journey around the mainland. Kent offers a lot of gravel pit fishing and every so often throws up a real big one. Sadly it's trout waters are not what they were. Bewl water could be a really good trout water pike fishery, but years of gill netting have reduced it to a shadow of it's true potential. Bough Beech as far as I know will ultimately be a carp water which reflects the poor economics of stillwater trout fishing. Yet in its day Bough Beech was one of the premier pike waters with many pike anglers catching their first really big pike there. Sussex has some surprisingly good river fishing, notably the Sussex Ouse, Adur and Arun. These rivers however fluctuate in the quality of their pike fishing, something that has to be expected in such a densely populated area. Another trout water as was is Weirwood. As I write it is unclear whether or not this is still a trout water. It did in the nineties offer some very good pike fishing and I spent many happy days fishing it. The nearby Ardingley is a well-managed reservoir fishery offering mixed fishing and some good sport with pike to 20lbs. There are also some interesting gravel pits and estate lakes in Sussex, but once again for that extra something anglers have to travel out of the area.

Hampshire of course needs little introduction. The Hampshire Avon and Dorset Stour though perhaps not quite as good as they have been in the past still offer pike into the low thirties, which is big enough for most aspiring pike anglers. Heading through Dorset to Somerset we have fenland type fishing on the Somerset levels and not far from Chew, Cheddar reservoir where I caught my first cormorant in the mid seventies! Devon and Cornwall are never likely to attract much attention from visiting pike anglers, but waters such as the Exeter Canal have produced big pike in recent years.

Over in Northern Ireland they have suffered from pike poaching for many years. Here is also a certain amount of pike killing and mishandling caused by our continental cousins, the Germans and the French. The two major river systems are the Erne and the Bann. If you are local you are going to catch lots of doubles, some twenties with the chance of a really big one. There are quite a few Stillwater fisheries in the North, many of which are put and take trout waters. There are going to be some seriously big pike from there in the future.

Eire itself was once the place where we all went for our holidays. It was also the place where many people felt that they had the best chance of a big one. Then the Germans and French tried to wipe the pike out. On top of that we had their own fisheries service intent on killing as many pike as possible in a vain attempt to do something about the decline in brown trout fishing. There is some good pike fishing in Eire, but you increasingly need to live there to capitalise on it. You'll read a fair bit about Eire in this book, but remember I'm writing about it as it was.

I am going to make an assumption that many readers are fairly new to pike fishing and they are looking to improve their abilities. Here is how I'd go about being more successful. First you need a plan! I would get all the Ordnance survey maps for an area of around 30 miles from where you live. (unless you live in a very poor pike fishing area, then read what I've written later.) You'll need an A4 sized file and access to a photocopier. Next photocopy all the bits of map with rivers, drains and canals on. These you'll keep in the file and on them you'll mark the areas you've fished, the areas you have caught from, hot match pegs and anything you can glean about the water from the angling press. This is all part of building up an overall picture and developing a strategy. You will note all the stillwaters in the area and again list what you know about each. Then it is a case of fishing around and building up as much knowledge as possible. Usually it is best to fish as intensively as you can to gain knowledge. Then in the following years you will find that information gained from intensive fishing will help you to success in later years without the same degree of effort.

The learning process enables you to reduce the amount of wasted time. You'll learnt to fish say a small stillwater on those windy days when fishing a large pit would be a waste of time. You'll visit your river or drain venue at the optimum time, usually just as they fine down. The methods you use will be refined so that you use the right ones for the venue at the right time. Only when you have gone as far as you can on your local waters will you feel the need to move on.

THE NEXT STEP
Unless you live in Norwich for example you will eventually feel the need to expand your area of operations. To do this you will need time and money. Though I enjoy my local pike fishing I also fish lot of waters as far as 200 miles from my home. It is an expensive exercise and each year I spend in excess of 700 pounds on permits and syndicate fees. Fuel costs probably creep into four figures and it is not surprising that I find myself short of cash from time to time! I am lucky that I have always had jobs,

which have a fair degree of flexibility. When I worked for the water authority I was on flexi time, which allowed me to get morning sessions in. I could also build up lieu time, which gave me extra fishing days. Since I became self employed it has become easier to get days off, but only if I was prepared to work all hours. Working in the evenings is pretty normal for me as well as 12 to 16 hour days. Luckily I enjoy my work so I have no problem with this.

You will also need reliable transport and if you are sensible the full RAC or AA relay cover. Time lost fishing because you couldn't get the car or van started is not my idea of entertainment. If you are single life will be much easier. Relationships are always going to be difficult unless the girlfriend or wife has a life of her own. There is little point in having a gorgeous looking girlfriend who cannot drive and who likes to go clubbing 4 nights a week. By the time you've finished two or three days long distance piking she will have long gone! It depends what you want from life. I'd be inclined to enjoy the gorgeous girlfriend for as long as possible and then get on with the pike fishing…

If you have a family then things get more difficult. I would not describe myself as he best father in the world because I do tend to give priority to my pike fishing. Very little gets in the way of this. No one should really follow my example, but neglect of the family can arise in many other sports and business. The pursuit of excellence does have a price, something that some of our keenest pike anglers have found to their cost.

Most of the long distance pike waters are well known. The River Yare in Norfolk is about 120 miles from me and a couple of years ago I sorted out boat launching and so on. Unfortunately (depends how you look at it of course). Masons Lake came along and I never did start my Yare campaign. Sometimes it is easier to have a week's holiday on a water. Then you will have somewhere decent to stay. It certainly beats sleeping in a car or a bivvy! In an ideal world we should all be discovering our own waters. Now these days it is difficult to find anywhere that has not been pike fished. Fortunately waters get forgotten or neglected so any of us can rediscover waters. Anything like this goes onto my top-secret list. I go to considerable lengths to conceal some of the waters I fish simply because competition once it reachs a certain level detracts from your own fishing. The rest of the time it is I'm afraid a case of hitching your star to the next bandwagon! It always pays to be one of the first to get onto a new water because pike do get harder to catch if they are given a good pasting by other anglers. The rest of his book is devoted to my trying to pass on my experiences on the various types of water I have fished over the years. Here and there I'll try to tell some stories which I hope the reader will find interesting. Tales of particularly good fish caught by other anglers has always inspired me. It is my hope that my writing does the same for you.

BROADLAND
There can be few areas of greater contrast than the Norfolk Broads. On one hand you have windswept reed lined waters, home to many rare species of plants and animals. On the other you have the constant disturbance of motor cruisers, motoring up and down

endlessly. Wroxham epitomizes the commercialism of the Broads, which is probably the commercial center of the Broads. Yet even in the midst of the worst of the every day hurley burley there is pike fishing which many pike anglers would be extremely envious of. My relationship with the Broads came later in life than I would have liked. As a youngster in the period 1963 to 1966 the papers were filled with the exploits of Dennis Pye. There didn't seem to be a week when he wasn't catching, 20, 25 or even 30lb plus pike. For a brief period he was my hero, but then *Prymnesium* wiped out the Thurne system and Dennis faded from the scene. Dennis was a controversial character, something that was not helped by his claimed catches. They were so far ahead of those of fellow Broadland pike anglers such as Reg Sandys and Bill Giles that suspicion was bound to arise. Dennis claimed about 312 twenty pounders and I think 12 thirty pounders. Whatever the truth of the matter, Dennis Pye has a place in pike fishing history. The history of the sport is important and everything should be recorded for posterity. I've tried in my own small way to record as much as I can, but in the end it is not my role to stand in judgment of any one angler. I can point out the obvious frauds that have turned up from time to time, but in the end it is down to that persons conscience whether they decide to carry on with the fantasy. I have always held the view that the Thurne at its peak could have given one angler the chance to catch a mind-blowing number of big pike. Whether Dennis Pye was that angler we will probably never know. A little bit of history helps us to understand why the Broads are so unique. The valleys of east Norfolk and Suffolk were formerly part of a large estuary connected to the North Sea. The mouth of the estuary was about 4 miles wide

Fishing Horsey Mere in 1986

100

and Great Yarmouth was established on a sandbank. The result of all this water and low-lying land is marsh and over thousands of years peat bog. Where trees were scarce early man has to find an alternative fuel source. Peat when dug and dried makes a fine fuel. This peat extraction is thought to have happened in Saxon times and continued into the 13th Century. Channels to the rivers subsequently connected many of these peat cuttings. It was not until the 16th Century that roads were built and reclamation of land stared with the building of dykes and the first windmills in 1853.

The Thurne system Broads differ from the others in that they are very shallow with uniformly hard bottoms of gravel, peat or clay cover by a thin layer of mud. The boundaries of these broads tend to be embanked so they stand higher than the drained marshes. There is very little undrained land between the broads. Probably in the 13th or 14th Century the fight to keep peat workings relatively dry was abandoned that then produced the Broads we are now familiar with. Interestingly the whole area has always been prone to flooding from the sea. There are records from 1287 of "nine score men and women drowned at Hickling and St Benets Abbey. Flooding is a fact of life in the area with for example 7946 acres flooded in 1938 due to a break at Horsey and of course the floods of 1953 (I was born on February 1st, the night of the floods!) I mention this so the reader can see that the Thurne in particular has always suffered from being wiped out and then recovering.

The extra problems that have afflicted much of the Broads are comparatively new, but not so new as to have not been experienced elsewhere in the country. It seems that we

Historical summer house on Horsey Mere (circa 1985)

are always slow to learn lessons! One of the biggest problems has been the disposal of phosphate rich treated sewage effluents. Phosphate is one of the nutrients, which is a limiting factor of plant growth. It was once a major ingredient of detergents and its large scale release into freshwaters causes massive amounts of plant growth and ultimately causes algal blooms which can be dangerous to fish and higher animals. Then we had the change in agricultural practice during the Second World War. Increased use of inorganic fertilizers and the conversion of grazing to arable fields further increased the input of nutrients. Then we have had the heavy exploitation of the area for tourism and the associated boat traffic. Luckily steps have been taken to reverse many of these changes and there is hope that the excesses of mans activities will eventually be minimized.

I think J Wentworth Day summed up the broads quite nicely "A bitter land of bitter spaces. A land of ghostly mists and sea fogs stealing like grey armies. A land of shouting gales and thunderous surges. A land too of wide quiet meres and secret waterways, of sighing reed beds and the whimper of endless wings, of old, small woods of oak and monstrous fens."

My first encounter with the Broads came with fishing the River Bure in I think 1982. The waters I was fishing had very little potential for me to catch a thirty pounder and at this stage that was something I very much wanted. The Bure probably was not the best bet for a thirty, but that was where I started. In those days everyone was trolling livebaits, but I followed the example of Dave Plummer and concentrated on static fishing with live and deadbaits. I didn't pull up any trees, though a brace of 19 pounders could be regarded as a near miss! I also did a bit of night fishing, which yielded fish to 17 pounds. You'd struggle to night fish around Wroxham now because all the areas you could get a car to are now built on. My experience of the Bure suggested that you needed to use all the methods at your disposal. Paternostered livebaits did not produce much for me but you needed to fish them. Most of my decent pike fell to float legered smelt or half mackerel. The biggest fish to anyone I fished with fell to Barry Kerslake at 29lb, but sadly for me I had already moved on to the Thurne so a Bure twenty pounder is something I've still not had. There is a lot of river to fish and I found it paid to be mobile, giving each spot no more than a couple of hours. Areas where boat dykes entered the river, moored boats, bends, overhanging trees were all worth look. Trolled livebaits have caught a lot of pike on the Bure, but did not yield anything for me though I did not do much of it. The interesting thing about the Bure is all the connected Broads. It is likely that pike move from the Broads into the river during the depths of winter following the roach and bream shoals. You therefore have a concentration effect, whereby fish from a much wider area congregate in smaller area. This is always a big advantage.

When John Watson and Dave Plummer moved to Norfolk it coincided with a revival in the fortune of Broadland pike fishing. Post *Prymnesium* * I think that Broadland pike anglers had developed a mindset that said that the Broads were finished. I even saw members of the Broadland Specimen Group as it was then (notable member Steve Harper!) fishing the Relief Channel for pike! Dave Plummer and Watto being mega

* *Prymnesium parva.* A tiny algae which when it dies produces a toxin which is deadly to fish.

102

keen turned everything on its head and soon everyone realised that there was still plenty of big pike to be caught from the Broads. Steve Harper, Martyn Page and Watto had been exploring and put in some effort on one of the Bure broads, Decoy Broad. Now Decoy is a beautiful water, but a pain in the neck to fish! Firstly it was and I presume still is a Norwich and District club water and you had to book boats and pay for them in advance. Also no anchors were allowed, you had to use mooring poles. Luckily for me Dave Plummer was good enough to sort the bookings out for me, not easy in my case seeing as I was living 140 miles away.

What really got me interested was the 31 pounder that fell to Watto's rods. So the following winter I along with Dave Plummer and I think Trefor West started to fish it. To say that it was slow was the understatement of the year! I certainly didn't catch anything before Christmas. I think Dave might have had fish to 16lbs. It wasn't until February that I summoned up renewed enthusiasm. Now follows a chain of events which until fairly recently I was in partial ignorance of. I was friends with Dave Phillips and most weekends when fishing in the Fens or the Broads I'd drop in to see him. I told him I was going to fish Decoy in a couple of days. This information was mentioned to Watto, who I then understood to have gone up to Decoy and hid all the oars! When I arrived I was faced with either fishing with no oars or going home. Being of fairly determined Norfolk stock I decided I could use the mooring poles to quant myself along. This I did and soon two deadbaits and a paternostered livebait were cast out. Swim choice on this broad was a bit hit and miss because of its uniform nature and of course I was limited as to my movement! I had a thirteen pounder straight away on a 12oz bream livebait, something I'd probably not use these days! Then I tried to move and the wind caught me and I ended up at the north end of the broad. The quanting wasn't working! My last resort was to take the two balers in the boat and attempt to pull myself back up the broad by hanging over the front of the boat. It was hard work, but slowly I made progress. Eventually I reached a spot I fancied and cast out exhausted. I had one run, my first thirty at 32-02! It took a smelt and a few days later I was at Dave Phillip's when the phone rang. It was Watto and when Dave told him I swear I heard the phone drop at the other end! There's a little saying " What a tangled web we weave when at first we try to deceive" Perhaps not entirely appropriate, but that day and events afterwards still make me smile. The key factor, which helped me catch that fish, was being there in February, always a good month. The weather was right mild and windy and fate, not pike fishing knowledge put me in he right spot. I never went back either which is a shame, because it really was a lovely spot. By the way I certainly do not hold it against Watto, I think I owe him!!!!

My experience on the Bure system more or less ended there except for a few night bank sessions. The Thurne then took my attention with the first surprising catches by the likes of messers. Coull, Tipple, Forte and Amies. Fortunately for me I was fairly quick off the mark and arrived on the Thurne for my first session. I fished between the two broads and lo and behold Mr. Tipple was on the North Broad. That sorted that out! I went on in the next few years to catch some good fish though probably not the numbers of big fish some people had. My compensation came luckily at the upper end of the weight range!

All the Thurne Broads are shallow, around 4 to 7 feet. The Rivers connecting them are also shallow and you'd be hard pressed to find 8 feet anywhere. Nearly all the fishing is from a boat which means something of a culture shock for those used to fishing from the bank. The first boat I had was a 9-foot thin-skinned glass boat acquired from a certain Pete Evans of Sheffield who owed the Tackle Shop for quite a few rod blanks. He still owes us for two, anyone know where he is? I painted the boat olive green, but really should have used "old reed bed brown" if I had really wanted to blend in! At the time I had a few bits of fisheries kit in my custody because of my job with Severn Trent water. One such was a 3.5hp Yamaha outboard. This was to be my motive power for a number of years. Armed with this cut-price kit I set about coming to terms with the Thurne.

I soon learned that the techniques I used on the Fens had to be changed. There was a lot of weed on Martham North and South Broads. Deadbaiting had to be carried out using float leger gear and strong line. There was little scope for float paternostering; instead all livebaiting was carried out using free-swimming tactics. Baits had to be fished under streamlined floats at as little as 2 feet deep. The pike definitely lurk in the big beds of Marestail weed and the best way to lure them out is for something alive or seemingly alive to swim over the top of the weed. The wobbled deadbait was and probably still is an effective method in this situation. I think my best on a wobbled dead from the Thurne was 25 pounds, though I had quite a few lesser fish. Initially much of the action on the Thurne was concentrated on the North and South Broad. Gradually the then

Ken Latham looks over his ornamental Lake at Potter Heigham

104

Norfolk Naturalists Trust closed down the fishing, first on the South Broad, then on the North. Unfortunately stopping people pike fishing on a water connected to the Thurne is easier said than done. Eventually regulated pike fishing was allowed on the North broad with most responsible pike anglers realising that the free for all was over. Actually not being able to fish the South broad is probably a great conservation measure. Pike anglers are very effective these days and a sanctuary area does no harm at all. There is always the temptation to fish a water such as the South Broad and I know some of us had our fun in the early 80s. However when you understand that restraint might be important for the survival of big pike in the area, then there is only one way to behave.

Ultimately it was other anglers not me that realised you could catch big pike off of the river itself. Eddie Turner with three thirties (two different fish) and anglers such as Dave Humphries, Martyn Page and Steve Harper started to explore further downstream and they caught North Broad fish from as far down as Martham Ferry. It was eventually clear that pike from both Broads ranged onto the river particularly when the Broads were frozen solid. Having realised this I changed my tactics and started to fish the river more from December onwards. The ultimate reward came in February of 1985 when three fish graced my net, a 19, 16 and a 41-06. The next day I added a 32-08 for a three-day session I'll never forget. In those days the river above Martham up to the big tree was weed less. This gave me the opportunity to fish as I would in the Fens. It was possible to float paternoster livebaits and you could leger deadbaits. Legering deadbaits is a sensible option on a water with boat traffic. Sunken rod tips are the order of the day here. I also started to pick a few fish up on float-trolled baits. The weedy nature of much of the Upper Thurne was ideal for tripping a livebait along just over the top of the weed. At the time I was float trolling I quite happily used my electric motor having no comprehension that it wasn't allowed. I think they are trying to sort out this unhelpful legislation at the moment. My best two days had an interesting result. On day one I float trolled a 26-10 from between the Broads at Martham. While I set the camera up I put a deadbait out and promptly caught a fish just over 20lb. This retaught me the lesson that where there's one big pike there is usually another. The next day in exactly the same spot I trolled out a 27-10, exactly the same pike!

It always paid dividends to keep your eyes open when going from A to B on the Thurne. I remember motoring along at dawn and spooking a pike near the surface. I stopped and fished and promptly had a 16 pounder. The same happened to me on Horsey Mere. I'm pretty sure that Dennis Pye would have located big pike in the same manner, the assumption being that because the pike were more numerous then, you could expect to spook a fair few fish. Dawn was also a good time to spot the shoal fish on the river itself. Pike would not always be associated with the prey fish, but sooner or later something would turn up near them. Eventually my area of operations extended further downstream to Candle Dyke and Potter Heigham. There the tidal influence make's itself felt and tactics have to bear in mind the need to use enough lead to keep baits in position. The pike on the Thurne below Candle Dyke were always a bit of a mystery. Where did they come from? The capture of a 37-10 by Peter Woodhouse who was fishing with Bob Morris showed the potential of what was to become the most difficult fishing on the Thurne itself. I always felt that the fish that turned up on this section of river dropped down from Heigham Sounds or even further up the system. Whatever the truth of the matter mobility was the key approach. While a lot of spots could be bank fished a boat is the sensible way to cover water. You take all your essential gear with you without having to trudge along difficult banks. These Broadland pike will generally take a bait if you can find them; therefore you have to go to them rather than the other way around. This is where the boat with a cabin comes in. If I were regularly fishing the Thurne I would definitely use a boat with a big cabin so I could in effect stay on the water. There is no need for a big engine because of the speed limits on the Broads (speeding fines are now in three figures!) Thurne pike are active at night and you would certainly catch bonus fish with the round the clock approach. The nice thing about the Thurne system is that there are plenty of safe anchorages so you know that you are not going to find yourself in trouble in the middle of the night. Night fishing can be abused so you must try to do it properly. Remote buzzers such as Delkims should be rigged up on brackets so you can fish two rods with good bite indication. (You'll have to make your own because no one makes these). You cannot expect to get undressed and then well zipped up in a sleeping bag. You need to be out quick and you should cast near to the boat, in that way drop back runs will be eliminated. With the advent of the bait runner type reel I now use this function for all my boat fishing.

The three large Thurne Broads have all produced their fair share of big pike. I think it is fair to say that Horsey Mere was the first of the three to be "rediscovered". Interest then moved to Hickling Broad and Heigham Sounds. Fishing them again requires a degree of mobility, my experience on Horsey suggesting that some areas are more consistent than others. Mind you if you look at other angler's logbooks you would probably find totally different good areas! I always found that in September and October on Horsey you would fish out in the middle or at least well away from the banks during the first two or three hours. Then when the boat traffic started to get intense you'd retreat to the edges. In March when the Mere reopened boat traffic was not a problem so you'd fish where you fancied. On my first ever day on Horsey I motored on, looked around and picked a spot at random between the entrance and the island (as was). I promptly caught two nineteen pounders, something I was going to be hard pressed to repeat. I spent a lot of time on Horsey for very little return and always found it a difficult water.

Horsey was a deadbait and lure only water though I think that plenty of livebaits had a little swim around on there. Livebaits never did me much good, the few twenty pounders I caught coming on baits such as smelt, lamprey and herring. Wobbled deadbaits only picked up the odd small fish. Despite trying all sorts of areas fishing close to the reed beds only rarely produced pike for me, the open water generally proving more productive. I only ever fished Hickling the once and dabbled on Heigham Sounds and Duck Broad. The local anglers have of course done it all by now and once in a while a thirty pounder turns up. It is however very hard fishing. The conservation and boating interests do not seem to be able to get their act together. A few years ago the weed came back with a vengeance on Hickling Broad. The conservationists were over the moon while the boaters were horrified. In the end a lot of the weed was cut, which resulted in the nutrients from the dying weed, being taken up by our old friend *Prymnesium parva*. The result was another big fish kill, just as the pike fishing was picking up again. It will always be worth fishing the system for pike, simply because some always survive. The reduced density of pike accelerates the growth of those left giving you the chance of an outsized fish. Unfortunately fish like my 41-06 are very rare and very special. I do not think there was any telling when Steve Harper caught her at 32lbs that she would just keep growing. There were quite a few similar sized pike around at the time and none of them had the growth spurt that the "41" had.

Feeding periods did exist while I fished the Thurne system. Most of the fish caught came out in the morning and on the days when the pike were not well on the feed, moves later in the day tended to be unproductive. Though there is a lot of speculation these days as to the influence of external factors such as the moon, it still remains unclear as to why two identical days can produce different levels of sport. The weather has always been highly significant. Mild windy weather was in my experience much more conducive to catching pike than flat calm, sunny and frosty. It was a fact that the sort of weather that stopped you fishing on the big broads could yield fish on the rivers.

There is of course a lot more to the Broads than the Thurne, but Broadland pike fishing history tends to start and end on this system. At least 15 years ago I did interviews with some famous Broadland pike anglers and these interviews have never been published. This will hopefully give the reader some insight into a golden era.

I can only mention in passing the other Broadland waters because in most cases I've only fished them the once, some not at all. The Yare has been in the press a lot of late and I was going to fish it seriously. Unfortunately events got in the way. The Waveney has a reputation as a difficult water to fish because of the tidal flow, but it has produced fish to 30lbs in the past. I've had one day on the Ormesby Group of Broads and regret never having had the chance to follow it us. If you had the Ormesby group on your doorstep you'd have enough pike fishing to last a lifetime. To have the Ormesby group in the middle of all the other Broadland waters is simply unfair.

There are a dozen or more really interesting stories that can be told about Broadand pike fishing, almost all of which involve the Thurne. I intended at one time to write a book, which would be called Hickling, Heigham and Horsey. It would cover the history of the whole of the Thurne system. The one co-author needed was Derek Amies, but Derek seemed content to plough his own furrow with his own book project, which may yet come to fruition. I doubt if this will happen though because I'm not sure I'd want to help Derek because he didn't want to help me! Steve Harper with his excellent Broadland pike has to some extent stole both our thunder. So rather than waste the interviews I did over ten years ago, I've included two of them here. The first I with Ken Latham the man who was part responsible for the first "lure revolution in the UK"

Ken was kind enough to give me half a day and I recorded this interview. Some of the questions I asked were in no specific order, but they probably reflected my priorities at the time!

NF Ken Dennis Pye was very active when you were fishing the Thurne. How well did you know him?

KL In actual fact I only knew him to wave to. I saw him a few times when I was fishing with Peter Collins, one time editor of Angling Times.

NF How did you become associated with the Thurne?

KL I used to come on holiday to the Thurne and liked the area. The area that became Lathams of Potter Heigham was just a marsh near the river. The actual shop was built near to Bridge Stores. It underwent several extensions. The store thrived, particularly its angling section. Around 1966 the fishing was so good that for example 5 anglers had 900lb of bream on deep dyke in a night. I remember Bill Giles coming in and buying a solid glass rod.

NF Where did most of the pike get caught?

KL On Hickling Broad they were hard to find. Hickling was a very big area. Heigham sounds was good, Duck Broad not so good though Dennis Pye was supposed to have had some big fish off of it. I recall Dennis catching some big pike to order off of there for an American magazine. Horsey in comparison was much easier. One good day saw me catch fish of 25, 23, 18, 15, 13 and 10lb all between the island and the reeds. My best ever pike of 27-08 was off of Horsey and fell to a plug. Heigham Sounds and Meadow Dyke were great areas for plug fishing before the advent of Wagstaffe and Reynolds. Yellow and black were the most effective colours.

NF Were you importing American lures at the time?

KL No not at the start. I used to make some of my own lures. I remember catching a 25 pounder first cast from Heigham Sounds on a rolling pin handle fashioned into a plug. A trip to Chicago with Fred Taylor got me hooked on American plugs. I started to import them along with Umco Possum Belly Tackle boxes. These boxes were the ultimate lure boxes of their day.

NF Ken showed me one of his boxes. You could add sections to them and Ken's was about 6 sections high! In it was the most marvelous collections of lures. Any lure angler would have sold his, mother, the cat and the dishwasher to get his hands on some of them. I was lucky because without prompting Ken gave me a Gudebro Sniper. An effective and also collectable lure. I asked Ken about Martham Broads.

KL. We only used to fish the entrances to the broad particularly the South Broad. We spent much more time on Heigham Sounds. The weed growth was so prolific that you could only get into the broad from the bottom bay, Potter end.

NF What happened in 1969?

KL We had always had mortalities, *Prymnesium* had probably been around all along. When the big kill happened in 1969 I went up to look. Pike were floating around everywhere. There were not many rudd dead, mainly pike, roach and bream. The river authority disposed of them. The *Prymnesium* outbreak was thought to have started at Waxham Cut, the filth from the marshes pumped in via Brograve pump. The effect on the fishing was disastrous. Sales of everything particularly groundbait dropped through the floor.

NF So many keen pike anglers gave up pike fishing after *Prymnesium*, it must have been a terrible blow, one that I've never had to experience. Ken's lure importing proved

Peter Hancock's Horsey Mere 40 pounder - a fish that inspired many a pike angler.

Reg Sandys with 22¼lb pike caught in 1962, held by an unknown angler.

to be a bit of a white elephant. Wagstaffe and Reynolds with the demise of the Thurne found that they could not repeat the level of fishing they had experienced on the Thurne. In-fact Fred's series Footloose was moved to the Fens around 1973 and proved to be a complete dead loss because his techniques just didn't work well for large fish on the waters at that time. With Wagstaffe and Reynolds no longer hyping up lure fishing the interest in this method once again faded. This left Ken Latham with a huge stock of lures, which were destined to remain in stock for many years. At one stage Ken had some amazing lures in stock. There were all sizes of Creek Chub Pikies all made from wood. All the famous lures were there, Cisco kids, Helin Flatfish and Swim Whizz's. I made regular trips to Latham to buy lures for the shop and Ken's stock kept us supplied with lures throughout the 80s! When the stocks eventually dried up, we were only a few years away from the second lure revival. Ken eventually sold his business and it remains today one of the biggest, if not the biggest in Broadland. It remains a general-purpose store with a large angling section. Holidaymakers can get everything they need there for their holiday and have the added delight of a look at a big tackle shop.

One of the most delightful pairs of anglers I ever came across was Reg Sandys and Bill Giles. Kathy and I interviewed them for the proposed Broadland book and again it's a shame for it not to see the light of day. I actually first met Bill in the Fens. I think post *Prymnesium* he was one of the pike anglers who did not give up. Instead he traveled West to fish the same or similar waters as me. In this interview BG stands for both Bill and Reg who were both present. We called at Bill's Norwich house and I asked him as many questions as I could think of. Bill and Reg were always great diary keepers and because of this there is more detail available than from many other pike anglers of the era. Bill started fishing aged 4 with his brother and his biggest pike before he moved to Norfolk was 3lb 9oz Bill has lived in Norwich since 1938. Bill served in the merchant navy during the war and taught himself navigation. There are many interesting stories Bill could tell about those desperate years and to someone of my generation it is hardly possible to imagine the cold and the fear that was constantly with the crews of the Atlantic convoys. Particularly in the period 1941 to 1943 you never knew if you were about to be sent to oblivion by a German torpedo. Reg came from Stafford originally. The two of them met in 1952 when Reg was in his early 20s. They fished together for over 50 years!

When the two of them were fishing the Thurne they virtually had it to themselves. A look in Bill's diary shows the following; 1950 25lb from Duck Broad, days on the South Broad for no result in 1954, a trip to Hickling for no result in 1959 and a day on Horsey Mere on January 24th 1964, fish of 17-12, 15 and 13lb. On Feb 1st a 23-05 and on Feb 9th a 25-08.

NF. I asked Bill if he ever had anything big from Martham Broad and when did Horsey get busy?

BG I never had a big fish from Martham, the best being 14b I used to do a fair bit of perch spinning there in 1965. By then the Norfolk Naturalist signs were starting to spread. Horsey Mere did not start to get busy until Hancock's 40 came out. Then you could see up to 20 boats a day on there. One chap stopped to ask me if this was "Hornsea Mere"! It actually became difficult to catch pike from Horsey when it got really busy, yet the pike were obviously still there when *Prymnesium* killed them. I had an interesting experience on Duck Broad. Ian Gillespie came with a couple of friends and I fished with one of them. I hooked a fish and it gave a good fight. Then halfway in the pike slowed up, no fight at all. Then it started to fight again. It weighed 17-08 and had teeth marks on either side of its body. Was this a monster? In actual fact after *Prymnesium* Frank Wright found 3 or 4 pike over 40lb dead on Horsey.

NF During Horsey's heyday you must have met some interesting people and seen some sights?

BG. We did see a lot, but not always things we could believe! One catch that was convincing was when Edwin Vincent the son of Jim Vincent had a big catch from Horsey, fish of 31-06, 23, 13 and 11lb. All came from between the island and the boathouse, not generally a good spot these days.

Then there was the famous 34/24lb pike incident. Edwin Vincent was fishing Horsey and Dennis Pye came on the Broad and anchors. 20 minutes later he rows over to Edwin saying that he had a 34lb pike and would Edwin witness it? Dennis wanted to get it photographed so went to the bank. Edwin reweighed the fish and it weighed 24lb! All this was after Edwin had already signed a witness statement. Dennis refused to give it back! Another story involved Reg who went to have a 25-08 set up. There was a second fish there that was supposed to be one of Dennis's thirty pounders. It was smaller than the 25-08! Dennis tended to fish midweek whereas we fished Saturdays. I think the idea of being "The fisher of big pike" rather got to him. He felt he had to always catch. Dennis's best year produced 29 twenty pounders and we always felt this was open to question. Jim Vincent's best year was 27 twenty pounders. Dennis was a one method man, fishing one rod, this taking no account of those numerous days when the pike would probably have preferred a deadbait! Bill always kept a detailed record of their catches so Bill has kindly allowed me to provide detail from his diary. I think it gives a wonderful picture of pike fishing as it was before many of us had even cast a deadbait. There is a key to the methods used.

KEY SL	Sardine on leadless leger.
SFT	Sardine on float tackle
SM	Smelt on float tackle
HM	Head half mackerel.
LRLL	Live roach on leadless leger.
LRP	Live roach on paternoster.
HLL	Herring on leadless leger.
MLL	Mackerel on leadless leger.
LB	Livebait.
TS	Toby spoon
IS	Intrepid spoon

Feb.	11th	1950	25-08	Heigham Sounds.	LB
Mar.	11th	1961	26-04	Heigham Sounds.	LB
Oct.	28th	1961	20-08	Heigham Sounds.	LB
Feb.	3rd	1962	23-00	Heigham Sounds.	SDR
Feb.	1st	1964	23-08	Horsey Mere.	HHL
Feb.	29th	1964	25-08	Horsey Mere.	SDR
Dec.	12th	1964	22-12	Horsey Mere.	HLL
Dec.	19th	1964	21-04	Horsey Mere.	HLL
Dec.	31st	1964	21-08	Horsey Mere.	HLL
Dec.	31st	1964	21-04	Horsey Mere.	HLL
Feb.	6th	1965	20-04	Private Broad.	SS
Mar.	13th	1965	26-04	Horsey Mere.	SH
Mar.	14th	1965	20-04	Horsey Mere.	SH
Nov.	13th	1965	22-08	Horsey Mere.	HLL
Dec.	11th	1965	27-08	Horsey Mere.	HLL
Feb.	5th	1966	23-00	Horsey Mere.	HFT
Feb.	5th	1966	20-00	Horsey Mere.	HLL
Feb.	19th	1966	27-00	Horsey Mere.	HFT
Mar.	5th	1966	21-04	Horsey Mere.	HLL
Nov.	26th	1966	24-12	Horsey Mere.	HLL
Dec.	3rd	1966	20-02	Horsey Mere.	HLL
Dec.	10th	1966	26-08	Horsey Mere.	HLL
Dec.	17th	1966	21-12	Horsey Mere.	HLL
Nov.	4th	1967	23-08	Horsey Mere.	HFT
Nov.	11th	1967	24-00	Horsey Mere.	HLL
Dec.	16th	1967	26-00	Horsey Mere.	HLL
Dec.	16th	1967	22-00	Horsey Mere.	HLL
Jan.	4th	1968	21-08	Horsey Mere.	HLL
Jan.	4th	1968	20-12	Horsey Mere.	HLL
Feb.	1st	1969	25-00	Horsey Mere.	HLL
Aug.	19th	1969	24-08	Loch Lomond.	HFT*
Oct.	26th	1969	23-12	Relief Channel.	HLL
Nov.	2nd	1970	21-08	Counter Drain.	HLL
Feb.	11th	1972	20-12	Private Broad.	HHM
Feb.	10th	1973	21-00	Private Broad.	HLL
Feb.	2nd	1974	25-12	Private Broad.	HLL
Mar.	11th	1974	28-04	Ranworth Inner Broad.	HLL
Nov.	30th	1974	21-12	Decoy Broad.	TS
Feb.	17th	1975	21-00	Decoy Broad.	IS
Feb.	19th	1975	25-02	Private Broad.	LRLL
Feb.	20th	1977	21-12	Private Broad.	HLL
Jan.	26th	1980	28-08	Lyng Trout Lake.	LRP
Mar.	11th	1980	20-04	Redgrave Lake.	LB
Feb.	6th	1982	23-04	Private Broad.	HLL

*Witnessed by Dick Walker.

Feb.	4th	1983	26-04	Private Broad.	IS
Nov.	12th	1983	27-08	Private Broad.	HLL
Dec.	10th	1983	22-06	Lyng Pit.	LB
Mar.	3rd	1984	21-12	Private Broad.	SL
Oct.	20th	1984	22-08	Lyng Trout Lake.	SFT
Mar.	1st	1987	31-08	Ranworth Inner Broad.	HLL
Mar.	7th	1987	31-00	Ranworth Inner Broad.	HLL
Nov.	17th	1987	22-04	Private Broad.	HLL
Jan.	6th	1988	21-00	Private Broad.	HLL
Mar.	2nd	1989	26-12	Lyng Trout Lake.	HLL
Nov.	25th	1991	22-04	Horsey Mere.	HLL
Dec.	27th	1991	23-00	Horsey Mere.	HLL
Jan.	8th	1992	23-04	Horsey Mere.	SM
Nov.	4th	1992	26-05	Horsey Mere.	HLL
Nov.	6th	1992	24-03	Horsey Mere.	HLL
Feb.	1st	1993	20-12	Private Broad.	MLL
Nov.	8th	1993	24-08	Horsey Mere.	HLL
Nov.	8th	1994	24-12	Swanton Morley.	HLL
Mar.	7th	1997	20-02	Private Broad.	HLL
Mar.	7th	1997	23-12	Private Broad.	HLL

What is very interesting here is the impact that Horsey Mere had on Bill's fishing. With the capture of Hancock's 40 it is clear that the fishing became much harder. After the *Prymnesium* out-break in August of 1969 Bill's fishing changed completely. I first met him myself on the banks of the Counter drain at Welches Dam, an indication that Bill was having to spread his wings. Bill got around a lot and the fact that he fished on Lyng Trout Lake and returned to Horsey showed that he was still keen after years of pike fishing. His first and second 30lb plus pike were the same fish and not from the water where he had the bulk of his twenty-pound plus pike. The fact that Bill's biggest Horsey Pike was 27lb showed that even in its heyday Horsey did not give up its 30 pounders to everyone.

The rediscovery of deadbaiting was also something that Bill and Reg were involved in. It was probably a case of parallel development because the Taylor brothers on Wooton lakes also realised that deadbaits caught pike. Bill recalls that one day on March 10th of 1950 he was spinning a dead roach when the line got in a tangle and it took five minutes to sort it out. He had just about finished sorting it out when the line was pulled from his fingers. It weighed 8 1/4lb. Trying herrings came later on a frozen Rockland Broad when they couldn't get any dead roach. Hence their buying some herrings from a fish shop in Brundall. The herrings also worked on Ranworth Inner Broad in March of 1951. After having been on Heigham Sounds and catching pike to 18lb on herrings Peter Collins wrote it up in Angling Times.

THE FENS
For me the Fens are home sweet home and though I no longer live there I still spend as much time fishing these waters as I can. The history of the Fens makes interesting reading and turns up in all sorts of historical accounts. The improvement of the Fens

was a major part of the early life of a certain Oliver Cromwell who ultimately became Lord Protector of England after the execution of Charles 1st. The Dutchman Cornelius Vermoyden was the man responsible for much of the drainage of the Fens and his legacy to us all is that list of familiar names such as the River Delph, Hundred Foot Drain and Middle Level. The evolution of the Fen Drain network has continued over the years with the last major flood relief scheme completed in the late fifties early sixties in the shape of the Great Ouse Relief Channel and later the Cut Off Channel.

The area that I would classify as Fenland is a big one. It extends from surprisingly far north with the Wainfleet River and Relief Channel near Skegness down through the drains of the Witham system. An extensive system of drains exists around Boston and further south around Spalding the Welland system boasts some very famous names such as Vernatts and the River Glen. The Nene drains include the North Level and then when you get to the Great Ouse you have the most extensive system of waters extending from King's Lynn as far south as Cambridge. Much of our modern pike fishing evolved in the Cambridge Fens under the tutorage of Barrie Rickards, Ray Webb, Bill Chillingworth and many others. After the Broads the Fens are probably the second best pike fishing area in the country. Truly massive fish are not on the cards, but the overall standard of sport is such that you are likely to become an experienced pike angler fishing in the Fens quicker than in most areas. Fen drains are artificial waters and the rivers associated with them are anything, but natural in profile. Because Fen Rivers and drains are both in the same area, I'll look at them both together. The initial problem you always face in the Fens is one of location. It is at this point that I rummage through the cupboard for all the Ordnance Survey maps of the area. In an ideal world nothing will be known about your chosen water save perhaps one press cutting from 15 years ago. That's what I really like, but sadly it gets harder and harder to find these days. When several of us set about exploring the Middle Level in 1971 we were really trail blazing because no one we knew pike fished it. The same applied to the North Level in 1974. I've since had the opportunity to explore one more drain system which though unlikely to turn into a mega water has still proved to be interesting pike fishing which after all is what we all want.

The Middle Level project was nearly ruined by a group of Coventry anglers, the Coventry Circus Specimen Group who just happened to stumble on one of the good areas and then have a two page spread in Angling Times. Luckily because the pike fishing on the Middle Level was not on par with that of the more famous drains little harm was done and the few of us fishing it were left in peace. The way we came to terms with the water was as a loose group of anglers. I drew a map of the drain and started to map the points of capture of all fish over 10lbs. There was Andrew Mack, Dave Phillips, Ian Reeve and myself involved. I also fished a bit at the time with John McAngus and he supplied further info from other anglers who had started to fish the drain, notably the late Terry Kaye (the Grafham bailiff) and those long-term big fish hunters Merv. Wilkinson and Phil Smith. The picture we built up was fascinating and until they dredged the drain in 1980 we ended up being able to fish a large number of holding areas, which resulted in consistent sport. I've used the term holding area for about 20 years now rather than hotspot because none of the Middle Level swims I ever fished qualified as a hotspot. Unfortunately in about 40 years of pike fishing true hotspots appear to be extremely rare features. I think the best way to explain the difference is to produce two examples one of a hotspot, one of a holding area. The only current hotspot I know is on the private Cut Off Channel in Norfolk. The reason it is hot is because of a huge aggregation of roach that occurs every year in the one spot. Needless to say I got to fish the spot a lot later than many other pike anglers, though I was one of the first to be asked. The chap who owns the fishing rights phoned me up and said he had some private pike fishing and he wanted to know how good it was. Being a cynic and busy I declined and suggested he contact Ashley Brown from King's Lynn. About 6 years later when I finally cottoned on I got to fish it and as luck would have it, it all worked out OK.

I had been asking for another day for a while (the first day yielded some doubles to 22lb away from the hotspot) and finally I got to go in February. The chap who opened the gate for me said that he'd had sixteen doubles in the day the weekend before which made my heart sink. It had been hammered so I was bound to struggle. Anyway I was there so I had to get on with it. The next day I was off to Ireland so I didn't even have a full day. Out went the three rods, two deads, and one paternostered live. I thought to myself that it wouldn't take long to get bored looking at stationary floats. My only option would be to leap frog along the drain. Luckily for me the frog didn't need leaping because I was busy right from the start. Five doubles up to 23-10 before 8 in the morning left me wondering what was happening. That day the livebait rod just sat there doing nothing. When I finally had a run on it I missed it! Everything came on static deads fished hard on the bottom. It didn't really matter what bait it was because they took anything. In the end the favourite had to be lamprey section because I got my bait

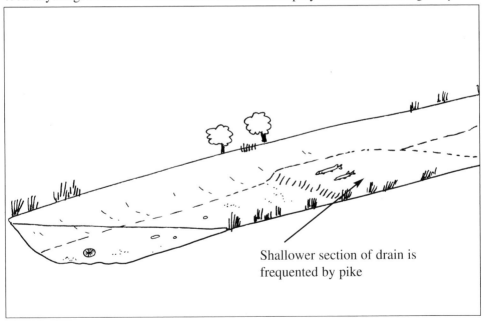

Shallower section of drain is frequented by pike

Fen Drain Hotspot

115

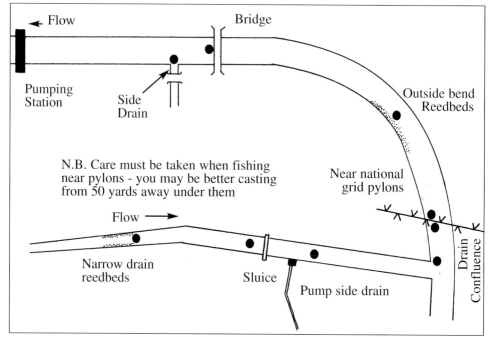

Flow ←

Bridge

Pumping Station

Side Drain

Outside bend Reedbeds

N.B. Care must be taken when fishing near pylons - you may be better casting from 50 yards away under them

Near national grid pylons

Flow →

Narrow drain reedbeds

Sluice

Pump side drain

Drain Confluence

Generalised Fenland River/drain swims

back each time and was therefore able to double and even treble up on each bait. By the time I had caught about 15 doubles the swim slowed down so I moved slightly along and caught the biggest of the day a 27 pounder. The actual landing of the pike was the hard bit. The banks are very steep and there are lots of brambles, which snag the landing net at the first opportunity. By 3pm I had caught enough. 24 pike, 22 doubles, two twenties. A whole seasons worth for most pike anglers in three quarters of a day. I went home having had my best days pike fishing ever as far as quantity of good pike is concerned. Dave Horton was due to fish in a day or two and I think I might have just taken the edge off of the pike's appetite!

I'm sure the same spot has produced similar catches to other pike anglers in the past. Therefore it was not a great feat of skill, just a case of fishing as hard as possible for a short period. It also helped to make the right judgment about moving along the drain slightly. Holding areas are a different ball game altogether. On a fairly wide drain like the Middle Level you'd think that you'd find the odd hotspot where you could make a big haul of pike. This was unfortunately seldom the case. We used to have one spot which for a while produced a similar sized brace each time we fished it. I remember myself having a brace of 15 pounders there and sharing the swim with Bruno Broughton for an 18-10 to him and a 19-10 to me. These holding areas would not fish the next day and not always the next week.

They were best fished at anything up to 4-week intervals, but this did not matter, as we all knew quite a few holding areas. When we tagged some pike we found the same pike turning up in different holding areas. It became clear that one swim would fill up with pike that took up temporary residence there. We caught them and the shock sent them somewhere else. Eventually they would return at some stage be it that season or the next. The holding area phenomena proved on the Middle Level at least to be more valid than the hotspot concept. In fact none of us ever really felt that we knew any hotspots. There was supposed to be one above Pingle Bridge, but every time I fished it I either blanked or caught the odd small one. It may be that other people were fishing the swim thus making it difficult for me to catch much. It occurs to me that hotspots may be a function of the number of pike in a water. You cannot expect to have a classic hotspot i.e. somewhere that consistently produces big pike unless there are a lot of big pike in the water. Though the Middle Level was a reasonable water I suspect that the pike population was not huge. They were in effect thinly spread over a lot of holding areas. On the Relief Channel in the late sixties and early seventies there were a lot of big pike but not that many good spots. You in effect have a concentration effect. So in reality the definitions I am trying to work to may well be artificial and simply a reflection of the density of the pike in a water. There is little doubt that pike favour setting up "home" in certain areas. These areas offer something that is usually attractive to one or more pike. The food fish may not be present in the exact spot, but they will not be that far away. It has been suggested that these pike move out from hotspots and holding areas to feed, sometimes ranging far afield, but returning to the same area or perhaps another to digest the meal or even wonder why it didn't catch one! This makes sense to me because even though the pike is a fairly primitive creature it obviously will have preferences as to where it spends most of it's time. The original definition of a hotspot (a Rickards and Webb concept, consolidated by Martin Gay) was an area where large numbers of good pike took up residence and though they were prepared to feed for short periods most days, for the most part they just used certain areas to hole up. I've concentrated here on Fenland type hotspots and holding areas, but they also exist on other types of water. The East valve tower on Grafham Water is certainly a hotspot, but because everyone knows of it and because it is hammered to death tends to produce best only if it has been left alone for a while. I'll look at other examples in later sections.

Certain sections of drain do look better than others. A change of width or a change of depth can if the rest of the drain is relatively featureless be enough to attract some pike. Bridges are sometimes useful, but because they are the first features some anglers come to they are frequently fished out. Where side drains come in is usually productive as is a stretch of bank, which is reedlined when the rest is bare. Man made structures such as pumping stations and electricity pylons frequently attract pike. The pylons probably work because dredgers have to work differently near them. This means that the drain bed is going to be different under or just to each side of the pylons. One of the best Relief Channel hotspots was on a bend where the old ox bow on the Great Ouse had been cut across while excavating the Relief Channel itself. The Channel's bed was probably gravel in one area or at least significantly different than that elsewhere. Whatever the reason the area was also famous for it's huge shoals of bream, which is why locals christened it "The Mad Mile". Even a row of Poplar trees was enough to make a holding area on the Middle Level. It might just have been coincidence, but it was also a good bream area. Some drains are so featureless that you cannot remember where you caught a big pike. I used to have this problem on Timberland Delph a side drain off the River Witham. Here and there, there might have been the odd bush on the far bank, but that was probably something like one bush every half a mile! The best holding areas of all had lay byes on the roads passing them by. How I hear you ask could that possibly influence a pike? Well it may be stretching a point slightly, but general roach and bream anglers tend to have lost the ability to walk these days. If they fish a convenient swim regularly it will probably we more attractive to the roach and bream because of the bait the anglers throw in.

Though we tend to look as Fenland Drains in linear terms, i.e. exploring them is carried out working along them, some also require looking at in term of the width of the drain. After all the Relief Channel is 100 yards wide and many other drains and rivers are 40 to 50 yards in width. We have the tackle to easily fish the full width of such waters and that is exactly what we must do. Sometimes you will find the bulk of the fish on one side of the drain and a bit of long casting beats the pants off of walking around to the other bank. Of course sometimes other anglers get funny ideas about what constitutes a drain, which is wide enough to be fished on both sides. About 10 year ago I was minding my own business on the Middle Level. I had three rods out, one in the edge, one in the middle and another on the far bank. To my amazement two anglers turned up on the opposite bank and proceeded to tackle up. I mentioned that I had a bait close to where they were standing. "Oh you'll have to wind in then" was the reply. By now I was seeing red as well as several shades of pink and ultra violet! I didn't mess about, I got the heavy-duty rod out with 18lb line and a big bomb and a treble. I cast across one of the anglers lines and made it impossible for him to fish. As darkness fell I was sure I'd be getting a visit, after all two against one, so I sat there with my stainless steel bank stick hoping I'd not have to use it. This is the sort of behaviour no-on wants to get involved in, but sometimes other anglers are so stupid that you have to make a stand. Luckily it hasn't happened again!

Location may be vital in the Fens, but when and how also counts for a lot. Two seasons ago I was pumped off of a favourite section of drain and moved ten miles to another drain. I'd only really played at fishing on this water so when I arrived I decided to walk a good way from the bridge. However as I walked down the bank two roach anglers told me there was a big pike striking at the surface that morning. I thought to myself, this will be nonsense as usual, but something in the back of my head said that the 3pm feeding period you often get in winter on the drains was only an hour away. So I dropped in near the bridge and sure enough at around 3pm I had a run and duly landed a beauty of just over 25lb. A 12 pounder followed. The move was made to the right spot at the right time. It often does not work like that, but that is no reason not to keep trying.

Most Fen drains are pumped or run off from time to time and at times of heavy rain can be impossible to fish because of the amount of debris on the move. A gentle pull is probably an advantage because the smell from your deadbait wafts downstream. I'm a great believer in trying to fish some of the better holding areas on Fen drains at the optimum time. One such optimum time must always be after the drain has been in flood.

It is particularly useful to be able to fish the really well known swim before someone else gets to them. I had my day in the sun a few years ago. The story actually starts with that rare creature a female Angling Times reporter phoning me to ask if a 29-08 pike was a record for that particular drain. Seeing as I'd never heard of the water I wasn't really qualified to comment. However it did lead me to investigate and on a trip out to the water I met the brother of the chap who had had the 29. He told me his best pike from the water was 19lbs. The story had the ring of truth to it so I set to work exploring the drain. I learned quite a bit that season, but for some reason never managed to get back to the water until February. The day dawned bright and windy, but I was still at home working! I kept humming and haring about going. I fancied the one swim and knew that the drain had been either frozen or in flood the week before. (I cannot remember which!) Bright windy days after grim conditions invariably see pike feeding well particularly in a month such as February. In the end, much later than normal I set out on the 50-mile trip to the drain. On setting up it took about 2 hours to catch two five pounders, a 14, a 23 and a fish of 30-08. All came from that one holding area identified the season before.

Being self-employed gives you the option of getting away on those rare magical days. Not everyone can do this, but even the weekend angler can move heaven and earth to make sure he gets out on these sorts of days rather than giving into domestic pressure. A posh meal out at a later date can do much to compensate for not helping with the shopping…

In pike fishing you can never say never, but as a rule of thumb I would not start my Fenland pike fishing until the end of October or whenever the first frost arrives. I do not think anyone understands why this should be, but it certainly does apply on many waters. Fenland Rivers present very similar problems to the Drains except that you have the luxury of bends in rivers. I've not really had much success on Fen Rivers. My best from the Witham was 18-11, the Welland 17-12, Great Ouse 17lb. So I'm no river expert. I missed out on some of the more spectacular river revivals such as the Little Ouse and in the last couple of years The River Lark has produced some big fish. It should be noted that both these revivals followed fish wipeouts! Always remember a water that has suffered a catastrophe will generally recover in 8 to 10 years. Most of my better Fen river pike have come from side drains that would normally produce nothing at all. Yet when the river is in flood, big pike often wander up to a couple of miles up the drain. My best in this situation weighed 25-14 and because it was really a Witham fish I'm not totally a failure on these waters.

Bait choice on Fenland waters would initially consist of the usual policy of chucking everything at them! I have found many drains to be virtually a waste of time on livebaits, brilliant on deads and sometimes quite productive to lure fishing. Why a water should produce on lures, but not livebaits escapes me, but I'm not going to try to buck any trends here! It is impossible to lure fish and live or deadbait fish effectively. The two methods require two totally different approaches. Dead and livebaiting are static or semi-static methods while lure fishing is best used as a mobile method. You can obviously lure fish around your live and deadbait rods and this can certainly produce fish that you might not have caught. However there is little point in flogging away in the same small area for half a day. Resting the swim is probably the best approach so doing a bit of lure fishing every so often is my approach. If you can leave the chair, the rod rests and the baits behind then lure fishing on Fen drains offers a host of opportunities. I tend to do about 5 casts and then walk 5 yards working along the drain. In this way you cover a huge amount of water during the course of a day. If you do not succeed in having a great days fishing you will at least gain some clues. Follows off of pike or even a few small ones can provide clues as to where the pike are. Though odd small pike can turn up anywhere, generally if you catch a few six and seven pounders in one stretch the chances are that there will be better fish present. They are just not falling to your lures. Lure choice depends to some extent on water depth and what you are confident in. I use Springdawgs a lot usually in fire, parrot or perch patterns. Flippers work and there's no need to ignore lures such as Spinnerbaits. All these lures are useful in shallow water. The bigger deeper drains and rivers respond to the Bulldawg proper and there's a host of diving lures and spoons you can try. The difficulty with diving lures is during the last few yards of retrieve when they tend to dive into the marginal shelf. All you can do is either wind slower or lift the rod tip as high as possible.

Deadbait choice follows my usual strategy of making sure that I offer a variety of baits. At least one oily bait such as sardine or mackerel and a "natural" type bait i.e. smelt, pollan, lamprey or coarse fish. Frequently oily baits are slower on the drains I fish, but do tend to produce the better fish. Using a variety of baits means that you will hopefully be offering something the pike want. I remember seeing Phil Smith on the North Level fishing three rods on half mackerel. He wasn't getting much (though he did catch a 30 the night before!). I dropped in below him and had quite a few runs on lamprey. My sardine remained unmolested. It may have been coincidence, but generally I think it has to be worth offering a range of baits.

If you are a bit younger than me you will have one advantage on some of us. I can still walk to the swims I want to fish, but it gets hard work sometimes. Younger pike anglers should be able to walk to any part of a Fen drain! I remember about five years ago when I decided to give the North Level a shot, walking about a mile just to try and find an area, which had not been flogged. I had just about staggered as far as I could when I put down my rucksack. Now I didn't drop it or throw it down, but a pike had heard me just the same. A big bow wave cut across the surface. I fished the spot and caught quite a few pike topped by a 22 pounder. That time the long walk had paid off. Unfortunately in subsequent visits the same general area proved to be disappointing, I eventually ended up near the bridge and catching fish to 17lb. So sometimes you can walk past them! Before I move onto other types of waters I ought to mention canals here. Now canals are even more artificial than Fen drains. They were designed for the transport of materials by boat. Today they are used more for leisure and this has resulted in the restoration of many neglected waters. Some neglected canals have been very good quality pike waters. The Leven canal north of Hull was very good until it was converted into a commercial fishery. This canal was actually the scene of my only pike on pike capture. (I have caught pike on live or dead pike baits). I had been fishing a small roach livebait when a tiny pike no more than 9 inches long took it. Before I could say, "What's going on here", a 9 pounder, which I somehow managed to land, had taken the little pike.

My experience of canal fishing is limited, but both waters I set out to explore turned out to be quite good waters after I had been unable to carry out the follow up fishing effort. One was the Stainforth and Keadby Canal. This is very much a match water in an area where pike have never been popular. Yet the water quality was very good and the past stocking policy of the controlling clubs suggested that it ought to be a good pike water. My first trip saw me pick a spot by a reed bed (on many canals reed beds are the only feature). I had two runs an 18 and a 12. Both fish were superb looking fish, probably never caught before. There then followed quite a few exploratory trips, but only the odd small pike turned up. I then put the boat on the canal and float trolled about 5 miles of it for nothing! My interest was then directed elsewhere, but the canal was then "discovered" and fish to 24lbs caught. My right hand man Bob Hopwood has since had three twenty pounders from that canal.

Further south of me is the Fossdyke navigation that connects the Trent and the Witham. The canal has produced pike to 25lbs in the past and I did give it a bit of attention. I found pike where side drains came in and near moored boats. The biggest was just over 10lbs and fell to smelt. I had hoped that the pike would follow the prey fish into the shelter of the couple of human habitations along the canal, but fishing these areas did not pay off. There are lots of canals around the country with turning basins, marinas and so on. All offer scope for pike fishing and should not be ignored just because they are canals.

SPECIAL WATERS. MASONS LAKE

Just once in a while lucky pike anglers get onto some very special fishing. There are a few such examples of such waters. Eddie Turners chalk pit (Lakeside at Thurrock) changed his fishing beyond recognition. Bill Flory on the Upper Thurne caught more big pike in a year than most pike anglers have had in a lifetime. The pike anglers who came to terms with fly-fishing on Blithfield had some exceptional fishing. The private section of the Cut Off Channel was unique. Going back years, the early days at Abberton and of course the Thurne pre *Prymnesium* offered special fishing. All pike anglers look for that certain something that is going to give then that pike fishing experience of a lifetime.

My quantum leap was (as I write still is) Masons Lake, a code name for a water, which had promise, which was subsequently fulfilled. It all started about 4 years ago. I used to spend quite a lot of time looking for promising waters, but in recent years the amount of time available for wandering around has reduced considerably. My pike fishing as a consequence had become less productive. Though I will at times jump on a passing

My first look at the Thurne

Bill Giles - Horsey 20¼ 14th March, 1965

My biggest pike of 25-10 Middle Level

This Masons fish really is a superb looking example. It weighed 24lbs

This Masons fish of 27-02 caught by Nige Williams is a
strange very light brown colour

Small rivers make for interesting fishing when they are like this and not in flood

Fast River Pike - The mobile approach led to the capture of this 21 pounder.

A 28 pounder landed at Weirwood

John Costellos's 41-08 from a West Country trout water

The new trout waters such as Chew have been kind to some people.
Duncan Pritchard with a spoon caught 25

Trout Waters produce big trout as well as pike! Bob Hopwood with a 12-08 brownie in a smelt

View of the Boat Inn at Lound.
A fascinating still water, now filled with gravel washing

25-01 gravel pit pike

Connecting pipes are nearly always good swims.

A beautiful 24 from Corrib just after spawing

Mark Ackerley with 32-12 May 1992 Maamtrasna Bay Lough Mask

Mark Ackerley with 30-12 from Lough Mask

Martyn Nelson's Mask 30

bandwagon and head for the latest "on" water I prefer to do my own groundwork. Groundwork however requires effort at times when you are not fishing.

Luckily for me I decided to follow up a hunch. I went or a walk around this particular lake, which was a bit naughty of me because I'd not, asked permission to do so. I looked at all sorts of likely areas, but found no signs to inspire me. Then in a corner with a load of driftwood was a shape that might have been a dead pike. It didn't look much, but unknown to me it was bent which meant that I could only really see the middle of it's flank. I searched around for a suitable branch or stick and tried to remove the debris. This didn't work so I went back to the car to fetch my landing net handle. With this I managed to get a better look at the fish. It was a lot bigger than I thought. I had no tape measure with me, so I marked off the fork length of the pike on the handle. When I got home I measured it, 42 inches, which is long enough for a 30 pounder, provided it is a fat pike. That pike looked fat. So there were or had been big pike in the water. Now because I want to tell you the story, but I do not wish to reveal where the lake is I'll not provide much detail about the water. A lot of people think they know where it is and the suggestions are fairly interesting, but of only academic interest to me at the moment.

I had to think of a plan, which would enable me to get access to the water. At the time I was convinced that money was the answer to most problems. I needed a couple of friends willing to throw a serious amount of money into the pot so I was able to make a serious offer. Dave Moore a friend of mine since I was 15 has quite a good job as a consultant radiologist so hopefully he could spare a fiver or several! Nige Williams had helped me get onto Blithfield a year or so ago so I owed him a favour. I also thought he would be keen enough to offer a decent amount of money to gain access to this lake. Now the next job was to make contact, something I'm sure other pike anglers will have done in the past. I phoned up and got the owner. Now I mentioned pike fishing and he was non-committal, however I wanted to actually meet face to face. I asked for 30 minutes the following week and luckily he said yes. The day I made my journey was bitterly cold and there was a lot of snow on the ground. I also had a cold of near flu proportions. I was received with due courtesy and given my 30 minutes. I made my offer of money to fish the lake, which was duly declined. However we could fish it as his guest from time to time! I was pleased, very pleased yet for some reason I didn't get around to asking for a couple of days until December the following year. We had agreed between the three of us that the number of potential swims was not enough for three anglers so we decided to fish it two people at a time. Dave could not book his holiday off at short notice so Nige and I were destined to fish the first day.

We arrived at dawn and put a couple of livebaits and a deadbait out. I did a bit of lure fishing, but nothing happened. However the livebaits evoked a response from fish up to about 12lb. Nige then had a jack which tangled one of my rods up. While I was sorting myself out he had a run that resulted in a very light coloured beast of a pike of 33-14. My emotions were mixed. I had to feel, "Why not me", but it was tempered by the satisfaction that my gut feeling about the water had been right. We fished all day and I picked up several more pike to 17lbs mainly on Bull and Springdawgs. We returned the next day, but it was clear that we had fished the swim out. We moved around a fair amount, but did not find any pike. We did find a big pile of pike scales in an area we have seldom caught pike from. The rest of the winter was spent fishing whenever we were allowed and to be frank it was hard work. I had a 23 pounder and the 37-08 mentioned in the lure fishing section. I also picked up a fish just over twenty pounds on a trolled Bulldawg, my first ever dragging the soft plastic lure. Nige and Dave had a quiet time, until in Nige's case I had a week in Northern Ireland. As luck would have it a wild windy period came in and Masons can fish well in this sort of weather. Nige had one hell of a day with the three best topping 20lbs, 31,25 and just over 20lbs. The following week when I returned he added salt into the wound with a 21 pounder from a new area. I mentioned the importance of windy weather and for the first year we were pretty convinced that the best weather for fishing Masons was just that. The following season though we had some good fish when it was windy we also had some when it wasn't!

To have one season on a new water was a treat, but to get the chance to fish it again was beyond our wildest dreams. If the 37-08 had survived we had the chance to fish for a very big pike never mind the other thirties. We all looked forward to fishing again and perhaps learning more about its pike. It was Dave's turn to start on opening day, and we prayed for a bit of wind. There was none at first, but it soon blew up. We had a few pike, but nothing huge up to 16lbs. The trouble with this fishing is you never know exactly what you are going to turn up. You expect far too much every day and sometimes your expectations are beyond what is reasonable. Dave kept flogging away with his Springdawg. I had finally convinced Dave that a proper lure fishing kit would be nicer and more effective than his 25-year-old glass pike rod! When he finally had a take it was the best fish of the day at 23lbs. The spot he had the fish from was interesting because it was just a bit deeper closer to the bank and sometimes you'd get the odd pike move into this little trench. Nige returned with me the following week and we opted to take the boat out after a less than exciting first day. We trolled Bulldawgs and Springdawgs and as we approached where I had caught the 37-08 I had a take on a Springdawg. Unfortunately it dropped off, only to almost certainly attack Nige's spoon, which was following behind. That fish went 27-05. We then caught a few more fish, Nige getting the better ones up to 16lb. I had to go home early so I left Nige to it. A few hours later when I rang him I learned that he had had a 30-12. The curse of the Williams had struck again! I have to take a philosophical view about these sort of events otherwise the only alternative is to stop fishing or put Arsenic in his coffee. Neither alternatives are viable ones, so I was happily consoling myself with the fact that I was lucky enough to get the big one the season before. That was until this season, but I digress!

The following week it was Dave and myself fishing and we started where Nige had had the 30-12. I do not miss many runs on livebait, but when I did and then saw the teeth marks in the bait I was not a happy man. Recasting the same bait the pike was kind enough to take the bait again. It was a big pike, but not in the best of condition. It should have weighed 30lb, but it creaked the scales around to 29-08. It really was a strange looking fish. Even when returned it just sat there on the bottom for ages. One assumes that not all pike drop dead when they are at the peak of health. It is possible that some go into a slow decline and that may be what I had just caught. You cannot complain about a 29-08, but I still wished it had gone 30lbs! Christmas came around along with a bitter freeze up. I managed to add a 24 pounder on livebait before all went solid and then we had a period when tons of snow water put the pike off. By the time things had settled down it was Dave and I again. This time he nobbled a 20lb 2oz from his now favourite spot. Dave tried the deeper water where we usually catch very little so I gave it a go as well. The Springdawg ever reliable fooled a 19 pounder that had a truncated tail.

The best two days so far was to come the following week. Nige and I met up at around 7am and set up on the bank. Nige was first with a 14 pounder to a livebait and then all went quiet. Nige was then a bit naughty and sneaked off to try one of the nearby spots without my help! He soon caught the same twenty pounder that Dave had caught the week before. There was then another lull and Nige then went off to try the spot again. Well once bitten, there was no way I was leaving him on his own this time. I joined him and pinched an 18-12 from under his nose. We went back to base and I could see what was coming, Nige was going to have a chuck in the trench spot. Luckily I was nearer and I got my cast in first. A 26-06 kindly chomped the Springdawg on the top. The day had a satisfactory conclusion! The next day we took the boat and headed up the lake. Despite having fished the water quite a bit we were still learning about the water. Despite trying livebaits we had nothing on them, but the Springdawgs did us proud with a brace of twenties each. The season was nearly over, but I had to go to Northern Ireland again and needless to say Nige nobbled yet another 30 at 31-12. My second from last trip with Dave saw him get a 21 while I had a 27-04. The end of season saw just a 17-12 and the odd small one fall to our rods. We had, had a more productive season that the previous one, but no sign of the real biggie. Hopefully we'll get the chance to fish again, but life has taught me one thing and that is, that nothing lasts forever. If we never fish there again I will pike fish somewhere else and perhaps there will be new challenges to take up. You have to move on eventually and who knows when that will be. Only then will it be possible to draw the maps and explain in detail why certain swims produce pike and others do not. Until then readers will hopefully forgive me for telling an incomplete story.

FAST RIVERS

Where I live we are not blessed with a large number of fast rivers, but if I extended my radius of operation to 50 miles I would have quite a few to look at. Locally I have the River Trent, a really big river. It is also a river that has changed a lot since I first pike fished it in the eighties. I only really fish the tidal Trent, though I have had a handful of trips further upstream. The only way to come to terms with a big river like the Trent is to put in lots of fishing effort. The one factor that increasingly throws a spanner in the works is when the river is in flood. This is one reason why I restrict my efforts on the Trent to September and whenever we have a very cold spell of weather when lots of stillwaters and drains are frozen over. My early exploratory trips on the Trent saw me fish live and deadbaits much as I would any other water. Then livebaits were miles more productive than deads. If you did get a run on a deadbait it would generally be on non-oily baits such as smelt. Sadly I was not a lure-fishing convert at the time and anyway we didn't have the lures we have today. Ten years later and the cormorants had done their job. The Trent was now a big fish water with a decided lack of small fish.

Pike survive despite this, but now they have an edge to their appetite. Deadbaits start to produce a lot more fish and now of course we have the soft plastics so our lure fishing is more productive.Fishing lives and deads on the Trent is harder work than on a drain or a stillwater. It takes a bit more effort to ensure that baits stay put when you cast them out. Float legering is not a lot of use here so running legers with 2 to 3oz of lead is the order of the day. Clip on bobbins have to be fairly tight and float paternostered livebaits require a minimum of 2oz of lead. Most of my Trent pike have come from weir pools while boat fishing. This is straightforward, simply anchor at the bows only and cast your two rods off the back. I tend to fish one sunken paternostered livebait and a legered deadbait. You need to watch the line carefully to watch for slack liners though fortunately most pike run away from the boat. I always carry a short handled landing net with a slightly smaller landing net because my 8-foot boat is very cramped. I've noticed many times that the better pike, i.e. those over 15lb tend to make off in a hurry when they take your bait. Bite indication is via the Baitrunner unless you are trotting a livebait, which is another option. Some pike anglers like to fish weir pools with good-sized livebaits on free-swimming rigs. I can see the logic behind the approach, but I've never been able to catch decent baits from the river so have to stick to paternostering smaller baits or plain boring old deadbaits. Deadbait choice has usually been confined to bait such as pollan and lamprey.

I've had a fair number of pike from the Trent on wobbled baits. Fresh baits are best and rigging them simplicity itself. I use 4 or 5 SSG shot to keep them down in the water. A boat really is a useful tool on a river simply because you have a lot of mobility. I've not had chance to do all the exploring I would like because there's never enough time in the week. I did have a morning trolling last year and having tried about 4 miles of river and only had one offer, was a bit disappointed. Perhaps another time. Bank fishing is viable, but you really do have to be mobile. One such example of mobility had an interesting outcome one September. I had walked upstream from Dunham to the famous "Dubbs" bend. I lure fished for a couple of hours, but all I had was an 11 pounder hooked in the back of the head. So I set out back, casting into every likely spot. As I approached an angler on the other bank I noticed that there were two people and they looked rather pink.

As I drew nearer I could see a very pretty looking blond stark naked except for some ankle boots bent over with a young man standing behind her. His trousers were for some reason at half-mast. By now I was watching with interest, but also ever aware that I might fall down a rabbit hole if I didn't look where I was going. When I looked up she was kneeling in front of him obviously attending to some poorly part of his body. Possibly she was kissing it better. Anyway they then saw me and rapidly got some cloths on. Later as I looked back he had just caught a bream. This all adds a new meaning to "Happiness is having a rod in your hand"!!! Another morning on the Trent was more exciting fish wise, but not so scenic. I had eight fish on Bulldawgs and Springdawgs including several doubles all from the same small area. It was so hectic at one stage that one pike tried to join me on the bank on it's own volition!

Small rivers are a bit easier to come to terms with because you can cover most of the pike from the one bank. In the bad old days there were not many big pike to be caught because the water quality was not very good and any pike lucky enough to get to a decent size invariably received the much favoured thrown up the bank treatment. Today despite the cormorants there are some good pike to be caught. Because I try to work in the shop on Saturdays I get to talk to a few customers. When one of them told me he had caught a 23 pounder from my local river I was interested. As usual it took me a while to get around to trying my luck. My previous two trips had spanned ten years and had been singularly unproductive. This trip was in a bit of a freeze up so stillwater venues were out. At first I leap frogged about 200 yards of river for absolutely nothing. Getting desperate I decided on another move. Soon I had a sardine, pollan and a paternostered livebait out. After about an hour the Delkim bleeped so I walked to the rod, but nothing seemed to be happening. Then I watched the line twitch slightly, not the normal behaviour of a very dead sardine. I wound down and found myself attached to a heavy weight. When the pike came up on the surface it looked about 15 pounds which was a good start to the day. In the net my hopeless weight estimation worked in my favour because it weighed 24 pounds.

It was a bit near to the end of the season to do much more on the river, but next season I gave it a much more serious try. It wasn't easy with the best fish in several trips a 14 pounder. I needed to try a different stretch and this is what I did. It looked interesting with some nice bends and better still no footprints in the margins. The first session yielded a couple of doubles and two small ones. Lives and deads produced fish. I returned the next week, but decided to try further along the river. Nothing happened so I moved back to the swim that produced the week before. Within 10 minutes the half herring float was off, crossing the river. It was a really good-looking 21 pounder and showed yet again the importance of being prepared to move. This is one of the reasons why you need to be organized as to what you carry when you go river pike fishing. A bivvy is not an essential for river fishing. I take a brolly should it rain or if the wind is particularly cold. Otherwise I can carry all the rest of my tackle to the swim in one go.

There are quite a number of fast rivers around the country and I must confess that I have fished few of them. From what I do know nearly all will produce pike on deadbaits, though some respond best of all to good-sized livebaits. Remember though what I said a lot earlier, you could get runs on big baits quickly, but you can usually catch the same pike if you persevere a while with smaller lives or even a deadbait. I think Nige Williams surprised a lot of people at the Parlor swim on the Hampshire Avon with a 30 pounder on lamprey. A classic case of a non-stereotyped approach to a new water.

TROUT WATERS

No single type of fishery has had the impact of trout waters. Though sometimes most of us wish we were somewhere else the draw of the trout waters is such that if you are serious about pike fishing you have to give them thought. John "Watto" Watson is not at all keen on trout waters, but he can afford to have that view living where he does in the middle of Broadland. Why then are trout waters so good? Well some of the pundits who write in the press like to use the classic phrase "The pike get fat on a diet of high protein trout". This shows a basic ignorance of fish biology. All fish have a high protein content because much of the swimming muscle is made of protein and most of the body weight of many fish is muscle. So trout probably offer little advantage pound for pound compared with bream or carp. The significance of trout is that in a put and take fishery they are stocked and provide a biomass of food fish over and above that which the fishery would normally support. All fisheries have a maximum weight of pike that can be supported by the prey fish. For example it is generally accepted that 100lb of prey fish in a water will support 10lb of pike. That100lb of prey may fluctuate, but in a balanced fishery will stay roughly the same due to recruitment of young fish and subsequent predation. The only time this goes wrong is when recruitment fails to keep up with predation. I saw one example of this on a gravel pit when a weed killer killed the weed the roach and bream had just laid their eggs on. The pike subsequently declined after this. They lost a whole years roach and bream fry, a vital food source.

Some trout waters stock in excess of 40,000 trout a season and even if there were no pike in a water a proportion of these will never be seen again. If only 20% disappear that is a lot of food for something be it the invertebrates and eels at the bottom of the water or more usefully from our point of view pike. If we consider 8,000 trout weighing 10,000lb going into pike this could support around 3,000lb of extra pike. That is a lot of 30 pounders. Most trout waters will also have a coarse fish population, which in turn will support a number of pike. So your average trout water would probably produce some big pike, but with the extra trout it will produce more big pike, bigger pike or both. Trout waters are as varied as any other waters. They range from quite small gravel pits to very big reservoirs such as the 3000-acre plus Rutland Water. Generally the smaller the water the more heavily stocked per acre a trout water will be. This obviously makes catching the pike from these waters very difficult. Fish that are not hungry are hard to catch! Some of the bigger waters have a comparatively low stock of trout. Rutland would appear in some areas to be devoid of trout (usually where the pike are!). Obviously it is impossible to stock a big water with the sorts of densities you see in small waters. It would make the whole exercise uneconomic.

Most trout waters have at some stage in their history been mismanaged. While there may have been reasons for removing pike on some waters, generally the policy of pike removal was carried out because it was the accepted truth. On Grafham Water in the seventies the death of a large number of perch caused the pike to feed much more heavily on the trout. This caused a crisis that was eventually resolved by pike removal. Sadly the pike removal on some waters such as Rutland and Pitsford may not have been required. In the end none of these waters ever recovered as pike waters to their previous glory and we must assume that pike populations always peak in the early years when pike had previously not been present. Some waters such as Chew obviously had some pike removal carried out, but the results from the first pike fishing there suggest that it hadn't done a lot of harm! Some trout waters had pike removed mainly by rod and line, which is a lot less effective than gill nets or seine netting when the pike are on the shallows. Blithfield was one such water and the selective removal of pike under 25lb has had a strange effect. Blithfield is now the countries premier big pike water, just on the basis of 30lb pike alone. It's pretty good for 35 pounders as well! Now whether Blithfield would have evolved into such a good pike water without this interference we will never know. Jason Davis has been collecting photographs of 30lb plus pike caught there and of 30 fish so far examined no repeat captures have been noted. This is obviously within the constraints of the quality of the photographs.

Some trout waters are not very hospitable for pike. Llandegfedd for example still has the best track record for 40lb plus pike in the country. This track record comes at a price though. Llandegfedd has very limited spawning areas, the two best locations in Green Pool and Sor Bay are easily exposed with only a small drop in water levels. This therefore makes recruitment to the adult population difficult. Even worse is the prospect for any female pike that have been unable to shed their spawn. It is possible for a female pike to survive failure to spawn, but generally there is probably a 50% chance that it will die. Many species of fish can reabsorb eggs but in the case of pike the best chance of shedding them probably comes with them trickling out over period of time. However if this does not happen the eggs tend to die and there must be a possibility of septicemia occurring with a possible fatal end result for the pike. We have certainly seen a number of dead pike in the summer on Llandegfedd and on waters I have been involved with spring is when you are going to get the bad news. The advantage of a high annual mortality of pike is that the available extra food is spread between much smaller numbers of pike. This must be the key to producing such large pike. The problem with mortality is that sometimes it can be so high that the pike do not live long enough to grow really large. The fluctuating fortunes of Llandegfedd may be partly to do with this and possibly to some extent due to anglers. We have seen some pretty desperate examples of pike handling on Llandegfedd, mainly due to fish being kept out of the water too long. Provided the environment remains the same and provided pike handling improves there is no reason why a water such as Llandegfedd should not produce big fish again.

Trout fisheries then tend to be water supply reservoirs or gravel pits. The water supply reservoirs can only really be fished from a boat while the gravel pits may offer a mixture of boat and bank fishing. Most water supply reservoirs are run directly by a Public Limited Companies such as Anglian Water and Severn Trent. A few are let to angling companies or private individuals. Generally where the PLCs are involved pike fishing is either actively encouraged or begrudgingly allowed. Most organizations such as Blithfield Anglers do their best to allow sensible fishing methods within the constraints of their lease. Where individuals run the fishing you will probably be allowed to livebait as well as use all other legitimate methods. The PLC standpoint is that livebaiting is not acceptable in the public eye. My standpoint is that the rearing of trout to be caught and then either killed or returned is not acceptable in the eyes of an angling anti. These are the only members of the public even remotely interested in what goes on at any fishery. So basically the PLCs are pandering unbeknown to them to the very types of people who would seek to close the fishing down! There is no doubt that the management of the PLC owned trout waters do a good job as regards the trout fishing (otherwise they would have had their P45 by now). They are a long way off the pace when it comes to pike fishing. Many of the pike in these waters live and die unmolested by anglers simply because lure fishing and deadbaiting are not effective enough. This is a shame because the viability of the pike fishing on these waters is at stake because of this. Some waters can be exploited successfully by lures alone but even on Blithfield we have no way of telling how many big pike would be caught if all methods were allowed.

How then do you catch these pike? Well the first problem that presents itself is the lottery syndrome. If you think you are going to be alone while fishing most trout waters you are gravely mistaken! The one factor that affects the individual's success is competition from other anglers. That competition may be benign or utterly cutthroat depending on where and when you are fishing. On Llandegfedd for example there are a few good areas and those boats that get there first have the best chance of catching something. Unless by pure luck someone moves out of a good spot and you move in and then convert what seemed like a duff spot into a good one. The key thing to remember is that you cannot trust all other anglers to behave, as you would do. When the fish are confined to small areas you have to expect boats to crowd into one area. However it is not fair to have someone anchor so close to you that you cannot effectively fish. A 50-yard limit is a normal rule, but some people cannot judge distances very well. Unfortunately the wardens on some waters are too busy watching for other potential infringements to bother with this.

Static anchored fishing is a feature of some waters and generally you have only lures and deadbaits to use. Lures can take a lot of casting before a pike finally gets fed up of seeing it and decides to see it off with a mouth full of teeth. My personal success at trying to "bore" the pike out has been very limited. In fact as I try and recall I cannot remember managing to do it! My boat partners have managed on very odd occasions, but any fish I've had have usually turned up very quickly. If I have a choice I try to avoid fishing waters like Llandegfedd because it is such a lottery. I will always have the odd go, but I'm not prepared to take up residence on the water mainly because there are other waters to fish.Where you have space to operate as you do on Rutland and Chew the use of the drogue enables you to cover lots of water and hopefully lots of fish. I can lure fish happily all day doing this because you are always doing something. Competition from other pike anglers tends to be less of a problem because unless you are the only person catching most boats will be busy doing their own thing.

Unfortunately as I write trolling is still frowned upon on the PLC waters in the Anglian region. Where it is allowed it can add a whole new perspective to fishing these waters. As for livebaiting, well this is limited to a few waters, but it does from my experience see far more pike caught in the long term. On the smaller gravel pit venues lure fishing can produce. A water I fish in Yorkshire produced a 33 pounder last winter on a Super Shad despite livebaits being allowed. However if I had to choose I'd stick with the livebaits. On these small waters swim choice can be critical especially when it is a walk off draw! My only solution to this problem is to wear my chest waders and fish the one swim which looks good that no one else wants to fish. These small stillwaters can be dreadfully slow. I remember having a couple of seasons when I had unlimited access to the then Cromwell trout lake. I never had a run of any sort despite having lots of livebaits out! Yet a few years later when it ceased to be a trout water it did produce a couple of big pike that had obviously not been caught earlier.

143

Some bigger trout waters exist in the Midlands. Harold Foster owns Elinor and Ringstead trout fisheries. Both offer some winter pike fishing at the time of writing organized by Derek McDonald. Ringstead is a weedy up and down water where free-swimming livebaits is the most productive method. You can find the odd areas to paternoster a bait and the pike you catch are invariably as fat as you can get them. My first pike from the water weighed 24lbs and was my 300th twenty pounder so all in all a good trip!

Location of pike on trout waters is a strange and perplexing affair. So often the pike turn up in areas that to us make no sense. On Blithfield there are lots of potentially good spots, but unfortunately they do not always hold pike. My secret seems to be to pick the wrong spots each time! My one decent pike caught during the Nige Williams organized fishing was a 27 pounder from one of the well-known spots. Mick Brown a few yards from me landed a 35 pounder on a twin-tailed jig. Mine took an antique lure, a Gudebro Sniper given to me by Ken Latham of Potter Heigham in Norfolk. It was cast out more in desperation than anything because the water was so coloured. Obviously that little bit of extra vibration the lure provided was enough to do the trick.

My advice would be to find out where the well-known areas are and head for them. If nothing is getting caught then you have to go and explore. Lure fishing allows you to be very mobile and this is your best hope of success. It does not always work, but often a good area is where the prevailing wind blows in. It is possible that the trout are attracted to a wave washed shoreline and this in turn is something the pike become aware of. One thing I have learned and that is spots that produce one day frequently do not always produce the next day. Also spots which have not produced sometimes do not produce later either! On Chew after having had limited experience it was clear that a good blow was better for pike fishing than a flat calm. Each water fishes differently and in an ideal world you'd only fish in optimum conditions. Unfortunately when you've booked six months ahead as you do on Chew there is not a lot you can do. You either fish or not fish! If you didn't fish it would be odds on that the weather changed and the pike came on!

The depth that you will find trout water pike in also varies. Esthwaite Water in the Lake District is one water where the pike are frequently caught from the top ten feet of water. Grafham Water on the other hand is somewhere where the pike are invariably well down. I had a 24 pounder out of 35 feet, which is deep for pike fishing. On waters such as Llandegfedd 40 feet is not too deep. Rutland pike tend to be in depths ranging from 28 to 7 feet, but willing to come up for a lure fished say 10 feet deep over the 20 plus depth. Weirwood pike were invariably in 20 or 30 feet of water except pre-spawning when they tended to come closer to the shore.

The time of year you fish is generally restricted by the concerns that run the waters. Lures will catch on some waters at all times of the year. Blithfield is one such water. Grafham is only open in October and November and can be very hard work if we've had lots of wind to churn the water up. Lure fishing effectiveness is reduced by poor water clarity and seeing as most trout waters open in October and November they are so often affected by the first autumn gales and heavy rain.

144

The biggest single move any pike angler could make would be to gain access to his or her trout water. It might seem hard to believe, but there are waters out there which have not been fished. These offer great potential for those who can get onto them first. Just as an example here is John Costello's story of two very big pike.

7/5/96

Dear Neville,

        I read your request in Angler's Mail dated April 13th for information on large pike so I am sending a few details of a pike I caught a couple of years ago. I have never publicised the fish for a number of reasons, the main one being that the water in question is private and I would not want to jeopardize any future fishing for myself and the two friends who also fish it. Good pike fishing, as you know is becoming harder to find in England and I owe a lot to the one friend who worked extremely hard to obtain permission to fish the water. My reason for writing is simply to help you record some of pike angling's history. I certainly do not claim any merit from the capture.

The water is a mature gravel pit of about 25 acres in the southwest of the country. It is a trout fishery, which has fairly heavy stockings of trout throughout the summer season. There are coarse fish present, though apparently not in huge numbers, mainly roach, perch and tench. We first fished the water a couple of times at the end of the 1991/92 season. We were limited to bank fishing and we blanked. The following season the owner would not let us fish the water. However in the early winter of 1993 the owner had a change of heart and gave us permission to fish from January to March. Most importantly he also allowed us to use a couple of boats.

The first trip on the water found the lake half frozen and very coloured. Not surprisingly we blanked. During the week the weather warmed up and the water started to clear. A friend managed a mid-week trip and had a couple of jacks. On Saturday January 15th I arrived to find the colour had changed to bottle green and naturally enough I was very confident. Two hours later a fish swirled next to one of the two livebaits I was drifting. I lifted the anchor and paddled across wind to get directly above the fish, leaving one of the baits out. The baitrunner screeched and a few minutes later I was paddling ashore with what I thought was to be my fish of a lifetime, 37lb 3oz! A friend managed a mid-week trip and landed a 32 pounder and on Saturday I arrived again. I only had a couple of jacks, but I returned the following morning, intending to fish until lunchtime. Conditions that day, January 23rd 1994 were ideal. Heavy overnight rain was just clearing at dawn and the freshening southwesterly wind brought masses of broken cloud and increasing sunshine throughout the morning. All in all brilliant pike fishing weather. Nothing happened most of the morning, but I kept moving, either drifting or trolling a couple of livebaits. Eventually having promised to be back for Sunday lunch I decided to troll down the lake and say cheerio to a friend who was in a boat at the other end of the lake. The last two livebaits were a bit on the small side so I stuck them tandem fashion on one tackle and started a slow troll down to the other end. A couple of hundred yards later I had a take, which I struck. The fight was nothing special and on netting the fish in a roughish swell my initial impression was that I had another 30 pounder, though smaller than the one I had caught the previous week. I rowed ashore with the fish in the landing net as I was less than a hundred yards offshore and it seemed more sensible if I wanted photographs. Into the weigh sling and the scales seemed to read 31 something. I lowered the sling and slowly lifting, counted the revolutions round. I thought to myself "This can't be right" The pointer appeared to have gone around four times. I lifted again and the same thing happened again. As you can imagine I was in a bit of a daze. I sacked the fish up and rowed across to my friend who had not seen anything because he was fishing with his back to the wind. On his "Happy Hooker" scales we recorded a weight of 41lb 12oz we returned the fish to the sack and I stayed with the fish whilst he phoned another friend who came out to witness the fish and bring another camera.

Reading the last paragraph it sounds like we messed the fish around, but it takes longer to write than it did to do. However she was full of spawn and whilst photographing I was extremely conscious of her bulk and the potential stain on vital organs through not being supported by water, so I simply held the fish in one pose for a few photographs and laid her on an unhooking mat for some others. Over the next few weeks we had half a dozen fish over twenty pounds and another thirty pounder. There were very few doubles in the water, possibly a case of an imbalanced fishery containing a lot of jacks and a handful of giants. As far as I know this fish was the biggest pike caught in England during the 1993/4 season. It is probably the biggest pike caught in the southwest of the country and, if it matters, may be the biggest pike caught on a float-trolled livebait. As I said earlier I do not claim any merit for the capture of such as monster. I was simply in the right place at the right time. Fishing is a compulsive hobby for me, but it is not the be all and end all. I felt privileged to catch such a fish, but it has in no way spoilt any challenges I may look for. Oh by the way in the excitement we completely forgot to measure the fish.

AUTHORS FOOTNOTE. This story has never been told before and I'm extremely grateful to John for writing it for me. The two large fish were subsequently found dead the following spring. This confirms what I said earlier in the book; very big pike are frequently at the end of their life. The difference between an angler's success and failure is often narrow and dependent on a few short months. A few short months when a monster pike may still be alive or may have died.

GRAVEL PITS

Of all the types of waters to make an impact on our fishing gravel pits are without doubt the most important. Some have now been established for as long as 50 yards while many have been with us for less than 10 years. The nature of the pit depends on how it was excavated. In some areas gravel seams are shallow and mixed in with the gravel is lots of waste material. Waste material will generally be left somewhere to the side of where the digger is working giving rise to bars, underwater strips or even islands. These pits are rarer these days, but if you find one it will be a lot more interesting to fish than your usual hole in the ground! Where the gravel is in very deep veins, your pit could easily be 25 feet deep. Yet it will still have some features because there will be spoil and topsoil some of which will either be left or in the case of topsoil used to cover up in-filled parts of the pit. Drainage trenches add to the features. I've been in the bottom of a number of drained gravel pits and even the least inspiring pit has had more features than I expected. An echo sounder or a self-locking float is required if you are to get to grips with the underwater topography.

Most young gravel pits will have relatively low fish stocks. Luckily because many of these waters are 10 to 50 acres in size (with odd ones up to 200 acres!) the sheer size of the water means that it can support one or two good pike. Readers must now excuse me if I give them a basic biology lesson, but once you understand this you will always be able to look at a fishery with some hope! The ability of a water to support fish life is related to its productivity. Productivity is a function of the amount of dissolved nutrients in the water and organic material on the lakebed. This is what produces food for the invertebrates, which are in turn eaten by small fish and ultimately, pike.

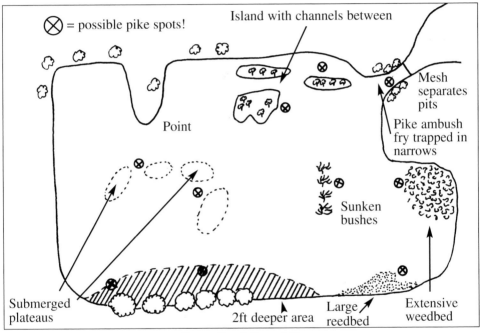

Generalised Gravel Pit

Each organism which consumes another is in what's known as a trophic level. To go from one trophic level to another i.e. if 10lb of invertebrates were eaten by a fish you would get say 5lb of additional fish. There is therefore a loss of material as you move up each level. The pike then eats the additional fish and you end up with an additional weight of pike. Looking at all the trophic levels together it is rather like a pyramid with the base being the algae and plant material the tip being the pike.

In many gravel pits perch become established first and because they are such voracious predators they tend to suppress all the other species. This means that many gravels pits contain this years roach fry, some larger roach, lots of perch and sometimes some decent sized tench or bream. Luckily for the pike its modest food requirements means that even the most dismal gravel pit will be able to support at least a 10lb pike! As a gravel pit gets older it matures and because of this it will support more fish. Gravel pits in some areas seem more productive than in others. Any pit with lots of limestone in the gravel will be more productive than one without it. This is because Calcium Carbonate is one of the essentials in the building of shells and exoskeletons. The more of it there is the more likely it is that there will be plenty of invertebrates in the water.

Another factor can influence the pike holding capabilities of the water and that is mans activities. Agricultural run off can fertilise a water. Sewage leaking into a water can in the long term be beneficial provided it is not excessive. Stocking with any species of fish can alter the pike population. The biggest single factor in favour of improving a pike water by mans intervention is converting a water into a heavily stocked water. Chucking 1000lb an acre of small carp into a water where there are a few pike is the quickest way to produce a big pike. Unfortunately most fisheries managers are not doing this deliberately so it is up to keen pike anglers to spot the opportunity before the pike gets removed. Eventually the value (particularly the economic value) of pike even in stocked waters will be realised, just as they have on trout waters.

It will usually take a pit about ten years to mature enough to support a 20lb pike always assuming someone has stocked the pit in the first place. You can usually tell how old a pit is by looking at the trees. Ten-year-old willows and alders will usually be 20 to 40 feet high. If they are only 10 foot high the water will probably be too young.

The fact remains that most gravel pits are low-density waters and only the really big ones will produce any number of pike. Most gravel pits are very weedy which can make some pike fishing techniques very difficult. This never worries me in the slightest because pike are very good at digging baits out of weed. Luckily static deads are very good baits on almost all pits. You just need to have confidence in fishing in weed. Your tackle obviously has to be up to the job because one big problem of fishing weedy waters is when lots of pike are lost with hooks in them. I cannot emphasize this strongly enough because this is one of the problems I had on one of my waters, Whitestones. Though not a gravel pit (it was a brick pit) lost fish were probably responsible for half the pike population dieing. Some pits have big pike, which survive mainly by eating very big prey sometimes small pike. I do not normally fish with large baits and so far I've avoided having to do so. However I'd never rule the tactic out just in case! Swim selection on a gravel pit depends on a number of factors; the most important being who else is on the water. The best swims always get fished first and needless to say this moves the fish around. Also some pike tend to spend most of their time in one area and are seldom caught from other swims. You need to be aware of this if you are targeting one particular fish. I like swims with variety i.e. corners, swims with submerged bars, casts towards islands, bays and points. Pipes that connect two pits frequently have a substantial through flow of water, which can attract food fish. Many fish are attracted by running water and some good pike swims that I have fished have been where there is flowing water. To say here that spot x will produce is obviously a case of my pretending that I know a lot more about every pit in the country than I do. If you fish a gravel pit regularly you will soon find the going areas yourself though I surprise myself by being able to pick the better spots more often than not. Except of course last week when four of us picked swims on a new gravel pit and two of us blanked. I with my superior swim sense was one of them!

On smaller pits you sometimes have very few features to look for. Overhanging trees can provide ambush points for pike. They can also provide shelter for fry, which in turn attract pike. One wonderful feature I came across thirty years ago did not do me any good, but I saw a twenty-one pounder caught because of it. A narrow channel connected two gravel pits at Chichester. One a small pit was full of fry, but a mesh fence prevented the pike getting into the small pit. The fry however not being very bright from time to time moved through the fence into a small tree lined bay. The pike in the big lake had the fry herded in the bay and every day it was carnage. My only problem was that I couldn't get there early enough at a weekend to grab a spot! Therefore my biggest pike from that water ended up as a 7 pounder! There are so many gravel pit situations; you have to judge each one as a separate matter. Regrettably big fry shoal gatherings are quite rare these days, which is a shame because, they make for really interesting fishing. There is nothing quite like trying to catch fry feeding pike and the sight as they crash through the fry shoals is spectacular. I've done a bit of fishing for pike that are fry feeding and generally all you can do is to fish free-swimming livebaits. Sometimes two small baits fished on one trace stands out better. I had a 5lb brownie on a twin bait in a fry-feeding situation, but there was no chance of any pike because there were none in that particular water!

Knowing which gravel pit to fish in which conditions is one shortcut to success. There is a definite relationship between depth and the weather. Shallow pits fish well in mild windy weather, deep pits can be reliable in this sort of weather and when there has been a frost. Shallow pits are killed stone dead by frosts unless you can fish towards the end of the day when presumably the pike have got over the initial shock of a bitterly cold night. Snow does not present a problem on a deep water; indeed my first pike over 25lb a 26-10 from Brandesburton in Yorkshire came while it was snowing. That particular pit was deep, at least 18 feet in the swim I caught from. On really windy days most big pits are a waste of time. The water tends to colour up and most pit pike do not like this unless the pit is always coloured. Head for a small water and odds on it will fish in a gale. Many gravel pit pike are nocturnal, but do not expect hectic sport. The average size can be high and if you are on a trip away from home a night session is a logical action.

Many of the pits I have fished are morning waters and this suits me fine because it allows early morning sessions. Some pits have definite afternoon feeding periods and if you can sort these out it is possible to move to different waters to capitalise on this. This only works if you do not have lots of competition. Remember the more competition the harder it is for you. As I write there has been a fish of 37 to 38lb caught from Bluebell Lake near Peterborough. Unfortunately everyone knows about it and the competition to catch it is intense. I do enough competitive fishing at the trout waters, so I'll not be fishing Bluebell unless they give me the water for a week! I reason that my time would be better spent elsewhere though the ultimate size of the fish may not be the same.

I have used the term gravel pit here, but much of what I have said applies to sand pits, brick pits and clay pits. You cannot nit pick here, just because of the strata the pits are dug from. All pits mature and become more productive as they get older. Unfortunately there is no simple relationship between age of the water and size of pike. Very old pits can sometimes be full of mediocre sized food fish. This leads to plenty of pike, but few big ones. Younger water may be full of 2 to 4lb tench and that's the one, which will do the big pike. Just spend time looking at the coarse fish catches from the pits you are interested in. If the food fish are 2 to 4lbs be they roach, rudd, tench, bream or even chub that's the one to look at.

One feature I've not mentioned is sunken trees. If a gravel pit has been worked a long time, sometimes trees get established. When flooded these trees become obvious holding areas for pike. Unfortunately they are also very dangerous areas as pike are easily lost in snags. If you choose to fish snags, please go geared up for the job, 50lb braid or 20lb mono minimum and be ready to strike immediately. The use of a boat can make things a lot safer for the pike because it I easier to correct mistakes from above.

DAMMED LAKES AND RESERVOIRS

Man has been damming river valleys for hundreds of years and though siltation eventually causes a lake to revert to dry land there are still plenty of estate lakes and reservoirs dotted around the country. Hardly any of the larger water supply reservoirs exist as ordinary coarse fisheries. Most of these are trout waters. Those water supply reservoirs that can be pike fished tend to have restricted access, i.e. on some you cannot fish the dam. Hardly any can be boat fished so catching pike can be very difficult. On some you cannot even use a radio-controlled boat. My experience of fishing reservoirs and estate lakes is limited however I have done a little bit of it over the years.

Estate lakes can be very productive and have a big stock of coarse fish. Because of this they can be good pike waters. They are fairly simple to figure out because the key features are the dam, the old streambed and the shallows where the stream comes in. Dams tend to be best when food fish gather after the first cold weather. Streambeds can be natural patrol routes for pike and positioning of baits there can be essential. The shallows are often where the pike are caught from at the backend of the season.

The biggest difficulty you face on many estate lakes is the shallow nature of the water. Paternostering livebaits is always difficult and a free swimming or drifted bait is much easier to fish safely. A radio-controlled boat would definitely be useful, but most anglers cannot justify the expense involved. My way around this has been to balloon baits out and luckily most of the estate lakes I have fished, fish well in windy weather. My best fish using this method was 18-10 and I'm sure it was essential on the day because it covered more water. The rods nearer to the bank certainly did nothing.

Action on the dam at Hollowel

An unusual hotspot - this emergency aeration pump at Chedder Resevoir in the 70's

At the time (1978) a personal best, this 27-00 from Hollowel

Our water supply reservoirs simply present the same problems on a much bigger scale. Reservoirs such as Staunton Harold and Abberton were where long-range techniques were first evolved. This was due in Staunton's case to the deep water being out of casting range and in Abberton's case bank fishing was so limited. Again balloons and drifting floats were the first line of attack until the radio-controlled boat entered the fray. If you are trying to cast long range then we do see a need for specialised rods and reels. A 13 ft 3lb test rod married with a big pit reel such as the Daiwa Emblem reels, a tapered shock leader and braid can see small deadbaits with 3 to 4oz bombs cast up to 100 yards. To cast further you'd need to take lessons from an experienced beachcaster! One thing is true about all fish species and that is that they try to avoid angling pressure. Pike in particular will always move away from areas where they are getting caught. On big reservoirs in particular this means that pike will frequently move out of casting range. This is the reason for the obsession with long distance fishing. On other types of waters long walks may be the answer or even a cast into an area you cannot legitimately fish!

MANAGED WATERS

I was not sure whether to call this section artificial waters, because it is a somewhat derogatory term in some peoples eyes. I opted for managed waters because this is probably a more precise description of the situation. In the UK the first managed waters were probably those run by Bill Chillingworth at the Woolpack Fishery. This is going back something like 20 years ago. Bill stocked a variety of waters with pike from waters like Grafham water, but unfortunately it soon became clear that you couldn't dump large numbers of trout water pike in a lake and expect them to thrive. His experiences taught me that the management of stocked fisheries required an input of food. I was not able to put this knowledge into effect until a few years later, but first I had already experienced a minor example of water management. In 1979 we were in the middle of the infamous Fenland pike and zander cull. I "rescued" a couple of pike a 17 and an 18 from a Fen drain and moved them to a local gravel pit. I put a fair amount of waste fish in over a period and both those pike ended up as 20 pounders. I doubt if this would have happened without this action.

A few years later when I eventually obtained my own water I stocked it with pike from Blithfield and proceeded to stock rainbow trout in the spring. A couple of friends joined in and actually enjoyed a bit of fly-fishing on the side. The project was a success with all the pike growing over the years. A 21 pounder eventually grew to 29-04 and sadly died that spring weighing in at 31-12. Another fish of 17lb turned up dead at 29lbs. Most of the fish in the pit grew at 4lb a year and this is near the upper limit for pike growth in this country. Eventually the sand pit was drained in order for more sand to be extracted. When I did the final count there was 100lb an acre of pike in the water, which is between 8 and 10 times what, you might expect. In later years several other projects were started and some went well, some did not. What I did learn was that stocking trout could enable a simulation of a trout fishery to be created. The pike ate the bulk of their prey in the period April to June with a further peak in the autumn. Generally finances did not run to stocking trout throughout the year so the big stocking of trout went in during the spring and waste fish were used in the autumn and winter. A calculation had to be made of the natural food production the water was capable of. Then trout and waste fish were provided to a level, which allowed each pike; about 3 times it's bodyweight of food. There were problems such as cormorants eating trout, but these problems were tackled in one case by covering the whole of a seven-acre gravel pit with criss crossed bailer twine. What a job that was!

At one stage when trout waters such as Grafham and Pitsford were being netted in the spring for pike large numbers of pike were sold to various waters. Because they were being moved pre spawn many of these pike failed to spawn and the loss rate was considerable. Luckily as far as I know this does not happen now, but if anyone does get offered large pike for restocking they should only take them during the autumn and certainly not in February or March. Mid doubles and low twenties survive better than larger fish. Hopefully most of our pike will end up staying put!

Managed waters provide the opportunity for good pike fishing in areas where there is none. They can however make you lazy and though I have enjoyed fishing such waters there is more of a challenge involved in fishing unmanaged waters. If you spend too much time on any one water you are not going to learn about new venues. You end up in a rut so be warned!

BIG WATERS

Perhaps the most interesting waters of all, but also the most difficult. I need to qualify that. When these big waters are fishing well or when the pike are concentrated they can be easier than most waters. However the rest of the time they can be very hard. You will not fish them half-heartedly! There are two ways of looking at big waters, one is as a local angler the other is as a visitor perhaps able to fish the water for a few weeks in a year. The vast majority of anglers fall into the later category and because of this I will approach fishing these waters from this point of view.

First I need to tell the reader which waters I have fished. Windermere in England (two days only regrettably). In Scotland Loch Lomond and Loch Awe. In Ireland Lough Allen. Lough Corrib, Lough Mask, Lough Gara, Lough Erne, Lough Beg and Lough Derg. In Wales Llyn Tegid. I have fished a couple of big waters in Holland, but they hardly compare to the natural waters mentioned above. I have not fished the Baltic, though I have fished for Baltic pike which run up one of the Swedish rivers entering the sea.

The big waters are inspirational. I think that if I were restricted to fishing just one type of water it would have to be a 5000-acre plus water. The fishing is not easy, but the challenge is part of the enjoyment you get from pike fishing. There is nothing like setting out on a calm sunny morning for a half hour journey to a distant area. Likewise there is nothing like battling back in a big wave when you have been caught out by a change in the weather. This is brown trouser weather and while you are doing it you do not enjoy it one bit. When back on dry land it doesn't seem so bad!

None of the big waters can be fished effectively without a boat. While I have taken my Orkney Spinner to Lough Corrib and Lough Gara, a 13 ft boat I not really big enough. The Lough boats that are available for hire are usually 19 foot long and capable of weathering rough conditions. Lough boats can be fitted with engines up to 15hp that gives you a fair turn of speed. However if you want to get from spot to spot really quickly you'll need a boat with a planeing hull and a 30hp engine. Better still the boat

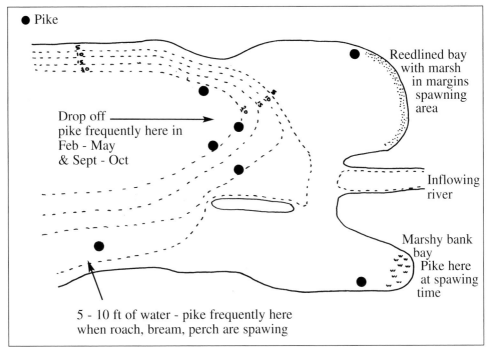

Generalised Loch/Lough - end of winter/spring and September

will have a cabin so when anchored up you can survive the worst the elements can throw at you. Most big waters are in the West of the country and because of this you get a lot more rain. In order to advise on how to fish these big waters I will take each one by one. Whichever water you fish mobility is vital. These big water pike are great swimmers and can easily move a couple of miles in a day. You have to be prepared to find the pike; they certainly will not be prepared to find you!

LOCH LOMOND

For many English anglers this is the nearest big water venue which offers anything like the true big water experience. (Windermere and the other lakes though nice waters are not quite as unspoilt as venues such as Lomond). The most popular time to visit Lomond is in the spring when the concentration effect of spawning themselves and then feeding on spawning roach and perch draws the pike into shallower water. Between the end of February and end of May any shallow area on Lomond will attract pike. The two best-known ones are Cromin Bay at Balmaha and Ardlui bay at the north end of the Loch. The pike get into these areas of around 6 feet and I've had 3 out of my six Lomond twenties from these locations. In May the roach tend to shoal up off the River Endrick drop off and this area is very popular with pike anglers. It tends to be a very much all or nothing area. It's either on or it's off! The roach also run up the Endrick River itself and this can produce pike. My best fish from the river itself was 19lb, but examples of that rare beast a Lomond thirty have been caught there in the past. You can also catch a stack of livebait if you go well up the river to where a dyke comes in. The biggest snag with the Endrick River is getting past the sand bars in it mouth.

Still my biggest Lomond pike a 26-00 from Ardlui

156

Roger Melbourne holds the net with a good Lomond pike. These were the early days at Ardlui

I've usually ended up getting out and pushing so chest waders are useful!

In the spring other areas do produce and you need to try them all. Portnellan is an area of shallow rocky bays with a drop off. Fish such as powan definitely swim into the shallow water in the spring and this must attract pike. The few pike I have had there have come off of the drop off in 20 feet of water rather than in the shallows. Over on the West side of the Loch you have Rhossdu bay and Slate bay. They all get fished a lot so do not expect miracles. Good pike turn up in all sorts of areas and you really should use your echo sounder to locate food fish shoals. I remember a couple of years ago fishing around for not a lot when Brian Ingrams mentioned a spot he had, had fish to 19lb from. Shane Garrett and I tried the spot, but it wasn't to be my evening. Shane had a 14 and a 21 pounder. The roach were clearly visible on the sonar and further betrayed their presence by topping as dusk fell.

The methods you use on Lomond depends on what you are confident in. I've only used live and deadbaits with success, my lure fishing only having caught small ones. Most of my pike have fallen to deads, but you must take a variety up there. They can be fairly choosey so you need sea baits and baits such as smelt, pollan, trout and roach. You never know when they are going to choose one or the other! There's plenty of roach to be caught up there and you really need to have a livebait out most days. Some pike anglers do well on there float trolling livebaits, but so far I've seen singularly unsuccessful doing this.

A few English anglers visit Lomond at other times of the year other than the spring. Unfortunately this is out of my scope, but if life were long enough I'd love to spend some time up there in the winter. Years ago there was a lot of nonsense about tackle having to be seriously scaled up to land these pike that can and often do fight really hard. I would suggest 15 to 18lb mono, 40 or 50lb braid, your usual traces and standard 3lb test pike rods will do fine.

LOCH AWE

A little further north than Loch Lomond, Loch Awe has had an interesting 25 years. I first fished it in April of 1979. It was a strange week when nearly all runs fell to livebaits and all the action was in the first two hours of daylight. I think Barrie Kerslake and I had about 40 fish with only one or two on deadbaits. Interesting the best fish a 17 pounder fell to a dead. I've been back a few times over the years and the water has changed a lot. The main reason for change has been the introduction of cage farming for rainbow trout. This has served to increase the productivity of the Loch due to the fertilizing effect of fish excrement. The mass escape of rainbow trout has also fed the pike, which means that Awe has in-fact produced bigger pike than Lomond in recent years. I have a photo of a 38 pounder from Awe and it looks like a big fish. With the escape of the rainbow trout has come an influx of fishmongers from places like Glasgow and the litter and damage to trees had to be seen to be believed. The result has been legislation to regulate the fishing on the Loch. I'm afraid this means that you are somewhat restricted in how you fish, so please note that my accounts here are pre legislation.

The Loch is long and narrow and has two really obvious areas, the bay at Ford, which is at the West end. This is a nice sheltered area and ideal for when the weather is not too clever. At the East end where the River Orchy comes in is Kilchurn bay. This large area of mainly shallow water is the biggest spawning area on the Loch. It therefore attracts a fair amount of attention in the spring. The river Orchy has a salmon and trout run and the mouth of the river is therefore attractive to pike which wait to intercept *salmonids* going upriver and returning. This happens in the autumn and winter. The visiting angler therefore has two key times, spawning and trout and salmon spawning. Again a water that is fished a lot tends to offer all or nothing sport. It is not hard to understand why this should be. On a lightly fished water sport can be consistent over a number of weeks. If they have been hammered you are not going to catch much most of the time. This is simply because most of the pike will have been caught and will have left the area. Yet they eventually have to return and it seems as if most of the pike get over their fright at the same time. No one yet has figured out what external factor controls this. So do not ask me how to predict it. You just have to hope it happens during your week on the water!

I always reckon high water levels and warm weather is the key to spring fishing on any water in Scotland or Ireland. You certainly do not want to see these conditions before you arrive! Odds on the water level will drop and it will get cold. I have had some dreadfully slow weeks on Awe. The memory of which are painful! My best Awe fish came well outside Kilchurn bay. I was fishing out on the drop off where the sunken trees are. The first fish I had was a 21 pounder on mackerel followed by another fish which wrapped itself round my front anchor. I sorted that out only to find that it had gone into a sunken tree. I lost that fish which wasn't very good for the fish. The actual bay itself is a key area and I've seen pike to 26lb caught there. Unfortunately by a chap with a forked stick for a rod rest! It was enough to make two serious pike anglers weep, with decent boat and all the gear!

Another time I had a week in September. I started at the Ford end and float trolled livebaits for miles on the electric motor. I never had a pull! The problem was that I didn't know the spots and I was probably miles away from them. When I went to the other end again float trolling the drop off I picked up 7 doubles up to 17lbs and ran out of bait. Unfortunately my deadbaits were a bit big and though I had the odd take on these I missed them. That was my last day, so it was a bit of a cock up. Like so many big waters to find pike there needs to be a reason for them to be there. Big weed beds are certainly worth a look and any drop off where there are lots of food fish showing. Your sonar will show you fish, but the best approach is to use your eyes at dawn and watch for roach rolling.

I never had chance to give lures a serious try on Awe, but when I fished it live and deadbaits were equally effective. As usual take mackerel and at least one of smelt, pollan or trout deadbaits. A good place to launch a boat was at the Orchy end, a place called Drishag Holdings. At the time he would trailer your boat in and out for a small charge. He might have better facilities by now. Trips away present certain problems and one of these is the freezer facility. For up to 4-day trips you can get by without a freezer. I put my deads in the one freezer I have that run at 26C so the baits are 8C colder to start with. I then pack the bait with plenty of freezer blocks in a high quality poly box. I use ones used for air mailing tuna from exotic locations. I then keep the box covered with an old sleeping bag at all times. Baits for the day are taken out and transferred to a small Coleman box. For longer trips you need a freezer. Nige Williams takes one with him! None of my freezers are that portable, but I do have an electric cool box, which can be run off of a 12V battery charger. That can give you a couple more days of semi frozen bait. I run it off a battery charger because it drains even a big leisure battery within a day.

LOUGH MASK

This one is probably my favourite water of them all. Though it has been raped by the gill-netters of the fisheries service, it may one day be worth fishing again. If the netting stopped in March of 2003, it would probably be worth fishing again in 2008. The only problem with this is some of us are getting a bit too old to wait 5 years! When I first fished it at the end of the 80s I had struggled to get my head around how to approach it. It was not like Lomond, Lough Allen or Loch Awe. Because of this we ended up fishing Lough Corrib, which was more like the waters we were used to.

Lough Mask is a mere 22,000 acres, but it can be divided up into sections, which are easier to cope with. At the North West corner we have what's known as O'Malleys bay of islands. The nearest slipway is at Shrah near the water supply intake. To the East is Ballygarry an area of channels and bays in amongst a lot of rocks. There's no proper slipway there and even a FWD could struggle to get a boat out. There is very little of interest down the whole West side except for the school bay at Tourmakeady and some islands near to Paedric O'Heehnahans hostel. The West bank from Shrah to Maamtrasna is ideal for a fast run with a good boat and a big engine. Mostly you are over 70 feet of water. Maamtrasna is the first of the Western inlets and because of the features and structure that you'll find there is one of the better pike holding areas. Round the corner and you have Upper Mask, almost a Lough on it's own. You have to launch your boat at the ferry bridge for Upper Mask as well as Maamtrasna. I love Upper Mask even though a sixteen pounder is the best I've had there. There are quite a few interesting features at the West end. Of course you also have the pool the other side of the Ferry Bridge that produced Eric Edward's 38-10 monster. The South end of Mask itself is not that exciting though there are odd spots, which have produced good fish. In the South East Corner is Dringeen, which never produced much for me, but Pete Haywood once had a 21 pounder just outside of it. As you go up the East side you are now in very rough ground with rocks all over the place. Cahir Bay and Cushlough were all once great pike spots, but the pike are very much here today gone tomorrow. Where the River Robe comes into Cushlough has produced many big pike up to 36lb. The best fish I ever hooked on a jerkbait came off at this spot. Unfortunately I didn't see it, but as far as I am concerned was not a mega pike! There is a good slipway in Cushlough.

Just a bit further north you have Keel bay, which has produced fish to 27lb while I was fishing it, but I never caught anything from it at all. One thing you will notice about Mask is that there are lots of rocks! It's not to bad on the West side, but the East is a nightmare. We struggled to come to terms with the rocks; not realizing that lure fishing in amongst them was one way of catching pike. We were too busy looking for grassy or weedy water where we could static deadbait or troll. Despite this those of us who fished it did have some good fish. A classic case was Martyn Nelson's fish of just over thirty pounds. We had split up into three groups that day and Martyn had gone with Carl Barber to Upper Mask. We had a few fish to I think 17 pounds out of Maamtrasna when I decided to try over the other side of the bay where Eric Edwards had caught his first Mask thirty. Needless to say there was nothing there. I headed back to the bay by the house, as it was getting dark. I was surprised to see Martyn fishing off of he bank because I had expected him to be on his way back from Upper Mask. Apparently they had come back early so Martyn decided not to waste the evening. He waved me over to photo and help weigh a big fish. It was indeed a big fish and though I struggled to remember the ounces thirty pounds something is all I needed to know! Martyn had been on a lot of trips to Mask and had not had a twenty pounder from there. Yet all his birthdays had come at once that day. That's how pike fishing can be, I had in effect moved away from that fish to try elsewhere. Sometimes the old judgment is suspect!! Generally on Mask mobility was the key. You could safely say that an hour or 90 minutes and that was it for each spot when static deadbaiting. Float trolling of course covers new water all the time so you can afford to cover the same spots twice just in case. The same applies with lure fishing. You certainly had to keep on the move when lure fishing, my only regret on Mask was that I never tried it very much. In the spring the pike moved into shallow water to feed on the perch and trout. You could never predict with absolute accuracy when they would arrive, but usually it was end of April first week of May. Unfortunately this coincided with the best trout fishing so the Lough tended to be a bit busy!

Then in August when the perch fry were big enough they would tend to shoal up in certain areas and the pike would descend on them in numbers. I always missed out on this because I only tried once in August and it didn't happen while I was there. I used to enjoy my winter fishing on the Lough, especially as you'd often have the whole Lough to yourself. The first week of December was often good because the trout were now returning from spawning up the rivers and of course the pike were there waiting. Mid February was also worthwhile in the areas close to the spawning bays. Mind you big female pike do not tend to hang around these areas until just before they are ready to spawn. They can easily swim a mile to these areas in an hour. So timing as always is a problem. You did not want to leave it too late otherwise they'd do a great trick and that was switching off just before they spawned. We watched them spawning on February 23rd one year, which is a long time before the end of the season in the UK!

Mask has the potential to be a very dangerous water if you do not treat it with respect. It is certainly not the place to learn to boat fish! Even in May you can experience the most horrendously strong winds and though with experience you can spot a squall coming you usually have to have a bad experience to learn from it! Luckily there are areas where you can get out of the worst of the weather. I had quite a few good fish while fishing sheltered inlets and bays in December. The best day produced 3 twenties to 29-08, which just happened to be a thirty a week before when Mark Ackerley caught it! Static deadbaits were very effective at this time, unfortunately some of the pike killers started to use them the last time I fished in winter. This was I'm afraid another nail in an already well-nailed coffin. I loved those days and remember not meeting another human being for 5 days! There is something I cannot define about the air or the atmosphere on Mask. It's that same feeling you get from long past experiences. I remember as a child of 4 or 5 walking along a dyke in Norfolk and there was a huge field of daffodils. That memory and the atmosphere will be with me forever. The same applies to December evenings on Lough Mask. A big pike caught and returned and nothing, but wildfowl and the odd otter for company!

I always believed that Mask was a use it or lose it situation. That is why I publicised what we were doing so much. The competition made my fishing harder, but it was worth the risk. Sadly it did not pay off. Mark Ackereley tells here of his own experiences. I personally feel this is one of the most inspirational stories I have ever read.

THE SECRET LIFE OF LOUGH MASK

My fascination with pike fishing in the West of Ireland was first stirred by Fred Buller's amazing Domesday Book of Mammoth Pike. Entries such as the account of the 46 pounder netted from Ballygary Bay enthralled me and I read them time and time again. If that book had never been written, I think the course of my life would have been very different! One lake stands head and shoulders over all the others mentioned, and that is of course Lough Mask in County Mayo. What follows is the full story of my exploits on Lough Mask and to a lesser extent Lough Corrib between 1989 and 1995.

When in 1988, my parents took early retirement and moved from England to County Clare in Ireland, it was just the incentive I needed to start my exploration of the western loughs. The fact that the Fisheries Board had recently stopped the infamous pike culling was further encouragement. Unfortunately, at this point Irish politics intervened when the Government attempted to introduce a national rod license. The western loughs were the centre of resistance to the licence and were declared a no-fishing zone by local anglers and boatmen as a gesture of defiance. Signs were posted all over the Corrib and Mask system proclaiming no-fishing. Anyone breaking the strike was made aware in no uncertain terms that their presence was not wanted. Not wishing to get involved in any unpleasantness I reluctantly kept away. It was not until late 1989 after some intense and at times heated negotiations that an agreement of sorts was reached and the no-fishing signs came down. During the strike I had been to Ireland on several occasions to visit my parents and had taken the opportunity to drive around Corrib and Mask. Using Fred's book as a starting point, likely looking areas were noted as well as access points and boat launches. One bay on Lough Corrib had particularly caught my eye. The bay was sheltered, luxuriantly weedy, and got a mention in the book. When I found out that some English pikers had fished the bay during the strike and taken some good catches, my excitement reached fever pitch. It was time to get the rods out!

Large lures fished from a drifting boat was supposed to be the killer method, so this was how I started off. From the boat, the bay really did look superb, the water being around five to ten feet deep, gin clear and incredibly weedy. My confidence was high as I drifted with the breeze across the bay, casting a large Epinger spoon over the top of the weed. Just as I was approaching where a river flowed in, the spoon was hit with a bang and a twelve pounder duly boated. Things were getting better and better. Second drift, and in exactly the same place a bigger fish was hooked. At this point, things started to go downhill. The breeze had by now picked up making it extremely difficult to control my large micromesh landing net and I was being blown fast into an area of solid weed. Struggling to control the fish with one hand, I managed to drop the anchor and eventually netted the fish safely. As I did so I breathed a sigh of relief and reflected that I still had a few things to learn about this boat fishing lark. On lifting the fish into the boat I was horrified to see that the fish was very badly hooked in the gill rakers and was bleeding profusely. Despite nursing the fish, which weighed in at seventeen pounds for several hours it never recovered and eventually died. Sitting in the boat feeling very low indeed, I made a mental note never to use a lure with large trebles again. At this point I was interested to see another pike angler turn up and commence fishing. The angler turned out to be NJF himself, the first time we had ever met. After exchanging greetings, I admitted that a fish had died on me, half expecting to get a telling off. In fact, Neville was most sympathetic, pointing out that any pike that was caught and put back in Lough Corrib was a lucky fish indeed. After a good chat we went our separate ways. The next couple of days didn't produce anything of note for me, and it soon became clear that only a few pike were present in the bay. The rest of the season I spent fishing Loch Lomond in Scotland but results were not fantastic and my thoughts kept returning to Corrib and Mask.

November of 1990 saw me once more in Ireland. Another area I had marked down as having potential was to be explored, this time on Lough Mask. It was a beautiful, sunny, calm winter day that saw me launching my boat on Lough Mask for the first time. After a forty five minute motor I arrived at the area I fancied. The sounder showed an average depth of six feet with considerable weed growth. Not knowing what to expect I got out the lure rod and selected a Kussamo Professor spoon. After a couple of casts I was pleasantly surprised to hook a fish, only a jack as it turned out, but it broke the Lough Mask duck. Half an hour later, I had taken another four jacks, none bigger than a couple of pounds and expectations were falling. I have fished so many venues in Ireland where pike killing has caused a jack explosion. Was this to be yet another such venue I asked myself?

Moving a few hundred yards in the boat, I resumed fishing and was very surprised when the spoon was taken with an enormous swirl. After a good scrap, a short but extremely fat fish was netted. The scales showed 20-08, my first ever lure caught twenty! Feeling very pleased with myself, I had a quick coffee then resumed fishing. Within ten minutes, another identical looking fish was in the boat, a 19-00 this time. That was the end of the action for the day. What a result for a new venue it had been! The condition of both fish was superb, they were immaculate, and definitely the fattest pike I had ever seen.

My father joined me the next day and we not surprisingly returned to the same area. Fishing lures and wobbled deadbaits I managed three different elevens but my father took top honours with a 21, his first ever over the magic mark. This day was memorable for another reason as well. When we were unloading the boat back at the launch an old chap wandered over and informed us that Mrs. Thatcher had resigned. I'm not sure what my father was more pleased about, that, or his twenty!

Back in England, I could not wait to get back to Mask. As well as being excellent pike fishing, it seemed I more or less had it to myself. None of the locals appeared to bother with pike and I was not aware of any other English anglers fishing Mask at that time. The few English pikers I knew of who ventured to the West all concentrated on Lough Corrib, a situation which I was very happy with!

It was the Christmas holiday when I managed to return and inevitably I headed straight for the site of the November success. Arriving at the area, I noted that the weed had died back somewhat and that the water level had risen. Two float legered deadbaits were soon soaking on the bottom and I sat back in the boat to await events. It was two hours before the first run, and unfortunately I missed it, as I did the next two! Eventually, contact was made with a fish and I was quite pleased to record another eleven pounder. A large smelt was quickly hooked on and cast back to the same spot. Within minutes the red polyball float started moving slowly away again and I picked up the rod before the baitrunner even had time to click. It soon became clear that this was a much better class of fish which proceeded to circle slowly and powerfully around the boat. I knew it was big, but when it finally came to the surface, my knees went weak. It was huge! I was starting to panic a bit at the thought of losing such a fish but it went into the net first time and I let out an enormous shout. Heaving the fish into the boat, I stood back and stared. This was the pike I had dreamed about for so long! I knew it was thirty plus and sure enough, the scales registered 32-04. Not wanting to photograph the fish in the boat, I pulled in the anchors and motored quickly to the bank which was only a hundred yards or so away. After a couple of very quick photographs I gently put her back and was pleased when she swam strongly away. The rest of the day passed in a complete daze. I was on a different planet! Driving home that evening I could hardly control my excitement and I remember being worried that I would crash the car and be killed before I had a chance to tell anyone about my catch! Fortunately for me, I made it back in one piece to my parents house and was able to tell the tale and enjoy a few celebratory glasses of Jameson's whiskey!

The next day was Christmas Day so it was not until Boxing Day that I was once more heading north to County Mayo. The weather had taken a turn for the worse and as dawn slowly broke I realised that it would be a waste of time. Arriving at the boat launch, I got out of the car and found that the wind was so strong I could hardly stand up! The boat was so full of rain water it was nearly sunk and it took me a good half hour to bale it out. Clearly it was madness to even think about fishing, so after securing the boat I drove back home to a warm fire. The storms continued for the next few days and although I managed to get out for a few hours one day, conditions were hopeless. This was just a little frustrating, but it is sadly, a fact of life with winter pike fishing in the West of Ireland.

At this time, I was working on a two weeks on, two weeks off basis on an oil rig in the North Sea. This is quite a good arrangement for the traveling pike angler, giving you much more holiday time than most people. After my next two weeks at work I could not keep away and once more found myself boarding the ferry at Holyhead, Lough Mask again being my destination. The first three days were quite slow, producing only two low doubles to static deadbaits. It was not until I tried a very shallow area that things picked up. Although it was only the end of January it seemed that the fish were already starting to move into the shallow spawning bays. This was confirmed when at the end of the trip I did see pike spawning in one shallow bay. The last two days produced six double figure fish, with the biggest going 18-10. What was very interesting was that I just could not get takes on lures, everything coming to deadbaits, either static or wobbled. This is a pattern that has since repeated itself time and again on Mask for me, to the extent that I now hardly ever bother with lures.

Studying the Doomsday Book, it was clear that most of the really big pike that had been netted from Mask had been taken in March from the spawning bays. Dringeen, Ballygary and Maamtrasna bays had all produced fish in the 40 pound bracket at that time of year. A serious assault on those bays with static deadbaits in true Lomond Cromin bay style just had to succeed. With this in mind, I booked two weeks off work in mid March, loaded the car with deadbaits and once more set off on the long drive westwards. I really thought I could not fail and was mentally clocking up the twenties and thirties. Eleven grueling days later I had to admit defeat. One eleven pounder taken on a lure was the pathetic total. Despite fishing from dawn to dusk every day I had managed only one run on a static deadbait. On several occasions I had been fishing in very large concentrations of fish but they just would not feed. After being given such a severe drubbing, I decided on a return to my old stamping ground of Loch Lomond for the next couple of sessions.

Lomond turned out to be a big disappointment. There were hordes of pike anglers and I rarely managed to get the swim I wanted. Also the number of cruisers and jet skis had increased to a ridiculous degree. Even worse was the fact that most of the fish I caught were in very poor condition, showing signs of bad handling. I soon found myself yearning once more for the tranquility of the Irish Loughs. At least in Ireland I was competing only with the pike and not other pike anglers.

June of that year, 1991 I managed to get over for a three day session and decided to fish Corrib by way of a change. At that time I was still a very keen lure angler and this visit was a lure only affair. Things were fairly slow but I managed one 22-06 on a spoon which was a lure caught personal best.

The frequent trips to Ireland were starting to cost me a lot of money in ferry and plane fares. I had spent more time in Ireland over the last year than I had in England. After some serious thinking I decided that it made sense for me to move and live in Ireland. I was young, single and in fact mobile, because the nature of my job enables me to live more or less where I wish. My employers were prepared to pay the cost of my flight every two weeks from Galway to Aberdeen. What did I have to lose? Enquiries were made and I found a cottage that I would be able to rent from October for six months at a very reasonable rate. The cottage was right on the banks of Lough Mask and even had its own private harbour for my boat. I would give it six months of intensive effort and see what turned up!

October and November in fact turned out to be rather slow. I was fishing as many different areas as I could, trying to increase my knowledge of the venue. A lot was learned but few fish came to the net. By mid November I was again fishing the area that had produced my thirty the year before. Several pike were seen swirling in the area and at last a take on a half mackerel produced a nice fat 21-04. It seemed that I had found a few fish, but sadly I had to fly to Scotland the next day so was not able to capitalise on it.

Returning two weeks later I was really keen to get back amongst the big pike. As an added bonus my good friend Peter Robinson was due to come over from England for a few days fishing. It would be nice to have some company for a change. I had four days fishing on my own before Peter was due to arrive and these turned out to be some of the bests days fishing I had ever enjoyed. Two twenties at 20-11 and 27-12 were boated along with three different 19s and three other doubles. All the fish came to static deadbaits fished from the boat in the same spot I had taken the 32. It was turning out to be quite a hotspot! Peter had been given instructions as to how to find me on the lake and he was due to arrive at midday along with his own boat. At exactly twelve I had a take on a half mackerel and landed a 23-12. This I popped into a pike tube so that I could show Peter when he arrived. About an hour later I had just decided that Peter must have been delayed and that I should put the fish back , when another half mackerel was away. That one turned out to weigh 27-00. What a brace of fish! A couple of photos of the two in the bottom of the boat were taken and I was just putting the 27 into the tube in place of the 23 when Peter turned up in his boat. He was just a little gobsmacked to see such a super fish and looking rather frenzied he quickly got some rods out to join in the fun.

No more runs occurred that day to either of us but dawn the next morning found us both anchored up in position, about a hundred yards apart in our boats. It was a glorious, calm winter morning, the kind when it feels good just to be alive. We both chucked out the usual assortment of deadbaits and sat back to watch our floats. Most of my fish had come from baits cast close to a large dying weedbed and I had instructed Peter that it would be a good idea if at least one of his rods was fished with a half mackerel cast close to the weedbed. This he did and I was not too surprised to see his float zooming away within fifteen minutes of us starting. I quickly picked up my binoculars to get a good view of the action. When Peter got the fish near his boat it swirled on the surface, and the Irish air turned blue! This was obviously a good fish. After wallowing about for a bit, the fish then decided that it was giving up and swam quietly into the net. When I saw Peter struggling to lift his net into the boat I realised that it was something very special indeed so I quickly reeled in and rowed over to give assistance. She was a huge, old looking brute of a fish and weighed in at 33-12. We were both amazed! A quick video and photographs were taken and back she went. Nothing more happened that day but we did enjoy a bottle or two of Ballinrobe's best sparkling wine that evening!

166

Things slowed right down the next few days and no more twenties were taken, though Peter did land a few good doubles. That was it for the year for me. Little did I know what 1992 was to hold in store.

My first session of the new year was on the third of January. The wind was near gale force so fishing from the boat was out. I would have to find somewhere sheltered that I could fish from the bank. My first idea was to fish the Clare river near where it flows into Lough Corrib. Driving there, it started to rain very heavily which made me think that the river would be coloured and a waste of time. The previous year, Neville had tipped me off about a couple of bays on Corrib from which it was possible to bank fish, so it was to there that I headed. Neville had taken fish to 27 from the area and another English angler had apparently taken a 36. Despite this, my confidence was low as I trudged across the fields to the bay I had chosen. Three deadbaits were quickly cast out into the shallow weedy water and I huddled behind my brolley, trying to shelter from the incessant wind and rain. I was more than surprised when one of the Backbiters sounded before I had even drunk the first coffee. The run was dropped, but I was considerably cheered up. Minutes later a half mackerel absolutely screamed off and this time the rod bent into something substantial. After a good scrap an obvious twenty rolled into the net. As it did so one of the other rods, also with a half mackerel tore off. The line was a blur as it left the spool. I had no choice but to drop the net and hope the first fish didn't escape. Bullying the fish as hard as possible I could hardly believe it when I saw it was another twenty plus. I am not a fan of hand landing big pike but this time I had no choice. Luckily, all went to plan and I was soon looking down at a lovely brace of fish. They were fin perfect, fat fish and absolutely identical in every respect. One weighed 23-02 and the other 22-14. I took a couple of shots of them lying together on my sling before popping them back. The photos later turned out very well and were in fact used by North Western Blanks in their catalogue, earning me a free rod for my troubles.

An eleven pounder plus half a dozen small fish completed the days catch. It was an excellent start for a new area and I was looking forward to what the future would bring. I fished the same area quite hard over the next couple of months but things got slower and slower and I never did as well as that first day. By mid March, action was almost non-existent wherever I fished. I had to move from the cottage at the end of March and decided it was time to take a bit of a break from piking for a while. The winter's fishing had produced nine twenties including the two 27s, a total I was more than happy with.

During my short break from fishing I took the opportunity to purchase a Volkswagen camper van. This I thought would be rather handy for the summer pike fishing. By mid May I was raring to get fishing again so I hitched the boat to the van and set off for Corrib once more. Fishing several different areas I managed a few doubles and one twenty at 20-04, taken on a drifted deadbait. It was fairly hard work though, so a change of venue was called for and back to Lough Mask I went. A large bay I had never tried before had been marked down as a likely looking area. The only problem, was that it was a long way from the nearest boat launch and it took me a good hour with the outboard on full before I eventually arrived there. A river flowed into the bay and there was a huge area of weed. It really did look the business. Anchoring up in about ten feet of water I decided to drift a shallow fished bait over the top of the weed. This was instantly successful and in quick succession two doubles of 13-14 and 17-00 were landed. No more action was forthcoming that day and after motoring back to the launch, the night was spent in the camper van by the lakeside.

The alarm woke me just before dawn the next morning. Still in the sleeping bag, I leant over and put the kettle on. It really was nice to be able to lie in bed sipping a coffee, looking out over the lake watching the sky gradually get lighter. Most of the gear was still in the boat so it didn't take long before I was on my way to the bay again. Starting off in the same spot as the day before I quickly took a fish of 16-06 on a drifted bait before things again went quiet. Thinking over events, I decided that what was needed was a method that would cover more water. The bay was vast and I was only covering a fraction of the likely looking area with my drifted baits. Float trolling was a method that I had dabbled in before and I knew that it was very much a favourite technique on the English trout reservoirs. I had my electric outboard and sounder in the boat, so I was fully equipped. Deciding it was worth a try, I rigged up a rod and set the float at about six feet deep. The bait chosen was a dead roach of around four ounces in size. Only a couple of hundred yards had been covered when the rod top slammed violently round and the baitrunner made a most alarming noise. Giving the motor a quick burst in reverse, I picked the rod up, engaged the baitrunner and held on hard. The rod took on a serious bend and I was forced to backwind straight away. It was a good ten minutes before I could get the fish within netting range and by that time I had drifted out into deeper water. Several attempts were made before the fish was safely in the bottom of the net. Parting the mesh, I knew I had taken my biggest ever pike. I had drifted very close to a small grassy island by now so I decided to do the weighing and photography there rather than in the confines of the boat. On the Happy Hookers a weight of 32-12 was recorded. My second thirty pounder. I just could not believe it! The fish was in good condition but fairly lean and I wondered what she would weigh in peak winter trim.

The action did not stop there though, several more good fish falling to the float trolled deadbaits, giving me a total of over a hundred pounds for the day. As well as a personal best, it was the first time I had ever broken the ton barrier. I was particularly pleased that it had come from what was for me a new area of the lake and to a new method.

The third day turned up three more mid doubles, all again falling to float trolled deadbaits. The weed was so thick in the bay that it was necessary to fish the baits very shallow. Takes were often accompanied by a large swirl. It was exciting stuff and a style of fishing that I took an instant liking to. Most of the fish got heavily weeded, but by pulling from directly above I was always able to get the fish moving again and didn't lose any at all. An 18-12 was the only result of the last day but I packed up feeling very pleased with events.

After two weeks at work I was raring to get back to the bay for a bit more float trolling action. I felt sure that after the rest it would once more produce the goods. Three days later I had been brought back down to earth with a bang. Despite fishing hard I had only managed a couple of jacks. What a contrast with the previous visit. I just could not understand what was going on as conditions appeared perfect.

At a bit of a loss as to where to try next I decided a change was in order and the next couple of sessions were to completely new venues. This was good fun and quite a few fish were landed including two 18s. None of the venues struck me as being mega pike waters though, and it was not to be long before I was studying the map of Lough Mask again.

I had read in an old copy of Trout and Salmon magazine about pike being caught from another bay on Mask during a trout fishing competition. It had to be worth a try, so in mid July I launched my boat on the bay for the first time. As I did so I noticed that there was a lot of weed, and even more encouraging was that there were enormous shoals of perch fry present. Things were looking good. After two days fishing, four nice doubles had been taken on my float trolled deadbaits. Not a bad result, but I felt that things could have been better. I had seen quite a few decent pike feeding on the perch fry but could not get them to look at a bait. It seemed that the pike were preoccupied with the fry and were not interested in my larger deadbaits.

It was three weeks before I could return. Looking around the margins I noticed that the perch fry had grown considerably and that the shoals seemed to be even larger than before. Numbers of terns and gulls were present also, no doubt feeding on the fry as well. It was with mounting excitement that I set off, the electric motor on tickover with a float trolled joey mackerel set at five feet deep. The first take produced a fat 13-14 and two more low doubles were added before the day was out . All the fish had come from a part of the bay where it dropped off sharply from five to twelve feet. There was thick weed growth along the drop-off and huge shoals off fry in the weed. A classic pike holding feature!

The alarm woke me at 6.30 the next morning, but the sound of heavy rain on the van roof persuaded me to switch it off and go back to sleep. When I woke up an hour later the rain had stopped, it was a glorious sunny day and mist was rising off the lake. I could hardly get out of the sleeping bag fast enough!

Expectations were high for the first troll of the day over the drop-off hotspot. When the sounder showed only four feet deep I realised that I had cut in a bit too far so turned the boat quite sharply to head back out to deeper water. Just then, the float plopped under and the Baitrunner howled. The fish was moving very fast and I hit it straight away. I was soon in no doubt that this was a good fish. At one point it got about a hundred yards away from the boat and kited fast through a thick weedbed. I really thought I might lose it but fortunately I managed to regain some line and eventually got the fish within netting range. The netting went without a hitch and I was once again staring down at a large lump of a pike lying in the bottom of the boat. She was incredibly thick across the back and I knew she was going to be close to the thirty pound mark. Onto the scales and yes! Thirty pounds and twelve ounces! After years of never even dreaming of catching a thirty, all of a sudden they just seemed to be giving themselves up. What a venue this was!

A large portion of the pike's tail was missing, presumably through an encounter with an outboard engine. Even more interesting was that there was what appeared to be a gaff wound beneath the pike's chin. Nobody gaffs and puts back pike into Lough Mask so it must have managed to escape from a bungled gaffing attempt. A very lucky pike! Apart from the battlescars, the fish was in pristine condition and on being returned she swam strongly away.

One problem with summer pike fishing on Lough Mask is the large number of trout anglers. Earlier in the year I had been witnessed catching a few fish by a party of trout anglers. They were not catching trout and in desperation turned to pike. Several dead twenties were the sad end result. To my relief, no trout anglers passed whilst I was playing and weighing the big one. It appeared that there was a big concentration of pike in a very small area and the last thing I wanted was a load of trout anglers to start slaughtering these pike. Pike protection laws are almost universally ignored on Mask despite signs at every boat launch. Fortunately, the day for most trout anglers begins at eleven a.m., so it is possible in the summer to get four or five hours of peace and quiet in the morning before the crowds descend.

This was the general approach I took over the next few days. An early start and fish to about eleven then a break of a few hours before going back out for the late afternoon and evening. It turned out to be the best pike fishing I had ever experienced. A further fourteen double figure fish were boated, two of which were twenties at 21-08 and 22-10. Every fish was taken on float trolled deadbaits. Lures were tried on a number of occasions but failed to even get a single take. The pike were really feeding hard and I managed to my astonishment to not miss a single take throughout the entire session. Anyone who does much float trolling will know how rare that is!

After resting the bay for a week, I returned and carried on where I had left off. Action was non stop with thirteen more doubles landed, including one twenty at 21-00. Several of the fish I recognised as repeat captures. Not wanting to keep hammering the samefish I decided on a break from piking for a few weeks.

Mid September saw me refreshed by the break and once more launching my boat on the perch fry bay. It was apparent that the perch fry had by now dispersed from the bay and so it turned out had most of the pike. Two days trolling produced three pike of 11-06, 15-04 and 21-05. Several other areas were tried with little result. It was now becoming clear that unless a concentration of pike was found, the fishing on Mask could be very difficult. There is after all, an awful lot of water for the pike to disappear into.

In the Autumn of 1992 I again decided to rent a cottage by the lakeside for the winter months. A busy spell at work however, meant that it was late November before

I next managed to get the rods out. It didn't take much thought to decide to try the scene of last winter's success. I had by now realised that the pike in this area were feeding on trout which were running up a nearby river to spawn. I had tried the same spot in the summer and it was totally devoid of pike. In addition the water level was much lower during the summer. The water level of Lough Mask varies by as much as 5 or 6 feet from summer to winter. This has a big effect on the pike fishing. I have caught pike from Mask in the winter in places that you will find cattle grazing during the summer!

The weather was bad for the first day of the session and it was touch and go to even manage to stay anchored in position. To my surprise, I had four runs on old faithful half mackerel and landed three good fish of 19-12, 22-04 and 24-06. A fourth big fish was lost when it ran through a snag. This was an incredible result considering the bad conditions and I hardly dared imagine what the next few days would bring. It was obvious that big pike were in the area in large numbers.

Day two and the action continued with pike of 13-00, 20-10 and 12-02 falling to my deadbaits. The next day I decided to give the area a rest because Peter was due over the day after and I did not want to hammer it to death before he got there.

More wind and rain greeted Peter's arrival. It was a case of extra anchors being needed and we both got blown off our swims on several occasions. I had noticed that one particular spot seemed to produce more runs than any other so I decided to leave a half mackerel there, all day if necessary. It really was rather grim and we were both huddled down in the bottom of our respective boats trying to keep warm. Nothing happened until three in the afternoon when I was pleased to see my half mackerel float moving purposefully through the waves. The bait was at long range and on winding down I was met with solid resistance. As I slowly pumped the fish towards the boat I reached behind me to get the net ready. To my horror, the mesh was caught by the wind and wrapped round the top of one of my other rods. I tried in vain to free the net, but without putting the rod down, there was nothing I could do. "Oh well" I thought, hand landing it is! When the fish surfaced near the boat and I got a look at it, I quickly changed my mind. Swallowing my pride I shouted at the huddled form in the other boat "Peter, I've got a thirty on and I need some help!"

Being the good mate that he is, Peter was soon alongside in his boat and quickly scooped the fish which was lying quietly on the surface, into his net. It was indeed a thirty, at 30-04 and was a typical, fat, fin perfect Lough Mask pike. That evening, it was my turn to buy the sparkling wine!

Over the next few days I managed fish of 20-06, 21-10, 24-04, 16-02 and 16-14. Peter also joined in the fun with fish to 28-00. What was very interesting was that action had been tailing off until Peter tried a dead trout as bait. A flurry of runs to trout deadbaits was the result and he took a number of good fish including the 28-00 on them. It seemed that some fish would not look at the seabaits and were totally preoccupied with trout. Since that day, whenever we are fishing Mask in winter we both make sure that we have a few trout baits in the freezer box.

A couple of weeks after this trip I sat down one evening and sorted through all my slides of Lough Mask pike taken over the previous three seasons. The results were fascinating. My 30-04 was the same fish I had taken the year previously at 27-12 and the 24-04 I had taken the year before at 27-00. One fish had come out on three occasions. We first met in January of 1991 when it weighed 12-14. By November of that year it had shot up to 20-11. A quite astonishing growth rate. A year later I caught it in the same spot again, weighing an ounce less at 20-10. What was also interesting was the fact that all these fish had been caught in the same place as their previous captures. indicating that even in a water the size of Lough Mask the pike return to the same areas every year.

What an amazing years pike fishing it had been for me. A check of my diary showed that I had taken seventy five doubles, eighteen of which were twenty plus with three over thirty. I was starting to think that something truly exceptional could be just round the corner. The fact that thirties were coming out quite regularly suggested that there must be bigger fish about waiting to be caught. I was quite convinced that there were forty pound plus pike in Mask at the time, as I still do today.

The full story of my 1993 season would not make particularly interesting reading. Where as the previous year, everything went brilliantly, 1993 I will remember as the year when everything, with one exception, went badly wrong.

I was off work throughout January and February and put an intense amount of effort in. Two twenties at 21-10 and 24-10 were recorded, but considering the number of days I fished it was a meager result.

The highlight of the year came in May when Peter joined me for a week long session. We hired a cottage by the lakeside and enjoyed a fabulous weeks pike fishing in superb weather conditions. Float trolled and wobbled deadbaits accounted for 20 double figure fish for me, with three over twenty at 22-04, 23-14 and 28-14. Peter also did very well, taking fish to 29-00.

An amazing result, but if I was honest, I would have to admit that my heart was not really in it. I had fished so hard over the last couple of seasons that I had burnt myself out and just was not enjoying it as much as I used too. Such had been my obsession with pike fishing that I had done virtually nothing except work and fish for the best part of two years. The decision was made to leave Ireland and move back to England, a decision which I have no regrets about.

After moving back to England in May I made only two trips over to Ireland during the rest of the year. The first visit was in July and I was expecting to hammer the fry feeding pike again. The pike had other ideas though and I failed to boat even a single double figure fish. Pike were present in the bay but were totally preoccupied with fry and would not look at my deadbaits.

The second and last trip was in November, timed to coincide with the trout moving up the rivers to spawn. Unfortunately, very low water levels meant that the usual spots were a waste of time. I did manage two twenties of 20-04 and 24-12 but it was very hard going compared with the bonanza of previous years.

1994 will be remembered by me as the year when work seriously got in the way of pike fishing. I in fact spent most of the year working on oil rigs in Brazil. Every time an Irish trip was planned it had to be canceled for some reason or other. It was not until July that I managed to escape for a three and a half day session on Mask. After last seasons disappointment with the fry feeding pike I did not know what to expect. This time for some reason the pike were feeding voraciously and the float trolled deadbaits scored heavily. In order of capture, pike of the following weights fell to my rod: 24-00, 21-08, 21-00, 12-14, 10-08, 15-04, 13-06, 24-00, 12-08 and 22-12. Quite a result, and it was pleasing to see the average weight of pike well up on previous years. My father joined me one morning, fished for a couple of hours, knocked out a 22 and left in time to get home for lunch!

That October I was back again on Mask for another three day session. Due to pressure of work it was all the time I could spare. I have always found the pike in October to be rather unpredictable as regards location and behavior. This visit was to be no exception and I struggled to find fish. A lot of water was covered but it was not until the final day that a few pike were located near to where a river flowed in. The sounder showed a lot of large marks on the screen and several pike were seen swirling on the surface. Despite getting quite a few takes to my float trolled deadbaits, only two were converted, resulting in fish of 10-00 and 20-02.

Winter on Mask is most definitely my favourite time of year. The lake is free of trout anglers and the average size of fish I have taken has been exceptionally high. To my disgust it was not until January of the new year that I made it over for a week long session. Two things were worrying me. One was that I might be a bit late and that the pike feeding on spawning trout may have dispersed. The second thing was that I had heard that some other pike anglers had sussed out what it was all about, and that my usual spots might have been hammered. Thankfully I was wrong on both accounts and in fact had my best ever session!

On two occasions I managed three pike over twenty pounds in a day, which was something I had never done before. A total of nine pike over twenty were recorded in the week with the icing on the cake being my fifth thirty pounder at 30-08. The other twenties taken weighed 29-02, 26-04, 20-06, 21-00, 25-00, 24-12, 20-04 and 21-10. A further half dozen doubles were also added. Virtually all the fish came in the first four days. Bad weather made the last three days a waste of time All the fish fell to float legered deadbaits fished from the boat. Seven of the nine twenties came to half mackerel, one took smelt and one a dead trout. Mind-blowing stuff and it shows just what Lough Mask is capable of when conditions are right.

173

The set up I use for deadbaiting from the boat is a bog standard float leger rig. I would normally fish two rods on half mackerel and one with either a smelt or trout. Half mackerel I have found to be far and away the most effective deadbait and it also casts the furthest which is a definite advantage.

My float trolling rig is perhaps worth a closer look. The double trace helps to reduce line twist and aids retackling. After a fish has kinked the lower trace it can be quickly unclipped and a new one clipped on. Trebles are two size six Terry Eustace Super Strongs and I find no need at all for the fancy hooking arrangements some people seem to require. Line twist with this setup is virtually non-existent. I also have no use for elaborate devices for stopping the float moving down the line. Using this rig, fished slowly with the electric motor, it just is not a problem. I have caught hardly any pike from Corrib or Mask on trolled deadbaits with the bait set deeper than about 12 ft. Most of the time I set the float at six or seven feet deep. On the rare occasions that I do fish baits deep, I like to use a larger float and increase the weight on the trace to about an ounce. Other pike anglers I have talked to have also found that shallow fished baits outfish baits fished at depth. Downriggers or wireline I have never found a need for. In addition, the thought of getting a wireline or dowrigger snagged on the bottom in rough weather is not something I have a great desire to experience!

Bait choice when float trolling is fairly important. There are times on Mask when dropped and missed takes are a big, big problem. When I first encountered this phenomena, different rigs and hooking arrangements were tried in an effort to convert more takes. Nothing that was tried made much difference. It was not until I obtained some perch deadbaits that things improved. All of a sudden many more takes were resulting in fish in the boat. The pike, which were feeding on spawning perch at the time, seemed to be preoccupied with perch, and on hitting a bait which turned out to not be a perch, were dropping it in disgust. Since that day my first choice of bait will always be a perch or trout deadbait and I have found that they consistently result in less missed takes. On some occasions seabaits are accepted with gusto, but if missed takes start to occur then a natural bait is definitely worth a try.

Line is of critical importance, and for all my summer fishing I use 20 lb. test Big Game line having been broken several times on 15 lb. test line in the past. Lough Mask pike in the warmer months really do battle hard. Most of my fishing is done in the vicinity of weed and snags so an abrasion resistant line is very important. For winter fishing I scale down to the 15 lb. test Big Game line.

A rod with considerable backbone is also vital because when a big pike goes for the anchor rope you have got to be able to stop it in it's tracks. I have used all sorts of rods but have now settled on 13ft 3 1/4 lb. test curve Simpson Eclipses for all my fishing. They are a quite awesome fast taper rod that will put a half mackerel out of sight. I can see no need at all for the short rods many people seem to advocate for boat fishing.Reels used are the inevitable Shimano Aero Baitrunners. The baitrunner feature is indispensable for boat fishing, and for float trolling in particular.

There is nothing revolutionary about any of my methods. Success on Mask is all about finding the fish. Once located, the pike are usually very easy to catch and a float trolled or static deadbait will do the job. Some people might be surprised that lures have virtually no place in my approach. This is quite simply because I have found mobile deadbaits to be vastly more effective. I also feel no need to be tempted to use livebaits. I am convinced that mobile deadbaits will nearly always catch you the fish you are after on Mask and that livebaits are not worth the hassle. Anyone caught using livebaits on Mask, particularly roach, would be liable to have their teeth removed by the local trout anglers. Believe me, it is not worth it!

The reason for lures not being effective, is I believe due to the large number of trout anglers that troll the lake during the summer months. Any pike that has a liking for small Tobys or plugs will get bashed on the head very quickly. Of course, the good lure angler should always be able to catch the odd pike and I do know of some very large fish taken on lures in recent years. For consistent results though, a float trolled deadbait wins hands down.

Anyone reading this account might be starting to think that Lough Mask was stuffed full of big pike just waiting to throw themselves onto the hooks. This was definitely not the case and I am convinced that pike numbers were low in relation to the size of the water. My experiences have shown that unless a concentration of pike was found the fishing could be very difficult. The results which I enjoyed were the product of intense research and an awful lot of days. I would expect even very experienced pikers to have struggled without some prior knowledge of exactly where and when to fish. The Angling Times sponsored Pike Hunt being a case in point. To be fair to the guys though, I was on the lake at about the same time and could not catch either. On several occasions, especially in early Springtime I have gone a whole week without a fish.

What is undeniable though, is that Lough Mask did produce some very big pike and at times the fishing could be second to none. I doubt that there was any water in the British Isles which offered a better chance of a thirty pound plus pike. My results in recent years suggested that the pike fishing on Mask was getting better and better. I did not fish on Corrib sufficiently to be able to say the same but I would not be surprised if that had been the case also. Sadly though, all the fun is over. The gill nets set in all the strategic areas at spawning time have reduced the Mask and Corrib pike population to such a level that it may no longer be worth fishing these waters. It is a sad fact that many trout anglers now also agree it is a waste of money culling pike and that the money could be better spent elsewhere. One question I have asked Lough Mask trout anglers and boatmen time and time again, and that is "did the pike culling in the past have a beneficial effect on the trout angling?" About half have replied "yes" and half "no"! All that effort and expense for something which has no definite result!

LOUGH CORRIB
Lough Corrib is even bigger than Mask and though they have gill netted it they do not seem to have done quite such a good job as on Mask. With 44,000 acres this is hardly

surprising. In some areas you'd have to have a lot of nets to get most of the pike. Obviously because there is a small chance that one of the b******s from the Western Region Fisheries Board is reading this I'll not be giving any clues at all as to where I fish at the moment. When they stared netting on Corrib they made a point of netting where I and a few other English and Welshmen were fishing. That was after one of their chief hit men Danny Goldrick declared that particular area as being not very good for pike!! Duplicity or what! Corrib has a larger coarse fish population than Mask. Both bream and roach are present and this obviously has the potential to modify the pike's feeding habits. Many of the bream are 7 or 8lb plus and of no use to pike as food. The roach are numerous in some areas, but the brown trout are probably still the most important prey of the pike. If you look at where the pike are at certain times of the year they are definitely influenced by the trout. All rivers that enter the Lough will at some time in the autumn or winter see pike congregate to intercept trout and possibly salmon smolts on their way to the sea. I had a bit of luck in 2001 because with a bit of help from a friend I dropped onto a good spot. I was on a family holiday in Ireland (I try to avoid Ireland as a pike fishing tourist because of what they have done over there) and sneaked off to have a couple of days on Corrib. I took the bivvy determined to camp out and get away from it all. I had a hand held GPS unit with me for the first time and I was determined to learn how to use it. My son had entered the co-ordinates for where I was going off of my O/S map. I launched the boat and was doing OK until I realised that I was struggling to find the approved or should I say safe route! Anyway I ended up going around in circles despite the GPS, but eventually I sorted myself and ended up in the right area. Alastair Rawlings turned up and we shared a fairly unexciting day. I think he had a 12 pounder and we both caught a small one or two. He went home and I spent an uneventful night with two rods out. Not even a pull off of an eel! I was back out in the boat at dawn, but by golly it was dull. I had the odd cast with the Springdawg, but even that was not doing the magic for me. Then at around 10am I had a follow off of something that looked about 18lb. I recast a float fished smelt that was drifting around just off he bottom. Lo and behold it went under and there then followed one of the meanest fights I've had off of a pike for a long time. It went everywhere! Unfortunately it was a bit of a scabby fish being covered in fish lice. At 25lb though it was most welcome! A little later I did a repeat performance with a twenty-four pounder. His was again lice covered. It is very unusual to get such heavy infestations of fish louse and one has to wonder what environmental degradation there was in the immediate area. Lice are usually a symptom of poor water quality. Unfortunately because we have zero regard for the Irish fisheries people we are hardly likely to ask them about it.

All this is a far cry from the fishing several groups of anglers enjoyed in the late eighties. For the time being this is just a memory, but while we were fishing Corrib we learned some interesting lessons. These were that big pike did not generally come into quite as shallow water as they did on say Lomond or Awe. Also because there were so many shallow bays on Corrib it was not always easy to find the ones, which produced the bigger pike. I think I know now which bays to fish, but it's a bit late now! Just as an aside a lot of years were spent exploring parts of Corrib and trying to come to terms with a new water. All this is now wasted effort. From my point of view it has actually set me back about five years in terms of coming to terms with big waters. If that effort had been spent on Derg for example I would now be reaping the rewards of that knowledge. No one ever said pike fishing always goes to plan!

Interestingly on our first ever week on Corrib Dave Moore and I experienced a week when the pike didn't want mackerel! Well it does happen sometimes. We had a lot of pike to nine pounds on smelt and trout and only dropped runs on mackerel. It wasn't until the last day that I had a storming run on half a mackerel that went eighteen pounds. I really appreciated that fish and I'm unlikely to forget it even though it's a long way from my biggest ever pike.

I subsequently learned that John Matthews, Phil Pearson and friends had some breathtaking catches from where I had started on Corrib. My mistake was not appreciating how good it really was. You do not get it right all the time. If I did I'd not need to go fishing so often!

Spring was a good time on Corrib, though the fishing was never all action. I did have one good day when I had seven doubles the biggest being 14lb. I think I was a bit unlucky that day. Another pike angler who wrote to me told me about his friend's catch of a 36, 26 and a 21 in a day from exactly where I had been fishing! On one hand I had that empty feeling you get when you've missed out big time. On the other was the feeling that if I renewed my efforts something would turn up. In the end the best Corrib pike I caught was 27lb, so not a total failure. I did fish it in October, but results were terrible. February is when I *should* have been there!

LOUGH ALLEN

I first started fishing Lough Allen in 1980 with a combined honeymoon/fishing trip. I caught my first pike trolling on a dead trout fished 10 foot deep over 22 feet of water. It weighed 21lb and was one of the strongest fish I had hooked up until then. Spring trips were soon arranged and for some time until Corrib and Mask drew me to them I fished Allen a lot, both in the spring and in October. We always stayed at the O'Dwyers on the shore of the Lough and in the eighties everyone who fished there filled in a log-book. The beauty of this was that an overall picture of how the Lough fished could be built up. It soon became clear that the third week of April was a good one and so was the first week of October. Interestingly some weeks in September were good for lots of pike up to 17lb, but no big ones. I based my visits on what looked to be the most consistent weeks. Over the years it paid off with some brilliant weeks fishing. Unfortunately the weather is different these days and since they connected the Shannon with the Erne system you now no longer have the large water level fluctuations that made Allen unique. We always found that mobility was the key in the spring and even 5 years ago the approach still worked. The weather was also important and warm weather equaled good sport while cold weather put the mockers on it. In late February the fishing would be very slow, but you could pick up some of the better fish then. The used of very fresh deadbaits if you get my meaning made a big difference at this time of year. Once you were post spawn i.e. mid April onwards you would catch well on float legered deadbaits and sometimes on lures. Everything was caught in less than six feet of water and in the space of a week you would end up trying every bit of water of that depth. It was fun and when the pike were in the shallows very productive. Our best ever week was 12 fish over 20lb between four anglers.

For the rest of the year we trolled lures and deadbaits and did quite well doing this. Interestingly we did not manage to take this approach to Lough Mask with any success. While fishing Allen we took the advice of the masters of trolling this water, people like George Higgins and Roy Smyth. That was not to try trolling too deep, 7 to 10 feet was fine. The idea being that pike if they are interested will come up for a bait. Though Lough Allen is a fair sized water it is not as big as the main Irish waters so you could easily troll a lot of it in a day. When not much is happening you do tend to cover a lot of water and if you do get takes it pays to cover an area several times. We always found the pike to be in different areas each time we visited Allen in October. Luckily in a day it was usually quite easy to find some concentrations of fish. You would then revisit the same area each day. We caught from submerged plateau, ends of islands, points that stuck out from the bank. All these are classic areas, which should work on any big water. Of course as I mentioned about Mask, sometimes you cannot make sense of some waters!

We also had some success bank fishing in October, but you can only do this on the larger Irish Loughs if you can find deep water where the food fish shoals hole up in the winter. Lough Gara because the lower Lough is mainly shallow is an ideal water to fish the prey fish holding areas in winter, simply because these areas are small in relation to the size of the whole Lough. Bank fishing and chucking half mackerels as far as you can is good fun. When you get a run they do not half move!

I think Lough Allen is probably still worth fishing. The problem these day is that the shallow areas in spring often tend to have less water in them than they did and this can reduce the amount of water where you can find pike. This might at times work in your favour, but we always used to do best when there was plenty of water about. We had three consecutive trips a couple of years ago and the first one was a good trip with the group getting a 28, 27, 21 and 20 amongst other fish. The next two spring trips were very poor mainly due to low water levels and cold weather. A lot of people's attention has now focused on Lough Derg, which still appears to be capable of producing good pike. I've been there for a few days, but apart from a possible twenty that threw the hooks I've not much to report.

CHAPTER 9

CONSERVATION AND POLITICAL ISSUES

I've left this section right to the end because most pike angers are interested in catching pike, not sitting at a desk writing letters of complaint. Yet by being politically active we are protecting our sport. That is why we have The Pike Anglers Club, which covers all of mainland Britain. For less than 20 pounds you are helping to support a group of volunteers who seek to represent pike anglers. Sometimes a lot of negotiation and persuasion has been carried out on YOUR behalf by these people to protect your sport. Closer to government where legislation is enacted is the Specialist Anglers Alliance which in turn represents all specialist anglers. Failure to support these organizations is a failure to support angling in general.

As far as pike are concerned there are still black spots around Britain and Ireland where pike are considered as vermin. The West of Ireland and the far North of Scotland are such areas. There's still a lot of negative thought towards pike when it come to heavily stocked small carp waters. I will not suggest that there are no situations where pike are decidedly unwelcome. An ornamental pond full of exotic Koi and orfe is the last place you need a pike! The same applies to the small village pond, which usually holds species such as crucian carp and rudd. Pike in this situation can be destructive because the pike is probably a better predator than the crucian is an escaper! Even in these extreme situations there is no call for killing the odd unlucky pike. A handful of pike moved to a local river where there are plenty of all sorts of fish is not going to be noticed.

Where it is more difficult to justify the presence is where there is no economic case for their being there. Take for example a southern stocked trout river where no one else but trout angers are allowed to fish. Now you and I know that you could probably get a pike syndicate on the river, but the snag is a club that has always killed every pike runs the next section downriver. There is no chance of sorting this out. The only real option is to remove the pike because the culling downstream makes it difficult to get enough pike anglers together to compensate for the trout eaten. Better to move them to a water where they might at least have a chance of living. This is a bit of a dire example, but situations like this do arise.

Generally however the economic argument is such that we can convince almost anyone that pike are worth having in a fishery. I've never been totally convinced by all the biological explanations as to why pike are good for your water. In a natural water where man is not manipulating fish stocks pike obviously settle into a predator prey relationship, which means that neither prey nor predator becomes ascendant over the other. There is an annual surplus of prey fish production, which can quite easily be consumed by pike without making any changes to the long-term population structure. You have to look at fish populations in the same way as capital and interest.

The capital is the standing crop of fish in the water. The interest is the production of fish from the standing crop. Just as you and I can spend the interest, we should not spend the capital. Pike eat the production without making inroads into the standing crop. Just once in a while this can go wrong usually due to something we have done. Then action has to be taken to redress the balance between predator and prey. Fortunately these situations are very rare.

We know that the salmon and the wild brown trout are really up against it and it is only right that efforts are made to conserve stocks of these fish. Unfortunately all too often the pike is the easy target. In the West of Ireland the fisheries people have decided that removing pike can improve the brown trout fishing (and presumably the salmon fishing). The debate has gone on now for many years and it is not my intention here to go into detail. Suffice it to say the improvement (if any) in the *salmonid* fishing may not be sufficient to compensate for the loss of winter pike fishing. Certainly the Western Region Fisheries Board has been very slow to produce any figures to indicate that their gill netting of pike has done anything to improve the *salmonid* fishing. Unfortunately Ireland is a republic and we in the UK have little influence on it even though EU money was being use to cull pike. It will probably be too late for some of us to again pike fish in the West should they give up their foolish campaign against the pike.

If we cannot get the blind to see, we can at least get our own act together. Catching pike has the potential to damage them. Carried out correctly catching pike can be perfectly harmless to them. You just have to obey some simple rules. Here's how not to do it. Mike has four rods out. Now Mike isn't the most confident of pike anglers so he likes to maximize his chances. Covering water is the name of the game and because he has no confidence he has to have a bait just about everywhere. Rods spread out over 60 yards though illegal are not a problem. The Environment Agency rarely patrols on this water. The fact that the rods are well spread out isn't a problem because Mike has the latest remote buzzers. Mike has a run on the end rod, he runs to it. Line is running out so he gives it another 15 seconds because he missed his last run. Eventually he strikes, well strike is exactly what I'd call it. He doesn't wind down jerks the rod hard at nothing a couple of times before he finds the pike has found a snag. In the meantime the rod at the other end of the rank goes. Mike panics and pulls really hard on the snagged fish. The line breaks. He runs to the other rod and line is running out. He repeats the effort he calls a strike, but this time luckily for Mike the pike has swallowed the bait so even he cannot miss it! He plays the fish which is pulling quite strongly as if it was a Marlin rather than a pike. This is despite the fact that he has a 3lb test rod and 15lb line. The pike is played to a standstill and then netted. He drags the fish up the bank and lays the net plus the fish down on his unhooking mat. He then takes five minutes to find his forceps scales and camera. He walks up to his mate 150 yards away to tell him he has had a good 'un. Returning he takes the pike out of the net and tries to unhook it. The hooks are out of sight so he tries to get his mates help. Eventually after five minutes of surgery and flapping about the hooks are removed. Then it is weighed and 10 photos are taken. Then out comes the video camera followed by the digital camera. Then it is reweighed just to make sure. After what seems an eternity the hapless pike is returned and Mike wonders why all it can do is swim straight down into the blanket weed with its tail waving near the surface. The pike will swim off eventually, but will probably pop up dead 10 days later. Then of course there was the one he lost.

Hopefully the reader will have got the picture! Here's how it's done properly. Rods should be as close together as possible, but not so close that a pike can do knitting with your lines when it is close to the bank. If you are boat fishing be sensible and do not try to fish four rods each between two of you. When you get a run consider this; we are fishing for sport. If we need to hook every pike that runs off with our bait and cannot face missing one, get a gill net. That works a lot better! If you have used sensible sized semi-barbless trebles you should be able to strike within 5 to 10 seconds of getting the first indication. Use two sixes on sardines, smelts, herrings, mini mackerel and lamprey sections. Use a couple of fours on 4 to 6oz live roach. Use a pair of twos on 4 to 6oz live trout. Suitably "tooled up" you should not miss many runs on a quick strike. The strike itself is so simple, but so easily done badly. You need to wind in all the slack line until you can wind no more then bend into the fish. On 15lb line and a 3lb test rod you can bend as hard as you like, nothing is going to break! Obviously you need to be pre-pared to give line if the pike decides to head for the hills, otherwise give it no slack and keep the rod well bent. You hook the pike when it releases its grip and tries to get rid of the bait. That is why you do not give slack. The strike is even easier with braid because there is no stretch and you connect very quickly with the pike.

Playing the pike will usually be fairly straightforward. The only situations where a pike fight will last more than 5 minutes will be in spring, summer and early autumn, particularly when boat fishing. Even then 10 minutes should be ample time to land a pike. I always backwind when playing pike using a fixed spool reel. On multiplier reels you have little choice other than to use the drag. Back winding works for me and I've certainly never been broken by a pike because I could not give line quickly enough. Even Canadian carp going off at full speed have not been a problem. I see no difficulty for anglers who prefer to use the clutch on a fixed spool reel, provided it is set to give line grudgingly.

Sometimes things go wrong and there's no telling why. I was boat fishing on Upper Lough Mask and had already caught 3 doubles, in itself a red letter day. I then had a run on a half mackerel in about 20 feet of water. The float was running towards me and I had the feeling that this one was the one. I wound down and bent into the pike, then the line parted just above the trace. On inspection it looked like a bite off. There is no telling how big or how small it was. I will never know, but I will always wonder! Landing pike is something that is not always given as much thought as other aspects of pike fishing. The landing of a pike is the last act you must carry out before you can say that you have caught it. I suspect that 80% of those pike lost are lost because of accidents at landing. A favourite is the flying treble. Now flying trebles are common when you are lure fishing, but you also get a fair number when bait fishing. Because I've done it loads of times I will always hand land a fish if it looks as if flying trebles are going to cause problems. Hand landing does offer the potential for getting hooks in your hand. It has happened to me twice. Luckily once it was the semi barbless hook, the other time the outcome was not so good which meant letting the wife loose on my hand! Both times I hooked myself it should have been avoided and a momentary lack of concentration is all that it took. To hand land a pike you obviously need it at your feet in preferably about a foot of water. You slide your finger under the chin and lift it out. If there is any sign of the pike being about to shake its head get your hand out of the way quick. If you really do lack the confidence to hand land fish then use the net, but be prepared to have to cut your wire trace in order to avoid the pike rolling up in the net and damaging itself. Lures with lots of hooks may have to have hooks cut with bolt cutters. Either way there is more risk of the pike getting damaged once it is in the net than if you can hand land it. Then the risk is transferred to you the angler!

Once unhooked if I am boat fishing I hang the net over the side and allow the pike to rest while scales and camera if required are sorted. On the bank I put two-rod rests in the edge and fit each end of the landing net arm in the rod rest head. There are risks associated with landing net retention, as pike have been known to jump out. I think it was a chap called Neil Hodgetts on Bough Beech who had a very big pike in his landing net while sorting the scales out. It jumped out and poor Neil must have been as sick as the proverbial parrot. It could have weighed 35lb, but now he'll never know. I happen to know that Neil is a very careful chap and tends to do things with great care. This probably slows procedures down and in the case of pike in landing nets it is a case of "More speed, less pike lost". It's the sort of thing that causes you to wake up at night in a cold sweat!

I'm not a great lover of retaining pike simply because once they have recovered after a couple of hours they tend to be too lively. Ideally you want the pike to have recovered enough to not damage its health when you photograph it, but not so lively that it looks as if you are a participant in the "International Pike Tossing Competition" Holding the pike for a photo again depends on how confident you are. I favour holding the fish under the chin and not putting it down at any time. As soon as you put a pike down it tries to swim and that is where damage can occur. Good quality unhooking mats or lots of soft grass are pretty pike safe, but learning to keep the pike off the deck is a good idea. I generally have my photograph taken with my finger under the chin to maintain control of the fish. If it struggles I either hug it or keep it away from my body so it cannot lever itself off of my finger. Whatever you do, do not drop it! In between unhooking, weighing and photography rest it in the landing net in the water. One of the biggest killers of pike is exhaustion. Exhaustion is caused by over exercise and subsequent failure to recover. The reason for this is as follows. The muscles are what allow a fish to swim. The energy for the muscles is supplied via the bloodstream and as that energy is produced oxygen is required. (for the biologists the energy production process involves the breakdown of ATP to ADP, but that's enough of that!). During extreme exercise not enough oxygen can get to the muscle. This causes a debit that can be corrected later. The by-product of oxygen debt is the production of lactic acid which when the fish is at rest is easily converted to a less toxic chemical. Now if you keep the pike out of water after a very hard fight it is going to struggle to get enough oxygen into its bloodstream. Its gills work much less efficiently when out of water. If the lactic acid cannot be removed its toxic effect will eventually be felt. A pike in this condition will swim off roll over and generally wallow on the surface. Because the swim bladder is distended by only a tiny change in depth it will appear that the pike is "gassed up".

This makes it difficult for a pike to right itself. The best cure for the problem is to stake the pike out in sheltered shallow water in a way that restricts its movement. Then wait for it to recover. Generally this will take a couple of hours, but once it took overnight, but thatpike did turn up a couple of seasons later.

With care there is no reason why a big pike cannot survive a number of captures. When you see the condition of some of the pike that are caught on some waters you can only assume that someone has trodden on them. Areas of flank lacking scales, badly split fins, damaged jaws and broken gill rakers all turn up. None of this is necessary. You can teach the worst pike angler in the world to handle his fish carefully. In fact it is probably just as easy to be good at pike handling as it is to be bad!

Earlier I mentioned the terrible situation in the West of Ireland where the big pike of Lough Mask and Corrib continue to be slaughtered. I have to put in here mainly for the record a short account of how things sometimes go well for the pike angler, then badly and then well again. (It went mainly badly for the pike, but turned out fine in the end.) Blithfield Reservoir in Staffordshire is an 800-acre water supply reservoir, which is run as a put and take trout fishery. My first involvement with it came when I worked with the fisheries section of Severn Trent Water. We were netting for coarse fish to stock elsewhere. We had variable results except for one afternoon when we managed to get the net around a huge shoal of roach that took us into darkness to tank up and transport. I think it was that autumn or the next that Blithfield Anglers announced that they were going to allow pike fishing. It was strictly members only and their guests and as luck would have it because we had netted coarse fish for Blithfield Anglers we were invited as well. I couldn't wait for the day to come, but because I caught very little I cannot remember much of the detail. All I know is I fished from a boat in all the areas you'd expect to catch pike from on any other reservoir, but the pike had not read the books I had read! Eventually we found some pike, but unfortunately they were near the causeway and were being caught! (And killed!) Fish to 21lb were having the last rites read to them and there was nothing we could do. We were equipped to take any pike we caught away to other waters, but had little joy getting other anglers to help us. A few more sessions and a few more seasons passed and gradually I did get to grips with some pike. I learned to cast Toby lures 60 yards and caught pike including a 29-15. Word of the good fishing got out and eventually there appeared a remarkable number of "guests" of members. Gradually the whole situation descended into anarchy and needless to say lure and deadbait only fishing changed into anything goes. There were very few innocent people fishing Blithfield by 1986 and livebaits definitely made a big difference when the water was coloured. My last fish came though on a Crusader Spoon and weighed 31lbs. By this stage I had moved so many pike in my official capacity to other waters I was running out of homes for them. I put the 31 back, which didn't endear me much to the trout anglers. Finally someone was caught livebaiting and it became a lure only event, which I felt I could live with. Everything was tightened up and I looked forward to the next season. As it happened the day before I next fished Blithfield I was on a netting that yielded about 10 small pike. These had to be removed and I was going to drop them in at Lindholme Lake. Now Lindholme was about 16 miles from my house and I didn't really have the time to go out there that day. It would be easier to keep them alive in the tank go to Blithfield and take them to Lindholme with any unwanted Blithfield pike. Some of you readers will already be ahead of me here; something was going to go wrong! Sure enough a Blithfield member looked in the back of my estate and that was it. On your bike! That was the end of my association with Blithfield until about 3 years ago.

During the years I didn't fish it, loads of pike ended up being restocked into other waters and some were killed. Fly anglers learned to catch them and some huge fish to over 40lb came to specialist fly anglers. Remarkably unlike every other trout water in the country that had been culled, Blithfield kept producing big fish. In the meantime Nige Williams because of his contacts had continued to fish the water as a trout angler's guest, but proved to be very unlucky when it came to catching a big one. He may not have caught any big pike, but he was there on the inside building up a relationship with the people who ran Blithfield Anglers. It should be realised that the people who ran Blithfield were not evil pike haters or idiots. They only knew one thing, the accepted norm that pike and stocked trout do not mix. Luckily at some stage they took fisheries advice and they started to return all the pike over 25lbs. I presume that the advice that had been given was that the indiscriminate removal of pike can see a large population of small pike remaining. Because small pike have a higher metabolic rate than large ones they need more food per 1lb of weight of pike. The risk then is that more trout will be eaten by the same weight of small pike as large pike. At Pitsford the reservoir is full of small pike and though I have no evidence regarding trout predation, the pike fishing certainly is not what it was.

Nige Williams continued to try to convince BA that the pike fishing was a lucrative sideline. Really when you think about it the financial advantages of allowing pike fishing are so obvious, but old habits die-hard and Nige had to convince a committee. There were also other pro pike people trying to get involved and their efforts were not always entirely helpful. Finally an agreement was reached and Nige was given the task of putting together a sub section of Blithfield Anglers. I think I was the last person who thought he was going to get asked to fish there. However Nige must have convinced someone that I wasn't Satan after all because I was asked. I was very pleased because I had never thought I would be able to go back after the pike in the tank incident. I think and I hope that logic suggested that it was unlikely that I had brought the pike to stock Blithfield and they were a bit big for bait! Subsequently Blithfield Anglers Norman Spiers apologized to me on the banks of the reservoir. He didn't have to do this and there was certainly nothing to be gained from it. I was very touched by the gesture and it made me feel doubly good about being there. However I had made my own personal mistake and was soon to find out that there was a price for fishing Blithfield.

When I signed up to fish the reservoir it said on the rules "All pike under 25lb must be killed". This I had on a slip of paper. I do not know how everyone else reacted to seeing this is print, but I know that at the time I'd taken on a new business and was very much engaged in that. I was also almost totally out of any political involvement with pike fishing. In short I was totally absorbed in my own world, which involved making a living. The killing pike bit would be sorted nearer the date, but it wouldn't be me who was sorting it out! A while late Nige phoned me up and asked me if I would be willing to buy the unwanted pike? I replied that I had no suitable waters for them, but if it came to seeing the pike killed I'm sure I could sort something out. Luckily this never had to be put to the test because John Davey who runs Rudyard Lake agreed to take them. This avoided my having to part with money for something I didn't really want!

As far as I was concerned everything went quiet until the first day of the fishing. Mick Rouse of Angling Times showed us a press release from the PAC which to put it mildly was not complimentary to say the least. Those of us fishing Blithfield had been condemned in no uncertain terms. Over the next few weeks there followed an almighty row that in the end saw me lose my life membership of PAC (awarded for being PAC secretary for 3 years) and several PAC members such as Mick Brown resigned. The PAC was due to change from a Scottish committee to a North West one and there was a quick rearrangement of future committee members. A lot of people were upset. At the center of the PAC in Scotland was Frank Gibbons, an authoritarian, possibly dictatorial figure. A man who's heart was in the right place, but who was incapable seeing things in any other shades other than black or white.

Needless to say I was bitter and hurt about being thrown out of PAC. I cannot change how I behaved after being thrown out, but with the benefit of hindsight I might have done better not to take PAC head on. At the time however I could see no other alternative so I thought back with everything at my disposal. A new committee came in and unfortunately they seemed trapped in the framework laid down by the Scottish committee. I continued to apply pressure by every means possible. I did have quite a bit of support for my cause, but equally at the time there were people who clearly enjoyed the thought of putting the boot in. (I still find it impossible to give talks for some people) Some of my supporters such as Neil Wheater ceased to be involved with PAC, which was a terrible shame because Neil had done a lot of work for PAC over the years. In the end to cut a long story short Chris Burt of SAA saw that the infighting was doing specialist angling no good at all so a meeting was arranged near Leicester between the PAC and myself. The result was an amicable settlement. I was readmitted to PAC and we all prepared to get on with out lives. Unfortunately some of the old committee in Scotland decided to resign their life membership because of this. This was sad news because they had served PAC well for most of the three years. They eventually set up a Scottish PAC, which I think was a mistake because there is strength in numbers and the real PAC still represents a lot of Scottish pike anglers.

Since all the problems I've been able to take someone on to help with my business and now I can get a little more involved in politics. At Blithfield it is clear that pike fishing has been of great benefit to the trout fishery. It is not my job to divulge their finances, but the pike fishing has allowed the replacement of outboards and the stocking of more trout. It is an example to hold up to other waters that have good pike in their trout fisheries. The Blithfield philosophy might even get through to the dinosaurs in Ireland!

CHAPTER 10
IN CONCLUSION

After all this time I have to admit that I still enjoy pike fishing. I know this is the case because each season I regret not having fished various waters, which I had planned to visit. There is always somewhere new to try. I have changed my outlook in the last five years because I'm looking for venues capable of producing 30lb plus pike. This selective approach hasn't been very successful because although lots of twenty pound plus pike come to the net, there's no sign of regular 30 pounders. Perhaps I'm hoping for too much. There is nothing wrong with having aspirations, provided you try to do it off your own bat. I fish a number of waters I have "discovered" and which I have worked on for a number of years. Though from time to time I've moved to waters that are producing big pike I try not to do it. I try to stay on my own patch and dread when one careless individual puts a photo in the press and other anglers descend on "my" bit of water. That is pike fishing I'm afraid, there is never enough of it to go around.

There are times when I get down and times when I give up. You pike fish because you enjoy it and when you stop doing just that then pack up! Sometimes you miss out on a fish you might have caught, but in the end there are days when you probably wouldn't catch however long you stuck at it. I'm glad I'm still a pike fisherman after 39 years.

FOOTNOTE: The title of the book "Everything You Need To Know About Pike Fishing will have given a few reviewers the chance to point out that no book could ever tell the reader everything he or she needs to know. I accept this completely. I enjoyed having a bit of fun with the title!!!!

APPENDIX

I have always felt that the reader should have as much access as possible to the inside information of catching big pike. Obviously there are restraints, which require me not to name all the waters. Pike fishing is only as good as the lack of competition! Here I have listed the number of 20lb plus pike caught by years and also the number of twenty pound plus pike by venues. Those of you with copies of my previous book Pike Fishing With Neville Fickling will if you compare the 20lb pike list note a degree of variance with the figures year by year published here. The actual total is correct, but I'll never know why the yearly results are incorrect. Everything is held on my computer, but the final counts year by year were made badly! I have checked the figures shown here 5 times!

20lb plus pike by years.

Year	Count		Year	Count
1968	3		1987	17
1969	0		1988	12
1970	3		1989	12
1971	2		1990	6
1972	1		1991	13
1973	2		1992	24
1974	5		1993	11
1975	1		1994	8
1976	0		1995	7
1977	4		1996	7
1978	2		1997	3
1979	6		1998	10
1980	5		1999	7
1981	7		2000	16
1982	20		2001	20
1983	23		2002	11 (as of April)
1984	26			
1985	16			
1986	18			

Readers might wonder why there is such a fluctuation in results. Well it is not because I've had years when I have not pike fished. It does however show that you are only as good as the waters you fish. From 1968 to 1972 I was learning how to catch pike, but obviously not that well. The waters I was fishing were good, but compared to those that were to come only mediocre. From 1973 to 1981 I knew a bit more about what I was doing, but still didn't have the waters to improve the results. Then from 1982 to 1989 I had the good fortune to have brilliant local fishing and the River Thurne. There was a bit of a lull in 1990, but things went well again from 1991 to 1993. The west of Ireland played its part here. Then from 1994 to 1997 I started to struggle. This happened because I had started to try and make waters that were not capable of producing big pike do just that! By 1998 I had got fed up of struggling and decided to get my act together. As luck would have it everything fell into place, particularly with Masons Lake. There will be furthers ups and downs I am sure, but I think this shows what you can catch even holding down a job!

20lb PIKE BY WATERS		30lb PIKE BY WATERS	
Cove Farm	35		
Boat Inn Lound	25		
Lough Allen	19	1	
Whitestones	18		
Weirwood	17		
Masons	15	1	
Martham N.Broad	15		
River Thurne	14	2	
Relief Channel	12		
Dool Lough	11		
Windsurf Lake	10		
Lincs Sandpit	9		
Glasslough	9		
Hollowel	6		
Cut Off Channel	6		
Loch Lomond	6		
Blithfield	5	1	
Lough Corrib	5		
Girton 2.	5		
Alder Pool	5		
River Bann	5		
Horsey Mere	4	1	
Middle Level	4		
Lincs Drain 1.	4		
Fosters End Pit	4		
Saundby Pit	3		
Ballyquirke	3		
Lincs Drain 2.	3		
Lindholme Lake	3		
Grafham	3		
Manton	2		
River Trent	2		
River Idle	2		
Dam Flask	2		
Lough Mask	2	1	
Martham S. Broad	2	1	
Yorks Pit	2	1	
Lincs Drain 3.	2	1	
Sandhills Lake	2		

20lb PIKE BY WATERS		30lb PIKE BY WATERS
Scooterplas	1	
Girton 1.	1	
Loch Awe	1	
Notts Pit	1	
Mill Basin	1	
Roswell Pits	1	
Barton Fabis	1	
North Level	1	
Nunnery Lake	1	
River Delph	1	
Ringstead	1	
Bough Beech	1	
Counter Drain	1	
Tyrham Hall	1	
Lound Back Pit	1	
Decoy Broad	1	1
Ardingley	1	
Brandesburton 3&4	1	
Burton Stather Pit	1	
Wissey Pools	1	
Menteith	1	
Lough Gara	1	
Rutland Water	1	
Totenhill	1	
Timberland Delph	1	
River Nar	1	

Looking at the waters you can see that there are a handful of waters that have produced a lot of pike for me. Unfortunately many of them are no longer places I visit. I might return though if I think it is worth my effort! Lets for information look at the bad news. Cove Farm was drained. The Boat Inn at Lound has been filled with gravel washings. Lough Allen I not the place it was! Whitestones is a syndicate, but it is hard work. Weirwood at the time of writing was no longer a trout water, but who knows what the future holds. There is some hope of a return to Masons. The Thurne is still worth a look, but I've not fished it for at least 12 years. The Relief Channel produced its last 20lb pike for me in 1974! The Windsurf Lake at Lound is an unknown quantity, I no longer fish it. You can see that good pike waters come and go so catch as many big pike as you can while you can!

FURTHER READING

Most of the books listed here are out of print, but many can still be bought second hand. Scientific papers can be obtained from the national lending library. Contact you local library for more information.

ALLEN, J.R. (1939) note of the food of the pike (*Esox lucius*) in Windermere. J.Anim. Ecol. 8 (1):72-75

BEUKEMA, J.J. (1960) Acquired hook-avoidance in the pike *Esox lucius L*, fished with artificial and natural baits. J.Fish Biol. 2, 155-160

BREGAZZI, P.R. & C.R. KENNEDY. (1980) The biology of pike, *Esox lucius L.*, in a southern eutrophic lake. J.Fish Biol. 17, 91-112.

BOUQUET, H.G.J. (1979) The Management of Pike Stocks. Proc. 1ˢᵗ British Freshwater Fish Conference. 176-181.

BUCKE,D. (1970) The anatomy and histology of the alimentary tract of the carnivorous fish the pike *Esox lucius L.* J. Fish Biol. 3. 421-431.

BULLER.F. (1979) The Domesday Book of Mammoth Pike. Stanley Paul.

FICKLING. N.J. (1982) The identification of pike by means of characteristic marks. Fish. Mgmt. 13 No. 2, 79-82

FROST, W.E. & KIPLING, C. (1959) The determination of the age and growth of pike (*Esox lucius*) from scales and opercular bones. J. du Conseil Perm. Lit pour L'Expl de la Mer. 24, 314-341.

FROST, W.E. & KIPLING, C. (1967) A study of the reproduction, early life, weight-length relationship and growth of pike in Windermere. J. Anim. Ecol. 36: 651-693

FROST,W.E. & KIPLING,C. (1968) A study of the mortality, population numbers, year class strengths, production and food consumption of pike Esox lucius L., in Windermere from 1944 to 1962. J. Anim. Ecol, 39, 115-157.

HICKLEY, P. & SUTTON, A. A standard growth curve for pike. Fish. Mgmt, 15, No. 1, 29-30.

HORTON, D. (2000) Ultimate Pike.

JOHNSON, I. (1966) Experimental determination of food consumption of pike for growth and maintainence. J. Fish. Res. Bd. Can. 23: 1495-1503

KIPLING, C. & W.E. FROST. (1969) Variations in the fecundity of pike in Windermere. J.Fish Biol., 1(3): 221-227

LAWLER, G.H. (1965) The food of the pike in Hemming Lake, Manitoba. J.Fish. Res. Bd. Can. 22(6) 1357-1377

MANN, R.H.K. (1976) Observations on the age, growth, reproduction and food of the pike in two rivers in Southern England. J.Fish. Biol. 8, 179-197

MANN, R.H.K. (1982) The Annual Food Consumption and Prey Preferences of Pike in the River Frome, Dorset. J.Anim. Ecol. 51, 81-95

MAUCK, W.L. & COBLE, D.W. (1973) Vulnerability of some fishes to Northern Pike predation. J.Fish. Res.Bd. Can. 28. 957-969

OTTO, C. (1979) The effects on a pike Esox lucius L, population of intensive fishing in a South Swedish lake. J. Fish. Biol., 8, 79-88

RICKARDS, B. & WEBB. (1971) R. Fishing for Big Pike. A&C Black.

THOMPSON, G.J. & BAGENAL, T.B. Pike gill netting in Windermere. Fish. Mgmt, 4, No. 4, 97-101

TURNER, E. (1989) Mega Pike. Beekay.